Identity in Democracy

AMY GUTMANN

Identity in Democracy

PRINCETON UNIVERSITY PRESS

PRINCETON AND OXFORD

Copyright © 2003 by Princeton University Press
Published by Princeton University Press, 41 William Street, Princeton, New Jersey 08540
In the United Kingdom: Princeton University Press, 3 Market Place,
Woodstock, Oxfordshire OX20 1SY

All Rights Reserved

Second printing, and first paperback printing, 2004
Paperback ISBN 0-691-12040-4

The Library of Congress has cataloged the cloth edition of this book as follows

Gutmann, Amy.
Identity in democracy / Amy Gutmann.
p.   cm.
Includes index.
ISBN 0-691-09652-X (alk. paper)
1. Pressure groups.   2. Group identity.   3. Democracy.   I. Title.
JF529 .G886 2003
322.4—dc21
2002029338

British Library Cataloging-in-Publication Data is available

This book has been composed in Adobe Caslon

Printed on acid-free paper. ∞

pup.princeton.edu

Printed in the United States of America

10   9   8   7   6   5   4   3

FOR MICHAEL DOYLE

CONTENTS

ACKNOWLEDGMENTS

I am thankful for thoughtful comments from friends and colleagues, including Anthony Appiah, Eamonn Callan, Henry Finder, Russell Hardin, David Kahane, George Kateb, Ira Katznelson, Helen Milner, Rob Reich, Nancy Rosenblum, Ian Shapiro, Yael Tamir, Daniel Weinstock, Melissa Williams, and Alex Zakaras. From my earliest thinking and writing about identity, Dennis Thompson has made invaluable contributions to the argument of this book by reading and advising as well as encouraging me along the way. Sigal Benporath was a godsend, offering creative suggestions and excellent assistance in preparing the final version. Ian Malcolm's editorial advice was exemplary. Deborah Tegarden contributed her time and expertise as production editor far beyond the call of duty. I am grateful to the Spencer Foundation for their senior scholar grant, which funded research, and to the Center for Advanced Study in the Behavioral Sciences at Stanford, where I was a fellow during the academic year 2000–2001, with funding from the Mellon Foundation and Princeton University. I learned from many people who offered insightful comments when I presented earlier versions of these chapters at the University of Chicago, Harvard, Michigan, Princeton, Stanford, and Utah, and the American Political Science Association Convention. The book also benefited from my being part of a diverse group on deliberative democracy, sponsored by the Social Science and Humanities Research Council of Canada. Colleagues at the University Center of Human Values have long provided intellectual and moral support. I am most grateful to Michael Doyle. This book would be far less without Michael, and so would I.

The Good, the Bad, and the Ugly of Identity Politics

Identity groups occupy an uneasy place in democracy. Critics emphasize how much group identities constrain rather than liberate individuals. When people are identified as black or white, male or female, Irish or Arabic, Catholic or Jew, deaf or mute, they are stereotyped by race, gender, ethnicity, religion, and disability and denied a certain individuality that comes of their own distinctive character and freedom to affiliate as they see fit. When individuals themselves identify racially, ethnically, or religiously as a consequence of being identified with groups, they often develop hostilities toward other groups and a sense of superiority over them. Groups frequently vie against one another in uncompromising ways, sacrificing justice and even peace for vindicating their superiority as a group.

If critics told the whole story, we would have little reason to doubt that identity groups are up to no good from a democratic perspective. Defenders of identity politics point out some of the problems with the critics' image of the autonomous, self-made person who neither identifies nor is identified with groups. Without any group identities, defenders of group identity say individuals are atomistic, not autonomous. Group identities help individuals have a more secure sense of self and social belonging. Moreover, group identity propels women and disadvantaged minorities to counteract inherited negative stereotypes, defend more positive self-images, and develop respect for members of their groups.

What the defenders and critics of identity groups have to say is significant, but each captures only part of the relationship between identity groups and democratic politics. The relationship is far more complex yet no less important than that suggested by these and other common defenses and critiques of identity politics. People identify with others by ethnicity, race, nationality, culture, religion, gender, sexual orientation, class, disability, age, ideology, and other social markers. No single group identity or even all group identities taken together comprehend the whole of a person, yet a commonly shared identification around any of the above characteristics of a person often leads to a group identity. Group identities are as abundant in democracies as they are controversial. Politically significant associations that attract people because of their mutual identification are aptly called identity groups.

Were it not for the mutual identification of individuals with one another, there would be no identity groups. Although mutual identification is basic to human existence, it has been neglected in democratic theory, where the language of "interest" and "interest groups" (soon to be discussed), rather than identity and identity groups, is far more common. Yet no one should doubt that identification with others makes a difference in how individuals perceive their own interests. Psychological experiments demonstrate that something as basic as self-image changes when individuals identify with others. And just as remarkably, a difference in self-image can be based on a seemingly, irrelevant identification with others. Experimental subjects who view a beautiful stranger report an increase in their own self-image of attractiveness when all that they learn about the stranger is that they share her birthday. The experimental subjects apparently identify with the total stranger by virtue of sharing the same birthday, and that identification alone is enough to enable her beauty to enhance their own self-image.[1] Conversely, a negative difference can arise from group identification when women students are reminded of their gender or African American students of their racial identity before taking tests in subjects where it is widely thought that women and African Americans perform poorly.[2] Democratic theory and politics clearly cannot afford to neglect the differences, both positive and negative, that group identifications make in people's lives.

What difference does the existence of organized identity groups make for democratic theory and practice? When is nationality, race, religion, gender, sexual orientation, or some other group identity a good or bad reason for democratic action? What identity groups should be encouraged or discouraged, and what actions based on identity can aid or impede democratic justice?

The analysis that follows suggests that organizing politically on the basis of group identity is not a good or bad thing in itself. When identity groups put the group above opposition to injustice or the pursuit of justice, they are morally suspect. Identity groups do better when they offer mutual support and help combat injustice for disadvantaged people. Even when combating injustice is justified, it can be ugly. A completely justifiable struggle against the rights violations of an identity group, such as the Ku Klux Klan, is often ugly, bringing with it unavoidable pain and suffering, or avoidable only at the price of appeasement. Resistance to injustice often itself encounters resistance, and people may undeservedly suffer as a consequence. By subjecting identity groups to fair-minded scrutiny, we come to recognize the good, the bad, and the ugly of identity politics.

Basic questions about the political ethics of identity groups in democracy have been conspicuous by their absence in both academic and popular discourse, for reasons that are worth noting. Because political scientists have tended to treat all organized nongovernmental political actors as interest groups, they have benignly neglected the role that group identity plays in defining and guiding many politically relevant groups in democracies.[3] At the other end of the spectrum, far from neglecting identity groups, popular political commentators often subject them to hypercriticism. Some claim, for example, that although interest groups are "an inherent part of the governing process of a democracy," identity group politics—by contrast—"is antithetical to the basic principle of one indivisible nation."[4] If one thinks only of identity groups that teach hatred of others, sometimes martyring their members who are willing to kill innocent people, then it is easy to condemn identity politics. But this line of thought misleadingly narrows the notion of identity groups.

Nationality itself is a group identity in the name of which injustices have been both inflicted and resisted. Both slavery in the United States and apartheid in South Africa, for example, have been institutionalized and then opposed in nationalism's name. The nationalisms have differed dramatically in content. Democracies have fought both aggressive and defensive wars by encouraging nationalist impulses among their citizens. People have rallied around a wide variety of nationalist identities in support of tyrannical regimes, yet tyrannies also have been resisted by many nationalist movements.[5] Nationalism is part of identity politics, and nations no less than other identity groups should be scrutinized according to considerations of democratic justice.

Identity groups are an inevitable byproduct of according individuals freedom of association. As long as individuals are free to associate, identity groups of many kinds will exist. This is because free people mutually identify in many politically relevant ways, and a society that prevents identity groups from forming is a tyranny. Associational freedom therefore legitimizes identity groups of many kinds.

Many political parties are identity groups, calling upon and cultivating shared identities around ideology, class, religion, and ethnicity, among other mutual recognitions. The myth that superior citizens are independent voters—citizens who do not identify in a stable way over time with a party as a partisan reference group—was an early casualty of survey research in political science.[6] "Far from being more attentive, interested, and informed," *The American Voter* discovered that "Independents tend as a group to have somewhat poorer knowledge of the issues, their image of the candidates is fainter, their interest in the campaign is less, their concern over the outcome is relatively slight."[7] The rise of independent American voters in the 1960s led many commentators to declare mutual identification around a political party to be an anachronism, but the revival of partisan political loyalty since the mid-1970s (matching its high 1950s level) underscores the importance of parties as identity groups.[8]

There now can be little reasonable doubt that mutual identification around a partisan group identity plays a central role in the official institutions of democratic politics. As the literature on party identification amply demonstrates, the relative successes and failures of political parties cannot be adequately understood without attending to the ways in which parties succeed or fail in calling upon and cultivating mutual identification among potential members.[9] This book extends the finding that mutual identification is a central part of party politics by examining and evaluating the role of identity groups outside of political parties and the formal political processes of democratic government. Not only within but also outside of the formal democratic mechanisms, identity groups act in ways that both support and threaten basic principles of democratic justice.

Three basic principles are equal standing as a citizen—or "civic equality"—along with liberty and opportunity. The interpretation of these principles varies across democratic views, but the variation does not detract from the fact that civic equality, liberty, and opportunity are core principles of any morally defensible democracy. The broad range of views compatible with these principles all can be called democratic. Identity groups act in ways that both aid and impede democracies in expressing and enacting these principles. The benign neglect of identity groups by political scientists and the hypercriticism of popular commentators are not terribly helpful in understanding or assessing their role in democratic societies.

To assess some of the major issues that identity groups pose for democracy, I consider various illustrative examples, most taken from the United States, a context that provides examples of the major kinds of identity groups. The issues that identity groups pose for democracy are best analyzed in their specific political context, but other inquiries, I hope, will concentrate on other democratic countries. To indicate how ubiquitous and varied identity groups are in contemporary democracies, I also occasionally draw on examples from other democratic societies. These analyses must be even more suggestive, since the context can be less taken for granted.

Consider three political controversies that feature identity groups from three different democracies.

- In Canada, often considered the home of multiculturalism, the Royal Canadian Mounted Police, for the first time in its history, decided in 1990 to exempt a group from a long-standing rule governing their uniforms. Sikhs were exempted from wearing the wide-brimmed hat that is otherwise a required part of the Mounties' official uniform. This exemption, while not in itself earth-shaking, had far-ranging implications for the accommodation of diverse group identities by public authorities in Canada. The accommodation of the Sikhs in Canada met with six years of protest and was appealed to the Canadian Supreme Court, which refused to hear the challenge, leaving intact the exemption based on identity group membership.

- In Israel, also in 1990, a group of conservative and orthodox Jewish women petitioned the High Court of Justice to be given the same rights as Jewish men to pray in public. A year earlier, these women had peacefully marched to the Western Wall in Jerusalem, holding a Torah, determined to pray there without male approval. They were attacked by a group of mainstream orthodox Jews who were defending their religious prohibition of women from praying as orthodox men do in public.[10] Ten years later, in 2000, the court recognized the women's right to pray at the Wall without abuse by other worshippers. The court also held that the fact that their prayer offends other Orthodox Jews must not annul their ability to exercise their equal rights in public. In response to this ruling, the Israeli Knesset (the unicameral parliament of Israel) introduced a bill that would impose a penalty on any woman who violates traditional Orthodoxy by praying at the Wall.

- In the United States in 1990, James Dale, an assistant scoutmaster of New Jersey Troop 73, received a letter revoking his membership in the Boy Scouts of America. Dale rose up through the ranks from cub to eagle scout to assistant scoutmaster. When executives in the Boy Scouts learned from a newspaper article that Dale was copresident of the Lesbian/Gay Alliance at Rutgers University, they revoked his membership. Dale brought suit against the Scouts on grounds of discrimination. The New Jersey Supreme Court ruled in Dale's favor on the basis of the state's anti-discrimination law. In a 5 to 4 decision, the United States Supreme Court reversed the ruling and ruled that the Boy Scouts may discriminate based on their expressive freedom as a group to oppose homosexuality.[11]

These controversies pit politically-engaged identity groups against each other: Canadian Sikhs versus other Canadians, Orthodox Israeli Jews versus "Women of the Wall" (some of whom are also Orthodox), Boy Scouts of America versus gay men, along with other individuals and groups, many of them also part of identity groups, who supported one side or the other in these political battles. The political interests of the major groups in these controversies are intimately linked to their group identities. These identity groups represent only a small fraction of the groups that organize around a mutually recognized identity of their members and pursue a political agenda at least partly based on that group identity. Although non–mainstream groups like Sikhs and gay men are more commonly recognized as identity groups than are mainstream Canadians or the Boy Scouts of America, all are identity groups according to any impartial understanding of the term.

Once we recognize all these groups as identity groups, we are in a far better position to engage in nonpolemical analyses of the problems they raise and the contributions they make in a democracy. Here, in a nutshell, is the dilemma that identity groups present to democracy:

- Identity groups are not the ultimate source of value in any democracy committed to equal regard for individuals;

- Identity groups can both aid and impede equal regard for individuals, and democratic justice, more generally;

- Some identity groups promote negative stereotypes, incite injustice, and frustrate the pursuit of justice;

- Others help overcome negative stereotypes and combat injustice in contexts of civic inequality and unequal liberty and opportunity;

- Identity groups can also provide mutual support and express shared identities among individuals whose lives would be poorer without this mutual support and identification.

Why are identity groups not the ultimate source of democratic value? Equal regard for individuals—not identity groups—is fundamental to democratic justice. A just democracy treats individuals as civic equals and accords them equal freedom as persons. If identity groups were the ultimate source of value, then they could subordinate the civic equality and equal freedom of persons (inside or outside the group) to their cause. Accepting an identity group as morally ultimate is inconsistent with treating persons as civic equals who are free to live their lives as they see fit. Living your life as you see fit therefore presupposes that self-appointed groups not impose their identity on you against your will.

Why, then, are identity groups not only legitimate but often also important, indeed even valuable, in democratic politics? First, because identity groups can significantly influence individual identities consistently with individual freedom. Freedom of association is a basic individual freedom. People freely associate (and express themselves) in, among other politically relevant ways, identity groups, which do not comprehensively define the identity of individuals but nonetheless influence their identities in important ways. People value identity groups in no small part because they value relationships of mutual identification and support. Second, numbers count in democratic politics as a legitimate means of exerting political influence, and individuals are most influential in groups. Third, the influence of identity groups includes their ability to play a critical role in combating civic inequalities and unequal freedoms and opportunities of individuals who identify and are identified in groups. Fourth, even when identity groups do not combat injustice, as long as they do not inflict it, they can be valued and valuable for the mutually supportive relationships that they provide their members, which is one reason why associational freedom is an important freedom for democracy to secure.

IDENTIFYING IDENTITY GROUPS

Identity groups may be organized or unorganized and may be inside or outside the official organs of government. This book concentrates on organized identity groups outside the official organs of government because they are of such great political significance yet neglected by political scientists and treated in a highly polemical way by popular commentators on politics.

What kind of group is an organized identity group?[12] Organized identity groups are sometimes thought to be a kind of interest group, but that does not tell us very much since all politically relevant groups that are not part of the official apparatus of government are considered interest groups. Simply to subsume identity under interest groups also tells us too much when it suggests that all groups coalesce around the shared instrumental interests of their members. By separately identifying identity groups, we recognize another way in which individuals relate to politically relevant groups in democratic societies: on the basis of mutual identification.

People often join a group because they share an identity and therefore identify with the people represented by the group and want to support its cause. They usually don't join because they want some instrumental goods from the group that they could not otherwise obtain. Many members of organized identity groups could obtain the same instrumental goods even if they did not join the group. Why, then, do they join? The answer to this question should not come as a surprise (except to those who presume that all rational individuals act—and therefore join groups—out of self-interest). Shared identity is connected to identification with a group and, as a large body of psychological literature demonstrates, is independent of the pursuit of self-interest.[13]

Identity groups are politically significant associations of people who are identified by or identify with one or more shared social markers. Gender, race, class, ethnicity, nationality, religion, disability, and sexual orientation are among the most obvious examples of shared social markers, around which informal and formal identity groups form. Social markers of group identity also include age and ideology and other mutually recognized features around which groups of people identify or are identified with one another in politically significant ways. Identity groups need not be based on largely unchosen characteristics of persons, such as race or gender.

What distinguishes social markers of group identity is that they carry social expectations about how a person of the particular group is expected to think, act, and even appear. Social markers therefore contribute to the creation of collective identities of both individuals and groups. Collective identities can change over time, and they are also open to varying individual interpretations. Yet because these identities are collective, they may be very difficult for individuals who are so identified to change, even if they do not welcome the identification.

In the paradigmatic case, when a sizable group of people identifies *as* and therefore *with* each other, they constitute an identity group. When they act in an organized fashion in politics on the basis of their group identities—whether for the sake of gaining recognition for the group or furthering its interests—they are part of identity group politics. Because people identify as and with other people, they can join a group out of identification rather than (only, primarily, or even necessarily) to pursue their self-interest. (Alternatively, one might say that identification with others becomes part of a person's self-interest, but in saying this we should realize we are stretching the meaning of self-interest so that it no longer signifies an interest *in the self* but rather any interest *of the self*, which can even be altruistic. Such a broad definition of self-interest may be more misleading than illuminating.)

It should be obvious that the mutual identification of an identity group—such as gay, lesbian, feminist, Jewish American, Irish American, or African American—does not exhaust the individual identities of its members. Group identification is socially significant but not comprehensive of individual identity.[14] Each of these group identifications is also subject to varying interpretations by the individuals who make it their own. A person may make a group identification more or less comprehensive of his or her identity. Individuals have multiple group identifications, and their individual agency modifies their group identifications just as group identifications shape individual agency. Individuals who mutually identify around a social marker often join together in a politically relevant and socially identifiable group.[15] These are the organized identity groups that are the focus of this book. (There are also unorganized, or what might be called nominal, group identities that are attributed to individuals in popular culture— the geek, jock, bimbo, and hottie, for example. Nominal group identities, like organized ones, can degrade individuals or elevate them above others. I focus on organized identity groups for the sake of assessing their political importance in democratic societies, and therefore I use the term identity group to refer to organized groups. However, the more philosophical parts of my analysis may apply to nominal identity groups as well.)

An illustrative example of an identity group can help illuminate our understanding of such a group. A social marker of the Women of the Wall—their Jewish egalitarian feminism manifested by their wearing of prayer shawls ordinarily reserved only for Jewish men—is publicly identifiable and it carries a set of social expectations about how individuals within this group identity, as religious, feminist, and activist, are likely to think and act as well as appear. The expectations attached to this group identity do not comprehensively define the mutually associated individuals: a feminist woman is more than a feminist, and a Jewish woman is more than Jewish, and a social activist is more than just that. The social expectations can also change over time and social context. In the United States, Jewish egalitarian feminists have manifested this identity in different ways from the Women of the Wall. More generally speaking, the expectations of feminism have changed over the past century and even today they vary, for example, from religious to secular feminists as well as among religious feminists. Citizens of a single democracy therefore have widely varying views of what it means to be a feminist today. Notwithstanding this variation, members of identity groups associate and are associated with social markers that partly but nonetheless importantly define them.[16]

When individuals organize together around a recognizable social marker on the basis of their own mutual identification, they are a paradigmatic identity group.[17] In other cases, which we can call negative identity politics, people are identified against their will by others by being given attributes of a particular kind of person, such as a "dirty Jew" or a "nigger," even though they disdain being so identified. (They might even prefer not to be identified at all as Jewish or black.) Historically, negative identity groups have rarely remained only or even primarily negative. When individuals are stigmatized because they are identified with a group, if they have the freedom, they often also publicly organize as a positive identity group to protest and transform their social markers from negative to positive ones. Since there are identity groups in the business of both negative and positive identity politics, to call a group an identity group is neither to praise nor to criticize it. The National

Association for the Advancement of Colored People (NAACP) and the Ku Klux Klan (KKK) are both identity groups, and praise for one is often associated with criticism of the other. The KKK is responsible for a pernicious kind of negative identity politics, which the NAACP exists in part to overcome. The NAACP's identity includes joining blacks and whites together in mutual recognition of their common humanity and equal rights. A person need not be a member of the NAACP to benefit from the instrumental aim of the organization—the achievement of equal rights. Mutual identification around its egalitarian ideology helps explain why membership in the NAACP is robust and not irrational from an individual perspective.

Individuals identify in groups around their gender, race, ethnicity, nationality, class, sexual orientation, age, physical ability or disability, and ideology. These social markers are open to widely varying inter-pretations and also vary over time. The social markers of paradigmatic identity groups—religion and culture in the case of the Canadian Sikhs, gender and religion in the case of Women of the Wall, sexual orientation in the case of gay men—are sufficiently differentiated to enable both insiders and outsiders to distinguish the group from others on that basis.

Mutual identification draws individuals together to identify with politically relevant groups, sometimes in pursuit of instrumental ends. Mutual identification therefore does not preclude a group's pursuit of instrumental ends for its members and nonmembers. Identity and in-terest are often closely intertwined.[18] Identity is an effective means of a group's organizing with the aim of pursuing instrumental goals, but identity groups are not reducible merely to instruments for such pur-suits. Because interests have so often been the focus of political anal-ysis, it is important to shift the focus in order to understand and evaluate the role that identity plays in democratic politics. Identity groups are sites of mutual identification and the pursuit of instrumen-tal interests that are informed by mutual identification. Moreover, many identity groups pursue interests (both morally good and bad) for nonmembers as well as members, and therefore we cannot define them as serving only—or even primarily—the self-interests of their membership.

DISTINGUISHING IDENTITY AND INTEREST GROUPS

The time is long overdue for understanding the distinguishing features of interest and identity groups and how they interact. An interest group organizes around a shared instrumental interest of the individuals who constitute the group *without any necessary mutual identification among its members*. The members are not drawn to the group because of their mutual identification; they are drawn to it because they share an instrumental interest in joining the group.[19] The political action of the group reflects the social identification of its members. Even when individual members dissent from some of the group's actions, the group's actions reflect back on the identity of its members because the members identify with the group (even when they dissent from some particular actions of the group). Whereas the defining feature of an identity group is the mutual identification of individuals with one another around shared social markers, the defining feature of an interest group is the coalescing of individuals around a shared instrumental goal that preceded the group's formation.

The pursuit of instrumental interests by identity groups must not be taken to mean that these interests preceded the mutual identification and that therefore the group is really an interest group, not an identity group. The contrary is often the case. For example, without their mutual identification as Israeli Jewish feminists, the Women of the Wall would not have an instrumental interest in breaking down the barriers that exist for Israeli Jewish women who wish to worship in public. This causal connection between group identity and individual interests is one reason why we should not be selectively skeptical of using the idea of group identity to understand the way people act in democratic politics. Speaking of the term "identity," one scholar rhetorically asks: "Do we really need this heavily burdened, deeply ambiguous term?"[20] If we want to understand an important set of political phenomena in democratic politics, the answer turns out to be yes; the term "identity" is useful and illuminating. To be sure, "identity" has various meanings, but so does the term "interest," and "interest" is far more ambiguously invoked—to the point of meaninglessness—to describe each and every political action taken by apparently reasonable people in democratic politics.

What can group identity explain better than a ubiquitous invocation of interest? The example of African Americans who could pass as whites but chose not to, even in the midst of rampant racial prejudice, confirms the importance of group identity in informing individual interests and actions. For African Americans who could pass, it was the mutual identification with other African Americans that explains their interests in the group, not vice versa. Just as some African Americans could satisfy their self-interest by distancing their interests entirely from the group and living as white, so too can members of many other disadvantaged ethnic groups who are able but unwilling to pass. Most people, of course, cannot pass for a different gender or white rather than black, hearing rather than deaf, or vice versa. The existence of individuals who can pass but who choose to publicly identify with a less advantaged group is important to note because it demonstrates that group identification is not derivative of the self-interests of the members of the group.

The phenomenon of identity groups is therefore both real and distinctive. It expresses the robust idea that group identity provides a basis for individuals to develop a sense of their own interests in democratic politics. This idea has been neglected because "self-interest" is so often taken to be primordial rather than informed by, among other things, group identity. Identity groups encourage people to join by orienting themselves around some mutual identification that is broader than the specific interests that they are pursuing at any given time. The greater the role that identity or solidarity plays in attracting, retaining, or mobilizing members in political efforts, the more a group is distinctively an identity group. The greater the role played by the pursuit of shared instrumental interests of individuals—regardless of their group identity—in attracting, retaining, or mobilizing members in political efforts, the more a group is distinctively an interest group. One of the neglected issues that identity group politics therefore poses for democratic society is the way in which recognition of interests often follows from group identification rather than being given simply by the pre-existing interests of individuals apart from their group identifications.

As the distinction between a paradigmatic identity group and an interest group suggests, the mutual identification of individuals and the collective pursuit of shared instrumental goals are not mutually exclusive. Identity groups are so-called because members join, support the group, and act out of mutual identification. Identity groups may of course act collectively in pursuit of an instrumental interest of the group. The mutual identification and the collective pursuit of an instrumental interest are mutually reinforcing. When identity groups pursue instrumental interests of their members, they encourage more people to see their identities as bound up with a group. Conversely, interest groups that originally formed to pursue a discrete issue may solicit more members by orienting themselves around some mutual identification that is broader than the original issue that they organized to pursue.

In paradigmatic form, identity group politics is bound up with a sense of who people are, while interest groups politics is bound up with a sense of what people want. This distinction is as clear as it can be in theory, and its theoretical clarity can also help make more apparent the close connection between group identity and people's sense of their interests in political practice. How people identify themselves—the distinctive organizing feature of identity groups—importantly affects what they want, the distinctive organizing feature of interest groups. *Democratic politics is bound up with both how people identify themselves and what they therefore want.* For this to be true, identity groups must be politically relevant and worthy of our careful attention.

People's identification with one another influences their sense of what they want. Moreover, individuals who identify with others are better able to organize politically, and organized groups can be far more politically effective than an equal number of unallied citizens.[21] Taken together, these two observations answer the question of why group identity matters so much in democratic politics. Group identification—whether it be focused on gender, race, religion, sexual orientation, ethnicity, nationality, age, disability, or ideology—provides people with motivating reasons of mutual identification to organize politically. Since mutual identification informs people's sense of their own political interests, group identity and collective interests are often mutually reinforcing in democratic politics.

ASSESSING IDENTITY GROUPS

In order to evaluate the broad phenomenon of identity groups in democracy, we must avoid defining identity groups so narrowly as to include only those groups that aid democratic justice or only those that impede it, but include both. By beginning with a nonpolemical definition, we are better able to understand what inclines identity groups, whether intentionally or unintentionally, toward or against democratic justice.

Mutual identification is central to the raison d'être of identity groups. When mutual identification entails putting considerations of group identity above considerations of justice—for example, by preferring people of one's own "kind" above others even when matters of justice push in the opposite direction—identity group politics is morally suspect. Putting a shared identity above considerations of justice means elevating what is not morally fundamental above what is. Group identity is not morally fundamental. If it were, as I argued above, groups could subordinate just treatment of individuals (member and nonmembers alike) to the identity and interests of their group. This is a description of tyranny over individuals, whether by a minority or a majority.

Identity groups should be suspect whenever they encourage their members to ignore considerations of justice for the sake of supporting the group, thereby disregarding any injustice of their cause. Putting a group above justice is a common phenomenon. Call it "making morally too much of group identity." The phenomenon is so common as to tar the entire landscape of identity group politics. Not all identity groups act this way, and few do all the time, but when any do, their moral myopia needs to be exposed. The source of the myopia is thinking, feeling, and/or acting as if group identity is an overriding public good, which takes precedence over avoiding injustice or pursuing justice for individuals regardless of their group identity. This myopia is the source of ongoing injustice in democratic societies and world politics more generally.

Even identity groups like the NAACP that act overwhelmingly for the good sometimes succumb to the moral mistake of making too much of group identity. When Clarence Thomas was first nominated to the Supreme Court, the NAACP hesitated to oppose his nomination because he was black, despite the fact that his judicial philosophy was inimical to that of the NAACP. Although, after a short period, the NAACP strongly opposed Thomas, it lost important momentum in the early days after the nomination, and its hesitation in opposing Thomas made his approval by the Senate more likely than it otherwise would have been. Making too much of Thomas's race gave conservative Republicans an easier success than they otherwise would (or should) have had. At the time, President Bush publicly claimed that race had nothing to do with his choice of Thomas, but that claim is not credible in light of available alternatives to the Thomas nomination. What is credible is that race was related to the nomination not because Bush himself thought it should be but because he thought others thought it should be, and those others would not normally support a nominee with Thomas' conservative qualifications. Group identity can be used—whether sincerely or cynically—in ways that are ethically suspect but politically effective.

Identity groups are ethically suspect when they elevate group identity over considerations of justice. Critics suggest three reasons why identity groups will systematically subordinate justice to their cause. First, they say that identity is harder to compromise than interest, and democratic politics depends on compromise. Second, they say that identity politics is inherently sectarian and therefore inimical to egalitarian reform. And third, they criticize the involuntary basis of identity groups.

Each of these criticisms merits closer scrutiny. Even if identity groups on average are less compromising than interest groups, it is not clear what follows, since there is no more reason to commend or criticize identity groups *as a whole* than interest groups as a whole. The differences in political behavior among and within identity groups are so striking as to call into question the usefulness of this generalization about the entire phenomenon of identity groups in democratic politics. The critical premise is that by virtue of being an identity group, the group must be less compromising than an interest group because people do not compromise their identities. By contrast, they do compromise their interests. This reasoning, however, is misleading because the aim of many organized identity groups is to *positively express* the identity of their members while pursuing various instrumental interests of the group. In the pursuit of instrumental interests—such as equal pay for equal work for women—identity groups can be just as compromising—or not—as traditional interest groups that organize for minimizing taxes, for example.

One problem with criticizing identity groups for being uncompromising is that it does not follow that identity groups are more harmful to democracy than interest groups, even if they are less compromising. Everything depends on the nature of the issue and—in the case of identity groups that are committed to just causes such as equal rights for minorities and women—how effectively groups that are not organized around identity would otherwise fight for these causes. Democratic societies can benefit from the presence of noncompromising groups on some issues such as equal rights for women and minorities. At the same time, there are plenty of reasons to criticize the uncompromising positions of those identity groups that push for benefits for their group regardless of the merits of the case and even at the cost of denying civic equality, equal freedom, or opportunity to members of other groups. The same criticisms, however, can be directed at uncompromising interest groups—such as some corporate organizations—when their causes are similarly unfriendly to democratic justice.

When we pick prominent examples of identity and interest groups and ask whether one is more compromising than the other, the generalization seems even more doubtful. Is the National Rifle Association (NRA), a large interest group, more compromising than the NAACP, a large identity group, on the issues that concern its members? One cannot credibly claim that the racial identity of the NAACP makes it uncompromising while the antigun control interest of the NRA makes it compromising. Identities and interests are interpreted by groups over time, and neither identity nor interest as the basis of an organized group lends itself more or less to political compromise. Everything depends on the content of the identity or interest along with the context within which it is pursued.

Uncompromising critics of identity groups also say that they block progress toward greater economic equality in democracies.[22] Is this true? The politics of multiculturalism often seems preoccupied with supporting particularistic identities and interests and therefore is either oblivious or hostile to egalitarian principles such as Rawls' difference principle (which requires income and other primary goods to be distributed so as to maximize benefits to the least advantaged).[23] The critics are rightly critical of relatively privileged identity groups lobbying for greater recognition of their own interests in disregard for those of far more disadvantaged groups. Even equal pay for equal work for professional women or minorities, a just and worthy cause, is surely not as high a moral priority as a living wage for all workers, regardless of their gender, race, or other group identity.

Has identity politics as a whole actually distracted democracies from these more urgent causes? Women who mobilize for equal pay for equal work also are likely to be among the same people who avidly support a living wage for all workers. The implication of egalitarianism is not a critique of identity groups per se but a critique of those that present their claims solely in terms of their particularistic identities and not in egalitarian terms. This criticism, however, must also be levied against interest groups that are as particularistic as identity groups in this respect.[24] Both identity and interest groups are suspect in this regard, and so is every other particularistic group that conceives of its collective interests as self-justifying rather than in need of taking other people's interests into account.

In the absence of identity politics, would democratic politics, as some critics claim, be more egalitarian in redistributing income and wealth and supporting equal opportunity? Alas, there is no evidence for this counterfactual claim. To the contrary, one credible explanation for the rise of identity politics in the United States in the late twentieth century is the failure of conventional interest group politics and government to concern themselves with the civic equality, equal freedom, and opportunity of disadvantaged women, people of color, and the disabled. Identity groups arose in the United States representing all of these groups—and more—and they have succeeded in bringing far greater attention to these egalitarian causes and in effectively lobbying for more progress along egalitarian lines than would have occurred without them. Many of these groups, moreover, defend the application of universal and egalitarian principles—nondiscrimination, equal pay for equal work, equal opportunity, civic equality—to correct long existing injustices that interest group politics have passed by.

The record of success of egalitarian identity groups in the United States falls far short of the aims of democratic justice, but this failure of American politics long preceded the identity politics targeted by egalitarian critics. The critique of identity politics is at best partial and polemical when directed at organized feminists, people of color, ethnic minorities, and gays, lesbians, and bisexuals rather than at the institutions, ideologies, and interest groups that actively oppose any egalitarian reforms. "The politics of identity," Todd Gitlin writes, "struggles to change the color of inequality," meaning that the affluent are now black as well as white, but inequalities of income and wealth are no less (and in fact even more) than when only whites were affluent.[25] This claim might appear less forceful to many as a critique of identity politics if it instead read "the politics of identity struggles to eliminate the gender of inequality." Eliminating the gender *and* color of inequality is no small moral accomplishment, even if it is not enough. It is also untrue that identity politics struggled *only* to change the gender and color of inequality. Feminists and many African American, Latino American, and other identity groups continue to lobby to equalize work, income, and educational opportunities for disadvantaged members of their groups who still encounter discrimination in the marketplace, workplace, and educational institutions. Gay, lesbian, and bisexual identity groups also have struggled—although not always successfully—for equal sexual freedom as well as equal opportunity in workplaces and institutions, including the military.

Affirmative action is another target of critics of identity politics who blame such politics for dividing disadvantaged groups, particularly whites and nonwhites, into "internecine warfare" to gain entry into selective colleges and high-level social offices.[26] If affirmative action changed the gender and color of educational inequality by admitting more African Americans and women to selective colleges and universities, the change should not be disparaged as ethically insignificant. Revealingly, far fewer critics disparage the use of affirmative action for women, which changed the gender of inequality, than disparage its use for African Americans. Changing the gender and color of inequality in higher education, while far from sufficient to satisfy democratic standards of civic equality, is not morally insignificant. Affirmative action in higher education, we learn from the careful empirical investigations of William Bowen and Derek Bok, has done considerably more than change the color of inequality.[27] It has improved the quality of education as reported by both whites and blacks who attend selective colleges and universities and brought more black professionals into community service positions in their communities.

Many of the same individuals and identity groups, moreover, defend not only affirmative action but also egalitarian causes such as raising the minimum wage, increasing job opportunities, improving health care and public health, and making taxation more progressive.[28] Following the lead of William Julius Wilson, many African American identity groups also give higher priority to improving economic opportunities for the least advantaged, regardless of their color, and ally themselves with labor and other economically disadvantaged identity groups. But success on these egalitarian fronts in the United States in recent decades has not been easy, to say the least. And Wilson does not make the mistake of opposing affirmative action as if it had been responsible for blocking these other, more urgent egalitarian reforms.

Other things being equal, egalitarian politics has been more successful in those democracies where working class identity has been more politically significant. The reason not to criticize identity politics per se is not because group identity is good in itself—it is not—but because group identity can make organization around almost any cause easier. Egalitarian critiques of identity groups often fail to recognize that some of the most successful egalitarian movements in modern democracies have been organized around class identity, mobilizing large numbers of citizens to ally with one another to support welfare rights, minimum wages, and other economic redistributions. Although the most successful political alliances are not purely made on class grounds, neither do they succeed without strong support from class-based organizations (including class-based parties like Labor in many democracies that build on class identity). Only by dismissing identity groups based on class can one say that identity politics is an enemy of egalitarian politics. Perhaps this criticism can be recast and redirected against identity politics that lacks a significant class basis. If identity politics neglects class and concentrates on group identities such as race and ethnicity, as is the case in the United States, then it is less likely to pursue an egalitarian agenda.

To blame identity groups for the failure of egalitarianism in the United States, however, distorts the larger picture of resistance to egalitarianism among a citizenry that overwhelmingly identifies itself—and with one another—as middle class rather than poor or working class. In the last three decades of the twentieth century, while the top four quintiles (80 percent) of Americans have grown better off, the bottom quintile (20 percent) has grown worse off. Even if identity group politics has not helped improve this problem, the critics of identity politics have not made a credible case that in its absence, life would now be better in the United States for the bottom quintile, and the country would be further along the road to civic equality, equal freedom, and opportunity for all. Have interest groups done any better? At one time, unions did better, but their decline, and their relative lack of success in the United States compared to in many European countries, is attributable in no small part to the weakness rather than the strength of identity politics: the considerably weaker identification of American workers with a working class group identity than their European counterparts. A working class group identity can help motivate individuals to join labor movements and identify their interests with this group rather than with the ubiquitous middle class, the group with which so many relatively poorly paid workers in the United States identify themselves.

When ridding democracy of identity groups is viewed as the path to egalitarian justice, we might paraphrase Madison's comment about factions in *Federalist 10*: It would be as much folly to try to abolish what causes identity groups to form—particularistic group identities of individuals and freedom of association—as "it would be to wish the annihilation of air, which is essential to human life, because it imparts to fire its destructive agency."[29] Far from being antithetical to representative democracy, identity politics is an important manifestation of individual freedom within it. Far better to address the bad effects of identity group politics in a way that is consistent with free association than to try to abolish identity groups. In significant instances, identity groups have been effective in addressing inequality. More often than not, feminist politics and African American identity politics have been prominent sources of movement in the direction of civic equality, equal opportunity, and other egalitarian dimensions of democratic justice. In some instances, however, the efforts of these identity groups have been misdirected, in a direction away from democratic justice.

The ideology of identity groups is so diverse as to defy the generalization that it is either antiuniversalist and antiegalitarian, or the reverse. There are certainly many identity groups whose philosophies and practices work counter to democratic justice, and they are worthy of political criticism. Brian Barry directs his relentless critique of identity politics against illiberal groups that oppose or undermine the protections of equal rights that liberal democracies should provide.[30] So directed, the critique is correct. But Barry chooses to ignore the fact that many identity groups, including many of those that support affirmative action in the United States, struggle politically for precisely the reverse: equal effective rights by means of better economic and educational policies.[31] To be convincing to open-minded people, criticism of identity group politics needs to be discerning. Identity group politics as a whole cannot fairly be said to undermine a politics of redistribution.[32] Many identity groups—most feminist groups, for example—do precisely the reverse: they strongly support a politics of redistribution, and they ally with many other identity groups that do the same. On the other hand, many other identity groups are highly sectarian and inegalitarian.

Better than both sectarian identity politics and sectarian interest group politics, as egalitarians have long suggested, would be a universalistic and united egalitarian political movement to raise the standards of all disadvantaged individuals, regardless of their cultural, ethnic, gender, racial, or national identities. The idea that such a universalistically based movement will be forthcoming in the absence of identity politics is doubtful in light of American history and the relative weakness of working class identification. The history of egalitarian reform in many European and Latin American democracies has been based in no small part on a politics of working class identification that is far weaker in the United States, where income and wealth inequalities are correspondingly greater.

There is also this irony in this egalitarian critique of identity group politics per se: an alternative that consistently follows from the egalitarian critique of identity politics is a democracy in which more individuals ally together politically as free and equal persons. Such a justice-friendly alliance based on mutual identification as egalitarian democrats would be yet another form of identity group politics. Democracies need more people to ally together politically and defend just causes, whether out of mutual identification as free and equal persons, or out of their commitment to justice, or both. (The identification and commitment are fully compatible.) The need for a politics that is more conducive to justice does not come any closer to being met, however, when critics condemn identity groups per se.

Critics of identity groups also focus their attention on the involuntary basis for some of these groups. The members of ascriptive groups of a particular race, gender, or nationality generally do not have a choice of being identified with the group. Involuntary ascription raises a set of distinctive problems concerning identity groups in democratic contexts that is worthy of extended analysis. But the involuntary nature of some group identities cannot be the basis for a wholesale critique of identity groups or identity politics for many reasons, the most basic of which is that involuntary identity groups are only a subgroup of identity groups and not necessarily the most prevalent or powerful subgroups at that. Memberships in many identity groups—most religious groups and all voluntary associations whose members are drawn to them out of mutual identification (in some cases because of their ascriptive identities)—are voluntary, as are memberships in many interest groups.

Nor would an involuntary basis of membership suffice for criticizing a group, as the defense of labor unions (some of whose membership is involuntary) suggests.[33] The membership of most democratic societies is involuntary: Most citizens do not have the effective freedom to pick up and leave and settle in another country that would accord them civic equality and equal freedom. On its face, the left-handed invitation "love it or leave it" presents a false choice for most citizens, who cannot leave their country any more easily than they can change their gender (which, after all, is no longer impossible). The absence of an effective freedom to leave one's country is not a sufficient ground for criticizing an otherwise just democracy. But it is a good ground for criticizing democracies that are unjust, as all democracies today are, in not according civic equality and equal freedom and opportunity to all their members. Something similar can be said of identity groups based on race, gender, and ethnicity, for example, the fact that they are involuntary is not a sufficient reason to criticize them, but the absence of an effective freedom to exit some identity groups renders them suspect in the same way that societies are suspect vis-à-vis their citizens who are not accorded civic equality and equal freedom and opportunity within the group. When identity groups are voluntary, for their members, as fraternal and soraral clubs like the Masons are thought to be, they have at least a partial moral defense of the way they treat their members—based on informed consent—that is absent from involuntary groups of all sorts. The fact that democratic societies are not voluntary associations may also make it all the more important for other groups within those societies to be voluntary. This issue is critical to considering both cultural identity groups and ascriptive identity groups, which are the topics of chapters 1 and 3, respectively.

Religious groups are also identity groups, and their politics is an important part of identity group politics in modern democracies. Many critics of identity politics exempt religious groups from criticism, and treat them as deserving of special treatment. In chapter 4, I ask whether religious identity groups should be treated with special consideration in democracies. I argue that they should not, but the reason many people may think that they should is instructive. The ultimate ethical commitments of individuals—which may be religious or secular in their source—are an especially valued and valuable part of individual identity. The contemporary shorthand for those ultimate ethical commitments—conscience—instantiates the identity of individuals as ethical persons. As such, conscience should be treated with a degree of deference in democracies out of respect for persons as moral beings, which is a basic principle of democratic justice. A degree of deference does not mean that conscience trumps legitimate laws. It means that democratic governments may legitimately treat conscience as special in democratic politics when so doing does not violate anyone's basic liberty, opportunity, or civic equality. By recognizing that conscience can be either secular or religious, democratic governments avoid discriminating either in favor of or against religious citizens.

DEMOCRATIC JUSTICE

Identity groups are suspect when they elevate group identity above justice, but they often fight against precisely this problem, as it is often unconsciously ingrained in discriminatory political practices that are well established and therefore taken for granted. Identity groups need to be assessed by the same standards that one would apply to any groups that make political claims and exert political influence in democracies. I apply the democratic standard of civic equality, broadly understood to include equal freedom and opportunity for all individuals. There is no ethically neutral place to evaluate the contribution of identity groups to democratic societies, nor would a neutral place be desirable if it were available. When I use the term democracy, it signifies a political commitment to the civic equality of individuals. A democracy also can and ideally should be a deliberative democracy, offering opportunities for its citizens to deliberate about the content of democratic justice and to defend their best understanding of justice at any given time.

A just democracy therefore respects the ethical agency of individuals, and since individuals are the ultimate source of ethical value, respect for their ethical agency is a basic good. Ethical agency includes two capacities: the capacity to live one's own life as one sees fit consistent with respecting equal freedom for others, and the capacity to contribute to the justice of one's society and one's world. All democratic theories that take ethical agency seriously also honor three principles in some form. One is civic equality—the obligation of democracies to treat all individuals as equal agents in democratic politics and support the conditions that are necessary for their equal treatment as citizens. A second principle is equal freedom—the obligation of democratic government to respect the liberty of all individuals to live their own lives as they see fit consistent with the equal liberty of others. A third principle is basic opportunity—the capacity of individuals to live a decent life with a fair chance to choose among their preferred ways of life. Of course other principles may be considered basic by other theories, but for purposes of assessing the place of identity groups in democracies in this book, civic equality, equal freedom, and basic opportunity serve as critical standards. Since civic equality also requires many equal freedoms and basic opportunities, I refer to civic equality as a shorthand throughout the book of a principled basis for assessing the relationship between identity groups and democratic politics.

Why is it important to evaluate rather than just to describe the role of identity groups in democracies? Much more work needs to be done in describing the role of identity groups in democracies, far more than I can do in this book. But no matter how thoroughly we analyze identity groups, our discussion will be incomplete if it is merely descriptive. Description alone is not even sufficient to describe completely the role of identity groups in democracies, and it is not even the prior task to considering how identity groups at their best can contribute to democratic justice and how at their worst they impede its pursuit. This, after all, is part of a description of the role of identity groups in democratic politics.

To describe identity groups in a value neutral way would be to misdescribe and misunderstand not only identity groups but the nature of democracy. Democracies are not neutral political instruments; they are worth defending to the extent that they institutionalize in politics a more ethical treatment of individuals than the political alternatives to democracy, which range from benevolent to malevolent autocracies and oligarchies. Some identity groups aid democracies in institutionalizing more equal treatment of individuals and others impede it. A critical part of a description of the role of identity groups in democracies must therefore be to develop a language that helps us to understand their role in both aiding and impeding the pursuit of democratic justice.

Critics who do not labor under a false sense of value neutrality still may shy away from judging identity groups by democratic standards because they realize that democratic standards are themselves often contested. But so, too, are empirical descriptions of groups, and therefore avoiding controversy is not a good reason to seek value neutrality. Judging from the depth of controversies over historical accounts that are ostensibly empirical, it is not even clear that disagreements about ethical values arouse deeper passions than empirical disagreements (for example, about the causes and effects of ending slavery or instituting affirmative action).

Reasonable contestation or challenge is something to be encouraged in democratic politics, out of respect for individuals as ethical agents. Mutually binding laws and policies should be justified to the extent possible for ethical agents; efforts at justification, even if unsuccessful (as they often are) at achieving agreement, express mutual respect among persons as civic equals. Whatever specific principles we defend in democratic politics to assess identity groups, we therefore can also defend democratic deliberation about those principles and their application out of a commitment to mutual respect among persons, which itself is a way of treating people as civic equals.[34]

The principles invoked in this book to assess identity groups—civic equality, equal freedom, and basic opportunity—are defended by a wide range of democratic theories. The three general principles are still subject to disagreement in their application, especially in difficult cases. Does civic equality, equal freedom, or basic opportunity, for example, require the Canadian Mounties to exempt the Sikhs from its uniform policy? Assuming that both religious freedom and separation of church and state are violated by the inability of Israeli women to pray as Israeli men do at the Holy Wall in Jerusalem, what other features of Israel's nonseparation of church and state violate the equal religious freedom of Israeli women who identify as Jewish? James Dale's challenge to the Boy Scouts raises yet another kind of principled question concerning the competition between two principles. Which is more basic to a democratic justice: freedom from discrimination on the basis of one's sexual orientation or freedom of expression for voluntary associations? What difference does the nature of the voluntary association make in how we compare what is at stake on both sides?

Some controversies concerning identity groups that I draw upon are not hard cases to assess whereas others are. It is important to consider both kinds of cases in order to understand and evaluate identity groups in democracies. When a case is hard, however, and there is reasonable disagreement among affected parties about how democratic principles should be interpreted and applied, there is also a special need to move beyond basic substantive principles and call for deliberation within as inclusive a group as possible of the people who are significantly affected by the decision. Substantive principles inform democratic deliberation, but they do not take its place. Conversely, deliberation does not take the place of substantive principles; it would be a politically hollow (and ethically senseless) exercise if it were not substantively informed.

Liberty, opportunity, and civic equality are defensible on grounds offered by almost all democratic theories, which converge in support of these principles from different starting points.[35] Yet some people identify democracy far more simply with one single principle, majority rule. Why join democracy to a defense of any principles other than majority rule? First, because majority rule is not a principle by itself. It is a rule of procedure that cannot possibly define a defensible democratic politics, since majority rule can be used by oligarchic decision makers. Any democracy that is defensible on ethical grounds— grounds that respect the ethical agency of all persons—must do more than establish order through a decision-making procedure, since order alone does not respect the ethical agency of all persons.

I use the word "democratic" in this book as a concept of political ethics to signify a public commitment to treating individuals as ethical agents. (Democratic justice does not view individuals as atomistic individualists; it views them as ethical agents, which is quite a different matter.) A just democracy helps secure for all persons the conditions of civic equality, equal freedom, and basic opportunity, principles that are preconditions of a fair democratic process but are also valuable in their own right as expressions of the freedom and equality of individual persons as ethical agents.

A democratic state that respects individuals as free and equal persons does its best to secure civic equality for every person. There is room for deliberative disagreements about what counts as civic equality, but there is also a broad range of reasonable agreement possible among democrats. For example, democrats today count among the equal liberties freedom from slavery, serfdom, forced labor, and other forms of subordination of persons and the correlative freedoms of expression, conscience, assembly, and association. Basic opportunities are broadly agreed upon to include adequate schooling, subsistence, and nondiscrimination in the distribution of educational and career opportunities. Civic equality refers to both a set of political rights of equal suffrage and political participation in a fair competitive process of democratic decision making and a set of civil rights including due process and equal protection by the laws.

Defending these principles that are widely shared by democrats does not require anyone to be what John Rawls calls a "comprehensive liberal" because these principles do not encompass the entirety of a moral philosophy or a cultural identity. Nor does the democratic perspective that informs them encompass the entirety of any moral philosophy or cultural identity. Many democrats committed to civic equality for all persons are, to use Rawls's term, "political liberals." There are many versions of political liberalism other than Rawls's theory of justice, just as there are many versions of comprehensive liberal and nonliberal perspectives. Although the perspective taken in this book may be seen as a kind of political liberalism, it is compatible with many comprehensive philosophies as well.

Democracy, as I understand it, takes all persons, regardless of their ascriptive identities, as deserving of equal *political* regard or respect. Because a democratic view of politics is committed to equal respect for persons regardless of their particular group identities, it provides a potentially critical vantage point for assessing identity groups. While the political landscape is often divided between those who assume that all identity groups violate democratic principles and those who assume the reverse, neither assumption is warranted by this analysis. Distinguishing among identity groups is critical not only to understanding but also to assessing their role in democratic societies.

FOUR KINDS OF IDENTITY GROUPS

Four kinds of identity groups—cultural, voluntary, ascriptive, and religious—are worthy of separate consideration because each highlights a different set of ethical issues raised by the presence of identity groups in democracies and the ways in which they can either aid or impede democratic justice. Although the four kinds are not mutually exclusive, by focusing on culture, choice, ascription, and religion we can more readily examine the most important issues revolving around the relationship between group identity and democracy. I therefore have devoted a chapter to each kind of identity group.

Identity groups call attention to both the extent and the limits of expression of free identity, and the tension between free identity expression and its limits is a central issue in chapters 1 and 2. Chapter 1 considers cultural identity groups. Culture is the most common category around which controversies over identity groups gravitate. This is because of a tendency to consider every identity group as representative of a culture and culture as constituting its members' identities. Although culture can be considered the universal glue that unites or divides people into identity groups, so broad a definition verges on the vacuous. Political theorists of culture are more careful in specifying what they understand a cultural group to be. Cultural groups, they say, represent ways of life that are comprehensive or encompassing, terms that are used interchangeably to refer to the provision by culture of a context of choice that determines the range of what is feasible for its members.[36] Cultural groups also can give their members a sense of security and belonging. In chapter 1, I question the comprehensiveness of culture and pursue some corresponding concerns about the claims of cultural identity groups vis-à-vis both members and nonmembers. The concerns follow from democratic principles such as equal freedom and civic equality to which many theorists of culture themselves subscribe.

At the other end of the associational spectrum from cultural identity groups are voluntary associations. They are so far at the other end that they are often not even considered to be identity groups. Voluntary associations offer the opposite of a comprehensive context of choice to their members. Each association offers one among many options, along with disassociation itself, within an associational diverse context. Chapter 2 focuses on the voluntary groups that inhabit a democratic landscape, which de Tocqueville described in his portrait of democracy in America as of "a thousand different types—religious, moral, serious, futile, very general and very limited, immensely large and very minute."[37] Contemporary theorists of choice eloquently defend free association in democracy, reminding us that "to be free, to live as one likes, includes associating on one's own terms, which means engaging in voluntary relationships of all sorts."[38]

However essential they are to the fabric of a democracy, voluntary associations are far from problem-free. They pose a problem that flows from the very nature of the freedom that they represent in non-ideal societies that have been ridden by systematic social prejudices. Freedom of association entails the freedom to exclude people from one's association, yet prejudicial exclusion of people because of their gender, skin color, or other unchosen characteristic exacerbates civic inequality in many forms, including unequal freedom and opportunity. Prejudicially blocked entries into voluntary associations may therefore be considered unjust. Yet the freedom to form an exclusive group and the freedom to join one are both valued freedoms. Whichever way a democracy resolves this conflict between the freedom to join and the freedom to exclude, the freedom of some people to express their identities as they see fit will be limited by the freedom of others. How a democracy resolves the conflict of freedoms is critical to the value of voluntary groups vis-à-vis democratic justice, which is the subject of chapter 2.

In chapter 3, our attention turns to those organized groups that explicitly bring people together based on unchosen characteristics: mutual identification by ascription. Many identity groups organize around unchosen social markers such as gender, color, ethnicity, sexual orientation, and disability. Groups that organize around ascriptive identities are themselves enormously varied in their relationship to democratic justice. Some are justice-friendly, actively promoting democratic justice by advocating equal freedom and opportunity for individuals who are disadvantaged because of their ascriptive identities. Other ascriptive identity groups—like the National Association for the Advancement of White People, which arose in response to the NAACP—impede the very same cause. Even with regard to justice-friendly ascriptive groups, special issues arise. Some people claim that women, African Americans, and other people of color have special moral obligations to their ascriptive groups because if they do not contribute to the cause they will be free-riding on the efforts of justice-friendly groups. Although these special obligations are not considered legally binding, they are publicly defended as morally incumbent on individuals, and they therefore differentially burden some individuals who are identified with certain ascriptive groups and not others.

An alternative view—the identification view—suggests that *all individuals*, regardless of their ascriptive identities, can live morally better lives by identifying with disadvantaged people and contributing to just causes out of that identification. Justice-friendly groups make it possible for individuals to contribute to just causes without undue sacrifices in their lives. The identification view has the ethical advantage of applying to everyone, not only members of disadvantaged groups, and it also extends beyond any single democracy. Identifying with others and contributing to just causes can help make everyone's lives better, morally speaking. This kind of identification—for the sake of our living morally better lives and contributing to democratic justice—needs more prominence in democratic cultures if democracies are to have their best chance of becoming more just.

Religious identification is among the most prominent grounds for identification in modern democracies, so much so that religious identity, the subject of chapter 4, often calls for special treatment by democratic governments. Religious identification seems to be one of the strongest and most persistent sources of mutual identification known to humanity. Perhaps this is because religions hold out the hope of immortality (although not all religions do so) or because religions are often also "thick" cultures that mark the human life cycle with holidays and sacraments with which families and communities can mutually identify. Recognizing how powerful religious identity can be, many people—religious and secular alike—have been concerned to separate the power of organized religion from the power of the state. Long before anyone coined the term identity politics, religious identity groups, or "churches," were both honored and feared as potent political forces.

In order to protect churches and states from one another, some democracies have tamed the political power of both by a settlement that I call "two-way protection." Two-way protection is committed to protecting the religious freedom of individuals in exchange for protecting the democratic state from the political power of churches. By contrast, one-way protection aims to protect religion from the state but not protect the state from religion. Defenders of two-way and one-way protection disagree as to whether and how religious identity is special, and with what political implications. Chapter 4 asks whether religious identity is special in democracies for the most commonly suggested reasons: its truth value, its contribution or threat to the public good, or its constitution of conscience, the ultimate ethical commitments of sincere believers. I conclude that religious identity is not special for its truth value, its contribution or threat to the public good, or its unique constitution of conscience.

The conclusion that religious identity is not special, however, has a significant twist. In considering the claims of religious conscience, I conclude that it is not special, although conscience, more generally understood as the ultimate ethical commitment of individuals, is special. Conscience has some special claim to be considered by democratic governments because democracies are supposed to be committed to respecting the ethical agency of individuals. Since religious identity is not the only source of binding ethical commitments, democratic governments cannot defer only to religious conscience without discriminating among citizens. Whether and when democratic deference to conscience is desirable turns out to be a separate issue from the question of whether religious identity is special, but its importance is inseparable from an appreciation of the centrality of ultimate ethical commitments, including those given by a person's religion, to individual identity.

Freedom of religion is a subclass of freedom of conscience, which is freedom to pursue one's ultimate ethical commitments within the limits of legitimate laws. Two-way protection suggests that the limits of legitimate laws should sometimes accommodate conscientious dissenters, when such accommodation does not threaten discrimination. A great advantage of accommodating conscientious dissent is that it respects the ethical agency of persons in democratically defensible terms. Accommodating dissent based on ethical identity recognizes a reciprocal relationship—of mutual respect—between conscientious citizens and the democratic governments that imperfectly represent them. Neither democratic laws nor conscience receive full rein: both are constrained by the other in principled ways that any liberal democrat can defend.

BEYOND GROUP IDENTITY

Are democrats also an identity group? A democrat is anyone who is committed to civic equality—public respect for persons as ethical agents. Democrats therefore need not be so committed out of identification with others. They may be so committed because they believe every person deserves respect as a civic equal. Some democrats, however, are so committed to these principles out of identification with other people. Their democratic impulse may emerge from a common human reaction to the suffering of others: "There but for good fortune (or the grace of God) go I." Logically speaking, democracy does not need to rest on mutual identification among people, but it may do so. Practically speaking, identification with others can be a path by which many people become committed democrats.

In light of the common philosophical view that justice should be based on impartiality, it is important to emphasize that there is nothing wrong (even from an impartial perspective) with supporting just causes out of mutual identification with those who are suffering from injustice or with others who are committed to organizing against injustice. Those whose ethical commitments operate independently of any mutual identification still need to join with others to be politically effective; therefore, practically speaking, there is not much to be gained by an extensive discussion about whether democrats are necessarily an identity group. They can be. What is important to recognize is that in identifying with other people, democrats may be better able to act effectively in democratic politics, since identification helps people join together in political causes. Democrats identity groups are therefore good from a practical as well as an ethical democratic perspective.

The idea of a democratic identity raises another question of political ethics. Is being a democrat a comprehensive identity, and if so, does it threaten creative human agency? As I understand it, a democratic identity is not comprehensive. I can identify as a democrat and also as a feminist, Jewish-American, friend, foodie, political philosopher, lover, mother, and lots more (or other). Democrats are not—or at least need not be—any single identity either exclusively or above all else. Multiple group identities coexist in individual persons. Democracy does not offer individuals a comprehensive template for making choices in life. Rather, it informs contributions to politics, and gives people great freedom to live their lives as they see fit, consistently with the equal freedom of others. Equal freedom includes the liberty to identify with many groups.

What, then, lies beyond group identity? Individuals have many identities that are not captured by any identity group. We have identities that are idiosyncratic to our own personalities, and we also have identities that are shared with others—who are wise or foolish, careful or careless, neat or sloppy, serious or light-hearted, and so on—but these shared characteristics, however important to our personal identities, are not the kind that constitute an identity group.[39] Identity groups are characterized by mutually recognizable social markers that draw people together in politically significant groups. Many important features of an individual's identity are not captured by identity groups. Even if all our personality characteristics have a social dimension— otherwise they could not even be expressed as personality characteristics—not all are group identities of the kind that are featured in this book or that are central to democratic politics. Yet individual identities that do not lend themselves to identity groups may be at least as central to a person's sense of self. It is important to keep in mind that the group identities around which political identity groups form do not encompass the entirety of individual identities or even the most important parts of people's identities, even if they are often among the most politically significant.

Corresponding to the coexistence of multiple identities in a single person (some group identities, others not) is the coexistence of multiple groups and individuals that play a role in democratic politics. Some groups are identity groups; others are not. Many are a mixture of both. Whatever the mix, we should also recognize that some individuals, sometimes acting outside of interest and identity groups, can be politically effective. This is consistent with our opening observation that most people can make a significant political difference in democracies only by acting in groups. There are exceptional individuals who can make a difference without joining any identity or interest group by following a personal calling that happens to have political relevance. When Albert Einstein spoke out about politics, he was heard. When Nobel Prize winners like Toni Morrison speak out politically today, they are heard more than most other individuals, even though they are acting alone. The same can be said about the many rich and famous celebrities like Jane Fonda, Charlton Heston, Robert Redford, Barbra Streisand, and Steven Spielberg, although it is significant that those who seek the greatest political influence create or lead identity or interest groups (as Redford has done for environmentalists and Heston for the National Rifle Association). Individual political action is just as variable in value vis-à-vis democratic justice as identity group politics, but generally it is less effective because the numbers legitimately count in a democracy. Since wealth also counts, often unjustly, rich people are less dependent on group identities for effective political action. Yet they, too, form and join identity groups for some of the same reasons as anyone else.

In democratic politics, most people are most influential in groups, and identity groups are a manifestation of a basic freedom of association. Democrats therefore need to think about the ways in which a politics that depends in no small part on identity groups can work to better secure equal liberty, opportunity, and civic equality for all individuals, not only for the most privileged or the most powerful members of disadvantaged groups. The relationship between group identity and democratic politics is far more complex than blanket critiques and defenses of identity politics suggest. A democratic perspective attends to the interplay between group identities and democratic politics and assesses their relationship on the basis of broadly defensible principles of justice.

Identity groups as such are neither friends nor enemies of democratic justice. They pose distinctive challenges that have been neglected by political theorists who overlook the advantages of organizing on the basis of mutual identity in democratic politics and by political scientists who lump all politically relevant organizations together under the rubric of interest group politics. It is the aim of this book to overcome both kinds of neglect. A democratic view recognizes the legitimate but also problematic parts played by group identity in democratic politics and therefore the importance of distinguishing between the good, the bad, and the ugly of identity group politics.

CHAPTER ONE

The Claims of Cultural Identity Groups

"To abrogate tribal decisions, particularly in the delicate area of membership, for whatever 'good' reasons, is to destroy cultural identity under the guise of saving it."
—*Martinez v Romney*, 402 F Supp 5, 19 (D NM 1975)

"The extension of constitutional rights to individual citizens is intended *to intrude upon the authority of government."*
—Justice White's dissent in *Santa Clara Pueblo v Martinez*, 436 U.S. 49, 83 (1978)

The most common kind of identity group around which controversy stirs is the cultural identity group. When the term culture is loosely used, cultural identity subsumes the entire universe of identity groups, and every social marker around which people identify with one another is called cultural.[1] Culture, so considered, is the universal social glue that unites people into identity groups, and the category becomes so broad as to be rather useless for understanding differences among identity groups.[2]

Some political theorists of culture such as Avishai Margalit, Moshe Halbertal, Joseph Raz, and Will Kymlicka are much more careful in specifying what constitutes a cultural group. They consider a cultural identity group to be a group that represents a way of life that is (close to) "encompassing" or "comprehensive" (terms that are used interchangeably). A culture, Margalit and Raz argue, provides the comprehensive context within which its members make choices.[3] Culture also offers an "anchor for self-identification and the safety of effortless, secure belonging."[4]

The groups identified as cultural in this sense, although various in their content, are united by distinctive features when compared to other groups. Tribes like the Pueblo, Navajo, Hopi, Inuit, Sami, and Maori, for example, are each distinctive cultures, yet they share the status of indigenous peoples, separated by their cultures from the larger societies of which they are a separate part. National minorities, like the Basques and Catalans, are another kind of cultural group whose internal differences are as striking as their formal similarity as national minorities.[5] Still other cultural identity groups are defined by a specific religion (as are some indigenous cultures), so the cultural categories overlap. Ultra-Orthodox Jews in Israel and the Old Order Amish in the United States, two very different religious groups, are both often considered identity groups that represent fairly encompassing cultures.

In light of such great variation among cultural groups, what makes them an important category to consider for democratic politics is that all make far-ranging claims on democracy in the name of their cultural identity. The claims are understandably great once a person's culture is considered "a constitutive part of who the person is."[6] The claims include rights of sovereignty for the group, exemptions from laws that disproportionately disadvantage the group's members, aid for the group's cultural institutions, and support for the group's cultural survival. Rather than simply applaud or condemn cultural identity groups, we need to evaluate these kinds of claims in order to understand the ways in which they can both aid and impede democratic justice.

The most common ground invoked in defending claims of cultural identity groups is the idea that culture shapes individual identity in a comprehensive way. Members of minority cultures are therefore decisively disadvantaged if democratic politics is connected to a dominant culture that is alien and therefore alienating to them. How can democratic politics be so culturally biased rather than neutral? Democratic politics typically depends on some dominant culture that includes a common language (or languages), school curricula, occupations, ceremonies and holidays, and even architectural styles that are not culturally neutral. Members of minority cultures are therefore denied equal freedom and civic equality, the argument continues, when democratic governments fail to protect minority cultures while effectively protecting the dominant culture simply by virtue of politics as usual. By using a particular language, history, education, architecture, and a host of customs to carry on politics, a democratic government supports some cultures and not others. It cannot possibly support all cultures to the same extent and still act coherently or keep a society together. Cultural neutrality is not an option for a lot of governmental action and expression. In recognition of the lack of cultural neutrality and out of fairness to members of cultural minority groups, democracies and democratic citizens are taking more seriously than ever before the question that forms the focus of this chapter: What kind of political claims on behalf of cultural identity groups are justified in democracies, and why?

Before proceeding, we need to be as clear as possible about what theorists of culture mean by a culture. A culture, as Margalit and Raz put it, "defines or marks a variety of forms or styles of life, types of activity, occupation, pursuit, and relationship. With national groups we expect to find national cuisines, distinctive architectural styles, a common language, distinctive literary and artistic traditions, national music, customs, dress, ceremonies and holidays, etc."[7] The ideal type of a culture, so understood, is comprehensive, but no single characteristic—such as a common language, dress, holidays, or territorial concentration—is absolutely necessary for an actual culture to be considered as such. Theorists of culture assume a rough approximation rather than a perfect match of the actual to the ideal type: a culture constitutes and constrains the identities (and therefore the lives) of its members by providing them with a common language, history, institutions of socialization, range of occupations, lifestyles, distinctive literary and artistic traditions, architectural styles, music, dress, ceremonies and holidays, and customs that are shared by an intergenerational community that occupies a distinct territory.[8] Actual cultures encompass the lives of their members in many of these ways but not necessarily all. That's not a problem, write Margalit and Raz, "that's life."[9] What turns out to be a problem, I will argue, is the extent to which some political claims of cultural identity groups for sovereignty and the like depend on their actually encompassing the identities of members and therefore limiting some people's freedom and opportunity in inequitable ways.

CLAIMS OF CULTURAL RECOGNITION

The political question that arises once we recognize the non-neutrality of democratic governance is: What claims of cultural identity groups should be politically recognized, and why? To answer this question, theorists of culture begin by asking a fundamental question: What publicly important goods can cultural groups provide?

One good is a context for choice: Cultures provide the contexts within which individuals exercise their freedom and opportunity. Depending on whether a person was brought up as Pueblo, Navajo, Old Order Amish, Basque, Catalan, Scotch, Welsh, Ultra-Orthodox Israel Jew, secular Israeli, Inuit, Québécois, or Anglophone Canadian, her cultural options will differ. Both the nature and the range of her choices will vary with her cultural upbringing and context. Free individuals should be able to decide for themselves how they want to live their lives among the options that are open to them, but "the range of options can't be chosen."[10] The range of options available to an individual—the context of choice—is said to be given by the comprehensive culture. Culture, so conceived, is therefore both comprehensive and the context for individual freedom of choice.

Because every person needs a context of choice, every person needs a culture. Freedom is possible because comprehensive cultures can give people a broad range of options of how to live their lives. The options are available *within the culture*, and therefore individuals do not need to range beyond a particular societal culture to live freely as long as the culture really does offer equal freedom to its members. What theorists of culture emphasize is that freedom is exercised within a culture. However, some theorists of culture, such as Kymlicka, are more attuned than others to the need for cultures to offer equal freedom to all members, not just to some.

Beyond providing the context of free choice, cultural groups also can provide their members with social security because of the givenness of culture. Cultural membership is "a matter of belonging, not of achievement."[11] Merit has nothing to do with cultural membership: "To be a good Irishman . . . is an achievement," as Margalit and Raz explain, "But to be an Irishman is not."[12] This unearned quality of cultural membership turns out to be a highly valued fact of human life for many people. When competition for careers, honors, and status abounds within a culture, the good of secure belonging may become even more valuable because it is scarcer.[13] Theorists of culture conclude that "it is in the interests of every person to be fully integrated in a cultural group."[14] Insecure selves are not the civic equals of secure selves. Moreover, if citizens are equally insecure, they are not well served by their societies.

Yet another social good that cultural identity can help secure is self-respect. Self-respect goes beyond security. It is the "sense that one's plan of life is worth carrying out." Without a sense of self-respect, activities and choices in life may have little or no point. Self-respect, so conceived, is a necessary condition for the meaningfulness of a person's life activities. In the absence of self-respect, the choices that people make—their freedom—would be far less valuable. With self-respect, people's lives matter that much more to them. To support self-respect among civic equals, democratic societies must also support the particular cultural contexts that orient people's lives. Particular cultures constitute the context within which particular people can be self-respecting and exercise equal freedom, depending on their cultural upbringing.

The need to be reciprocally recognized fuels a democratic politics of cultural recognition.[15] A politics of cultural recognition connects self-respect and cultural identity. Charles Taylor argues that free individuals "can flourish only to the extent that [they] are recognized. Each consciousness seeks recognition in another, and this is not a sign of a lack of virtue."[16]

Why does the need for reciprocity require political recognition rather than toleration of all cultures that respect the freedom of individuals to pursue their own philosophies of life as long as they do no injustice to others?[17] Reciprocity may not be limited to being recognized politically as an "abstract" free and equal person with a shared general capacity to choose a good life consistently with the demands of justice. Reciprocal respect may depend on public recognition of the value of some cultural particularities that are not universally valued, such as the particular language, history, and customs that help constitute the context of choice for people who identify with that culture.[18]

All modern democratic societies contain multiple cultures within them. This is a straightforward sense in which democratic societies can be called multicultural. Some cultural identity groups come closer to providing a comprehensive context of choice for their members than others. Since minority cultural groups in a democratic society must compete with the dominant culture to provide a context of choice for their members, they find themselves at a disadvantage. The context of choice for their members is not the one favored by governmental institutions and practices. The democratic state protects the dominant culture, whether intentionally or not, through the language it uses, the education it accredits, the history it honors, and the holidays and other customs that it keeps. The state and the dominant public culture that it supports, both indirectly and directly, cannot be culturally neutral in this sense. Government conducts its business, public schools teach, and the mass media broadcast in the dominant language and in conformity with a culturally distinctive calendar. Family law conforms to the dominant culture. The civic associations with the highest social status favor people who identify with the dominant culture. Distance from the dominant culture also carries with it economic and educational disadvantages through no fault of the individuals whose cultural upbringing differs from the dominant one.

This is the context in which minority cultural groups make claims upon democratic governments that most theorists of culture support in the name of equal freedom, opportunity, and civic equality. (Later we will also consider demands made in the name of survival of the culture itself, which some theorists of culture also support.) To ensure equal respect for persons, democratic governments are asked to exempt cultural minorities from laws that impose disproportionate burdens on their cultural identities. The claim of Canadian Sikhs to be exempt from wearing the traditional hat of the Canadian Mounted Police so that they may wear their traditional turban at work is an example of this kind of demand, rooted in a distinctive cultural identity. While the Canadian Mounted Police exempted the Sikhs so that they might wear their turbans, the United States Air Force refused to exempt American Orthodox Jewish men from their uniform policy so that they might wear their yarmulkes (and the United States Supreme Court upheld the military's right to refuse).[19]

Other claims by minority cultural groups include asking for public support for their language alongside the dominant one in governmental institutions and schools, seeking state aid for their cultural institutions ranging from art museums to old age homes, seeking inclusion of their group's history, art, and literature in the public school curricula, and a host of other claims to acknowledge the equal civic standing and inclusion of their cultural identity in the larger democratic society.[20] What all of these claims tend to share is a call by (or on behalf of) cultural identity groups to be supported by the larger democracy not despite their cultural identity but on the basis of it.

Claims by members of cultural minorities for equal freedom and respect, taking into account rather than disregarding their cultural identities, need not be seen as threats to create culture wars. Some claims, as we shall see, can be justified by democratic principles. The claims still may be controversial, but controversy alone is no reason for minorities to shy away from making just claims or for democratic governments to pursue their promise of equal liberty and justice for all rather than for only those who identify with the dominant culture.

A CHALLENGING CASE

Many minorities that are commonly considered cultural, however, do not come close to fitting the ideal type of a comprehensive or encompassing culture. The Canadian Sikhs who sought exemption from wearing the official Mounties hat—and gained it through the defensible workings of democratic politics—integrate different cultures in their lives; they are far from a comprehensive cultural group. Theorists of culture differ in what groups count as cultural in the comprehensive sense. Indigenous peoples like the Pueblo in the United States, the Inuit in Canada, and the Maori in Australia are often considered cultural, but how close any single culture comes to being comprehensive, thereby constituting the identities of its members, needs to be subject to more questioning than it has yet received. A challenging case in point is Julia Martinez's attempt to gain a right to equal treatment from her Pueblo tribe and the United States government. The case raises the twin issues of where political sovereignty should rest, and wherever it rests, what its limits should be.

Julia Martinez lived at the Santa Clara Pueblo reservation almost all her life (with a brief absence to further her education). She married a Navajo man, and they raised their eight children as Pueblo, speaking Tewa (the traditional language) and practicing Pueblo religion and customs. Yet her children and those of other intermarrying Pueblo women—unlike those of intermarrying Pueblo men—were denied the full rights of the Pueblo, including residence as a matter of right, political rights such as voting, and sharing in the material benefits of Pueblo membership, such as using land and hunting and fishing rights.

The governor of the Pueblo claimed that respect for Pueblo cultural identity required deference to the authority of the group. This deference would allow imposing unequal membership rules on Pueblo women, just as deference to the authority of the United States government has allowed imposing unequal membership rules on women in the past. The fact that the Pueblo tribe denied equal protection for women was not under dispute. Pueblo women—but not Pueblo men—are denied membership if they intermarry; only women lose residency rights (for themselves and their children), voting rights, and rights to pass their tribal membership on to their children, along with related welfare benefits that are tied to tribal membership. Under dispute is whether a group right to preserve its culture takes precedence over equal protection of women in such a case.

Equal protection was explicitly included as a constitutional right of all members of Indian tribes under the Indian Civil Rights Act of 1968 (ICRA): "No Indian tribe in exercising powers of self-government shall . . . deny to any person within its jurisdiction the equal protection of its laws. . . ."[21] This is the constitutional right that Martinez sought to vindicate for herself and other Pueblo women. It is the right that the United States Supreme Court denied them, despite the fact that they are American as well as Pueblo citizens. The Pueblo tribe is not accorded *absolute* sovereignty by the Supreme Court, but it was accorded the sovereignty necessary to deny equal protection to half its members and to deny it undemocratically. Martinez lost her appeal for equal treatment because a majority of the Supreme Court defended the claim that sovereignty be ceded to undemocratic tribal authorities even if it means abrogating the equal freedom and civic equality of Pueblo women. Ironically, it was ultimately not the Pueblo tribe or a democratic majority in Congress (which had passed the ICRA) but the Supreme Court that prevented Pueblo women from vindicating their equal rights. In the name of sovereignty that had already been significantly limited for the sake of protecting the cultural majority in the United States, judicial deference was paid to denying equal protection of fully half of the cultural minority.

Why cede the Pueblo tribe the authority to abrogate the civic equality of its women members? The District Court concluded that "To abrogate tribal decisions, particularly in the delicate area of membership, *for whatever 'good' reasons*, is to destroy cultural identity under the guise of saving it."[22] The idea that requiring the Pueblo authorities to provide more equal protection to Pueblo women would destroy the cultural identities of the Pueblo is a particularly suspect argument in the context of a case brought by women to claim their civic equality as *Pueblo*. The District Court's conclusion is revealing of an illogical and dangerous way of thinking about the connection between culture and sovereignty. It supports absolute sovereignty for cultural groups and equates such sovereignty with preserving the cultural identity of members, even when many members favor changing the practices of their cultural group in the direction of more equal freedom and civic equality. How ironic that a court sworn to uphold a constitution that is committed to equal protection should deem that saving the cultural identity of Pueblo women—who are also United States citizens—requires those women to give up either their Pueblo identity or their constitutional claim to be treated as civic equals.

Respect for culture cannot mean deference to whatever the established authorities of that culture deem right. If the established authorities of American culture, whoever they may be, deem it right to discriminate against Catholics, it does not follow that anyone should defer to the authority. There may be reasons of prudence to put up with injustices, for example, when trying to resist injustice would likely be futile or counterproductive. If some discriminatory rules cannot be changed peacefully, then there may be prudent reasons to put up with them. But putting up with unjust rules should not be confused with respecting them as just or even legitimate. The Martinez case was not decided on grounds that the unjust membership rules could not be changed peacefully. It was decided out of deference to the sovereignty of the Pueblo tribal authorities. That deference should not be confused with respect for the members of the Pueblo tribe. In the Martinez case, deference to the Pueblo's tribal authorities meant not respecting Pueblo women's right to civic equality and their identification as the civic equals of Pueblo men.

What, then, becomes of the claims to political sovereignty made by cultural groups, whether they are minority or majority cultures, in multicultural democracies? Legitimate political authority needs to rest somewhere. Minority cultural identity groups have no less claim than majority groups to political sovereignty. But what degree of sovereignty should any group be granted, and by what standards may its sovereignty be limited? If legitimate political authority has limits, then pursuing the equal protection of women is a principled reason to limit sovereignty, whether the authority to be limited represents a majority or minority culture.

The call for group sovereignty often amounts to a license for the dominant members of a group to impose injustice on others, even (as in the Martinez case) on a majority of others.[23] Because cultural group sovereignty (again whether the group is a minority or majority culture) can conflict with respect for equal freedom and civic equality, a critical question of political ethics that arises in multicultural democracies is what limits should be placed on the sovereignty claims of cultural identity groups that are part of a larger democratic society. A corresponding question needs to be asked about the larger democracies themselves: What limits should be placed on their sovereignty out of respect for individual rights?

QUESTIONING CLAIMS OF SOVEREIGNTY

A cultural perspective goes awry at the start if it rests on the premise that a single culture encompasses the identity of the individuals who are its members. Questioning this premise leads to rejecting it. Rejecting it results in a far more qualified defense of cultural group claims and a correspondingly stronger defense of pursuing equal freedom and civic equality for individuals. This pursuit calls for qualifying the political sovereignty of groups, whether they represent minority or majority cultures, or a concatenation of cultures in a multicultural democracy.

At the extreme, the idea that a single cultural membership encompasses the identities of its members implies that individuals cannot think, act, or imagine beyond "their culture," which is singular, not multicultural. Maybe there is such a singular isolated culture in the world today, but it surely is the exception and not the norm, especially in contemporary democracies. It is therefore misleading to say "a culture" or "our culture" provides the necessary context for freedom and civic equality because it implies a singularity of cultural identity that largely does not exist.

Not only is a single encompassing culture unnecessary to have a context of choice within democracies today, it is undesirable because the claim that individuals cannot think beyond a single culture is threatening to individual freedom. Individuals do not need to depend on a single encompassing culture to enjoy their freedom. Julia Martinez could and should have been free to marry a Navajo man and remain a member of the Pueblo if only the United States Supreme Court or the Pueblo tribal counsel had let her. If the Pueblo are paradigmatic of encompassing cultures, then they undermine the ideal type. If the Pueblo are not paradigmatic but cultures like those found in Quebec or Puerto Rico are, then encompassing cultures are multicultural and they leave lots of room for their members to think, act, and imagine beyond their cultures.

The cultural argument can be modified in recognition that actual cultures do not conform to a comprehensive ideal type. Cultures may be more or less comprehensive in the contexts of choice they provide for people who identify with them. Should cultural groups then be granted sovereignty *to the extent* to which the culture is encompassing? If so, the rule would then be: The more comprehensive the culture, the greater its political sovereignty should be. This rule correlates political sovereignty with the degree of comprehensiveness. The rule is deeply problematic from any ethical perspective that takes equal freedom and civic equality seriously. The degree to which a cultural group is encompassing is not necessarily the degree to which it takes equal freedom and civic equality seriously. Yet it is taking freedom and equality more seriously that makes a group safer to exercise sovereignty. To defer to the sovereignty of groups to the degree that they encompass the identities of their members is to subordinate individuals to the dominant authorities in their culture, even if appealing beyond them is necessary to securing equal freedom and civic equality. "The more encompassing a culture, the more absolute the sovereignty of the group should be" is a rule that does not respect individuals. Cultural theorists like Kymlicka must reject this rule and therefore defend the idea that the sovereignty of minority and majority cultures alike should not be upheld at the expense of the civic equality of individuals.

The fact that Martinez wanted to marry someone outside her culture is an existence proof that cultures are not as comprehensive as many claim them to be. No culture has ever been shown to be so comprehensive as to preclude the possibility that some members can and will—using its resources—imagine beyond it. That the culture itself may inform such imagining does not make it comprehensive. There is no logical connection, moreover, between the degree of political sovereignty and the comprehensiveness of a culture. Sovereignty is power wielded over people. Just as absolute power corrupts absolutely, so does absolute sovereignty.

Many theorists of culture support the Supreme Court's decision in the Martinez case, but they are not thereby respecting persons in their cultural particularities. Respect for Julia Martinez and other Pueblo women in their cultural particularity requires recognizing that no single culture completely comprehends and constrains their thinking, imagining, and hoping. (All cultures combined may not completely comprehend individuals either, but that is another issue.) To say that cultures provide contexts for choice is not to say that any single culture or context is necessarily comprehensive. It is similarly misleading to say that cultures provide a sense of secure belonging. This is true for some but not for all or even most. Pueblo women who wanted to exercise their equal freedom to intermarry were deprived of their sense of secure cultural belonging. Their sense of secure belonging could be had only by abrogating their equal freedom and civic equality with men.

Theorists of culture defend democratic justice when they criticize restrictions of civic equality and equal freedom by democratic governments or majority cultures that try to repress minorities. When minority cultures and their claims to sovereignty are involved, however, some culturalists seem to think that respect for the "other" entails deference to such inequalities as long as they are supported by the cultural minority, as if such minorities were homogeneous wholes. Kymlicka is an important exception, but even he defends the Supreme Court in deferring to the Pueblo's denial of equal protection for women, on the grounds that any attempt from the "outside" to protect Pueblo women would be counterproductive and constitute an imposition of foreign culture.[24] It is hard to see how we say this or know that the imposition of constitutional law would be counterproductive when Pueblo women themselves were pleading with the Court to support their claim to equal protection, as legally enunciated in the ICRA.

Respect for persons entails not respecting tyranny by cultural majorities or minorities and not treating cultures as homogeneous wholes. Each individual is not encompassed by a single culture. Martinez clearly was not. This means that "outside" opposition to a particular cultural practice within a democratic context need not entail disrespect for those who identify with the culture. Did opposition to the Pueblo's unequal membership rules entail disrespect for Pueblo women? The contrary claim is far more credible: opposition entailed respect for Pueblo women as civic equals who should be given equal freedom and opportunity with Pueblo men. The lack of effective outside opposition to the unequal treatment of Pueblo women is far more plausibly attributable to indifference to the plight of Pueblo women than to respect for the Pueblo culture. Indifference to the unequal treatment of Pueblo women is the opposite of respect for them as persons.

Outside opposition to a discriminatory practice, especially when that opposition finds allies within a culture, demonstrates respect for members of the minority culture as fellow persons who can reciprocally recognize the basic freedom and civic equality of all persons, regardless of their gender, ethnicity, and nationality. The refusal by the larger democracy to support oppressive parts of a minority culture is therefore consistent with a commitment to supporting the self-respect of people who identify with that culture. The refusal of a minority culture to defer to oppressive claims of the larger democracy is similarly consistent with a commitment to defending the self-respect of its members. Only when sovereignty claims—whether on the part of majority or minority groups—are not permitted to supercede those of justice can the claims of freedom and civic equality be given their democratic due.

Equal freedom and civic equality are also fundamental to the arguments made by theorists of culture like Kymlicka and Taylor, who recognize that cultural rights should not take precedence over the basic rights of individuals.[25] Basic human rights do not include every right ever claimed as such but those necessary to respect individuals as civic equals, purposive agents with equal freedom to live their own lives as they see fit.[26] Kymlicka clearly agrees that basic rights include a women's right to civic equality, which was violated by unequal membership rules like those that denied American women the franchise prior to the Nineteenth Amendment (1920) and those that deny Pueblo women (but not men) the right to intermarry and remain members of the Pueblo culture. We all also need to recognize reasonable disagreement about the precise content of basic rights, and some of that disagreement is reflected in cultural differences as well as in differences within any culture. Yet when we think that a basic right is violated, we cannot consistently defer to the sovereignty of a group without making a mockery of the meaning of a basic right. We will be far less tempted to defer to the sovereignty of a group if we see that group sovereignty cannot be justified by the encompassing nature of cultural membership.

The assumption of the encompassing nature of cultural membership is so common that it is worth pausing to ask why we should not accept it. There are, of course, conspicuous examples of individuals whose identities draw upon many cultures, people like Salman Rushdie whose identities are deeply affected by the culture of their upbringing but by no means comprehensively constituted by a single culture.[27] Rushdie aptly called his *Satanic Verses* a "love-song to our mongrel selves." Even if Rushdie is the exception that proves the rule, such exceptions illustrate another rule: individuals are capable of thinking and imagining creatively beyond a single culture, and some do so even at great peril to their lives.

Exceptions to the rule of cultural comprehensiveness are far more common than the Rushdie example would suggest. Amartya Sen, himself an exception to the idea that single cultures comprehend all individuals, calls our attention to the equally compelling example of Cornelia Sorabji, who immigrated in the 1880s from India to England and described herself as feeling at home in England as a Parsi Christian woman lawyer and barrister-at-law who wore a sari, fought for women's rights, supported the British Raj against Gandhi, and taught at an exclusively men's college. As Sen writes:

> Sorabji chose her plural identities under the influence of her background, but through her own decisions and priorities. In making her own choices she was not unique, despite the spectacular uniqueness of her chosen combination of identities.[28]

Sorabji's cultivation of multiple cultural identities permitted her to feel more rather than less at home in England, despite the fact that it was not her homeland.

Many people exemplify the noncomprehensive nature of cultures. The Muslim adolescent girls in France who went to public schools wearing their headscarves were combining cultures in a way that would be impossible if any one of the cultures were comprehensive.[29] The Israeli Ultra-Orthodox women who demand to be taught the Torah also illustrate the openness of even supposedly closed contemporary cultures as they are experienced in democratic contexts.[30] Pueblo women who demand equal protection do not have only a single cultural identity, nor are they bound to imagining only what the combination of their cultures would suggest is possible.

Another irony of deferring to the Pueblo out of respect for a minority culture is that the very law that Martinez challenged, a 1939 amendment to the 1935 tribal constitution of the Pueblo, did not represent the Pueblo tradition.[31] The law required approval by the United States Secretary of the Interior. Prior to 1939, intermarrying Santa Clara women were admitted to the tribe, as were intermarrying men, on an individual case-by-case determination.[32] Writing in dissent in the *Martinez* case, Justice White suggests how the Supreme Court could have justifiably upheld Martinez's constitutional right without substituting its own judgment of the precise course of action the tribe should take to vindicate the right: "The federal district court's duty would be limited to determining whether the challenged tribal action violated one of the enumerated rights [of the ICRA]. If found to be in violation, the action would be invalidated; if not, it would be allowed to stand. In no event would the court be authorized, as in a *de novo* proceeding, to substitute its judgment concerning the wisdom of the action taken for that of the tribal authorities."[33]

What if the law in question in the Martinez case had been exclusively Pueblo in origin? It would be no more credible to claim that the identities of members of a minority cultural group like the Pueblo are insulated from "foreign" cultural influences, television being only the most obvious, which can partly constitute their identities as much as can their "native" cultures. Had the United States Supreme Court done its best to peacefully, lawfully, and constitutionally protect the civic equality of Pueblo women, it would not have been intruding into an encompassing culture. It would have been helping Pueblo women to vindicate their equal freedom and civic equality as individuals and Pueblo and American citizens.

If the identity of individuals is more than any single culture comprehends, then the sovereign authority of a group cannot be based on the assumption of a one-to-one correspondence between its cultural group identity and that of its members. There still may be good reasons why the Pueblo should be a self-governing group within the United States, with (nonabsolute) sovereign authority over those people who remain within the group. But an argument justifying any group's sovereignty should not be based on the false assumption that the group constitutes an encompassing cultural identity of its members.

DANGERS OF NATIONALISM WRIT LARGE AND SMALL

A history of broken treaties and atrocities suffered at the hands of the United States government supports a large degree of sovereign authority for Native American tribes—like other indigenous groups that have suffered egregious injustices—to protect their members against oppression and their culture against illegitimate intrusions. The political authority of a group, however, does not justify the oppression of individuals within the group when peaceful, legally legitimate ways of protecting basic rights are available. Nationalism, whether writ large or small, does not justify absolute authority or the violation of basic rights of individuals. Conversely, to limit the power of nations does not deny national groups self-governing authority. It denies them absolute authority, which no nation should have over individuals. The authority of legitimate governments is therefore limited, and one legitimate limit is the "extension of constitutional rights to individual citizens." As Justice White wrote in the *Martinez* case, this extension "is *intended* to intrude upon the authority of government."[34]

Intruding on the authority of government in the name of protecting individual rights applies far more extensively than we have yet discussed to nations writ large and small. An important concern of cultural theorists like Kymlicka is that, in the name of protecting individual rights, members of a dominant culture are willing to authorize intrusions in minority cultures but not in their own culture or sovereign government. The sovereign authority of all groups—small and large nations alike—must be constrained in order to protect the civic equality and other basic rights of persons. Neither minority nor majority cultural groups can justifiably claim such unconstrained sovereign authority as to systematically violate the basic rights of individuals. Nations writ large and small therefore should constrain themselves, or otherwise be constrained in prudent ways, to protect basic rights.[35]

All democrats can consistently defend constraints on the sovereign authority of small and large states alike in the name of protecting some basic rights. How best to put such constraints into practice is an increasingly important question for political scientists. Practical politics is often a matter of picking the least bad alternative and not letting the utopian best be the enemy of the good. We therefore might ask whether there is a better alternative, for example, to creating an International Criminal Court (ICC) that could bring charges and try people for crimes against humanity. The ICC, if ratified, would become the world's first standing court with "jurisdiction [to try individuals for] the most heinous abuses that result from international conflict, such as war crimes, crimes against humanity and genocide."[36] It is reasonable to oppose the ICC on grounds that there is a better available alternative—in which case the opponents need to say what it is.

A great deal of opposition to the ICC treaty, however, is couched in terms of a violation of the principle of national sovereignty, as if national sovereignty is an unqualified principle of political morality, which it is not. The idea of nationhood—whether writ large or small—should not entail the absolute authority to violate basic rights.

The empirical question always arises in politics as to whether there can be an effective institutional alternative to what now exists, with all its imperfections. The answer to this question, when directed toward the conflict between group sovereignty and basic individual rights, does not rest in a sovereign right of comprehensive cultural groups, whether or not we call them nations, to determine what individual rights should be recognized and respected as such. Such a right to sovereignty would beg the question rather than answer it. More troubling still, assuming a right to absolute sovereignty unnecessarily threatens the basic rights of individuals. This threat is both unnecessary and unjustifiable whenever an institutional alternative exists or could be created to help vindicate the basic rights of individuals. No society has yet fully vindicated these rights, which are also subject to reasonable disagreement. But the existence of reasonable disagreement should not be an excuse for the failure to urge vindication of those basic rights that one recognizes as such. Moral perspectives of democracy are aspirational but not therefore utopian.

There are also times when we can recognize human rights violations but do nothing about them—or when doing something beyond criticizing the violations would be worse than doing nothing. Imposing basic rights from outside a group when no one in the group is mobilized to defend those rights often can be a recipe for failure. We therefore should recognize when attempts to impose individual rights are problematic and counterproductive. In his defense of national sovereignty, Kymlicka writes: "In the end, liberal institutions can only really work if liberal beliefs have been internalized by the members of the self-governing society, be it an independent country or a national minority."[37] Liberal democrats like Kymlicka can and should emphasize that autocracies and theocracies are not "self-governing societies" in the democratic sense of the term. To call an undemocratic theocracy, for example, a self-governing society is misleading in that it implies that all members are equal citizens, which they are not.

Strictures against imposing basic rights on a self-governing society should not trade on the idea that there is a democratic will against the acceptance of basic rights in autocratically governed societies that deny their members rights as basic as equal citizenship. In politically sovereign groups where people are not treated as civic equals with equal freedom, the internal resistance to basic rights cannot be considered the free will of the people. Autocratic governments block the formation of a free popular will by refusing to protect rights such as free political speech and religious freedom. If nothing can be done from the outside that makes things better, we should at least not make a virtue out of a necessity by calling a group of people who are autocratically governed and denied equal citizenship "self-governing." They are not self-governing in any remotely democratic sense of the term.

Unlike the extreme case in which there is no internalization of support for equal citizenship within a national group, there obviously was support for equal protection among Pueblo women. Martinez and other Pueblo women went to considerable lengths to bring suit against their patriarchal tribe. Their claims were effectively resisted by the all-male tribal authorities with the aid of the all-male Supreme Court, which granted the tribal authorities absolute sovereignty over determining these undeniable rights of Pueblo women. Martinez lost her case in the Supreme Court not because anyone denied her principled right to equal protection but because those who were capable of granting it subordinated it to the sovereignty of the group, thereby refusing even to try to vindicate the equal rights of Pueblo women. As we have seen, it is misleading to say that the cultural identity of Pueblo women requires them to have fewer basic rights. Political authorities have required them to have fewer rights, and nationalist claims to absolute sovereignty often support such authorities to the detriment of the equal freedom and civic equality of individuals whose identities are not encompassed by their national groups.

A GROUP RIGHT TO CULTURE?

Cultural groups make many kinds of claims in democratic societies. Among the most defensible are claims to be exempt from laws or policies that impose unfair burdens on their members and claims for special aid to overcome unfair disadvantages faced by their members. Among the most problematic are claims to enforce laws that violate the basic rights that would otherwise be guaranteed by the larger democracy.[38] Some critics resist all claims that are couched in terms of a right to culture because they oppose group rights as such. Individuals, not groups, are the ultimate moral claimants in a democracy, but this is consistent with taking culture into account in considering the moral claims of individuals and groups that speak on their behalf.

When considering the fairness of laws and public policies vis-à-vis members of cultural minority groups, culture needs to be taken into account. If there is a right to culture, on democratic grounds, it must be an individual right to shape one's own identity, partly through cultural affiliations. Some cultural affiliations are inherited and affirmed over time. These affiliations can be considered politically free as long as they are not imposed on adults by political (or quasipolitical) authorities. (A quasipolitical authority is any group that exercises the equivalent of political power over its members who are not genuinely free to leave the group.) Other cultural affiliations are not inherited at all but chosen despite one's inheritance or as a consequence of rebelling against one's inheritance. There are also cultural affiliations in both categories—the inherited and the newly adopted—that are not simply found out there in the world but are the product of the creative agencies of individuals.

The challenge for a multicultural democracy is not to be culture-blind but to be fair to all individuals, whatever their cultural inheritance. Fairness, in turn, favors democratic support of cultural practices that are compatible with respect for individuals while rejecting those practices that are not. Fairness does not claim to be a culturally neutral standard, but neither is fairness specific to any single culture (or fully realized by any culture). Many cultural groups in democratic societies couch their claims in terms of fairness.

Claims based on fairness—such as the claim to be treated as a civic equal—need not be individualistic. People who are treated as civic equals share this status with their fellow citizens. Fairness, therefore, supports claims that are "shared with and pertain to us as members of the community."[39] Civic equality is such a claim. It is a right that can only be jointly held by individuals; it cannot be held by any individual in isolation (because the very content of the right is to be treated as a *civic* equal). The right presupposes the inclusion of individuals in groups, but the intended beneficiary and ultimate claimant of the right is the individual, not the group.

Although civic equality can only obtain in a group, it is fully consistent with the fundamental moral standing of individuals. Groups that support the moral standing of individuals also have moral standing insofar as they serve to support individuals. A democratic perspective refuses to give fundamental moral standing to a group *qua* group.[40] Why? Because once we treat a cultural group as having fundamental moral standing, we are logically led to subordinate the claims of individuals to the morally fundamental group. If the group has fundamental moral standing, then individuals as civic equals do not. They are subordinated to the group. When we give the group basic moral standing, we are led down a road to repression:

> [We must] discover whose voice we should treat as the authentic or authoritative voice of the group. Once we have discovered that voice, other voices that express dissenting views will be of no account; if the relevant moral standing lies with the group qua group and with no-one else, it is only to the single authoritative voice of the group that we should respond.[41]

When democratic states respect authoritative voices for each cultural group, which typically are internally undemocratic, they then authorize groups (and *a fortiori* themselves) to violate the basic rights of individuals that are subordinated to the group's undemocratic and antihumanist authority.

Group rights to culture that subordinate the basic rights of individuals to the group are what give rise to the greatest conflicts between defenders of individual rights, on the one hand, and defenders of group rights, on the other. Kymlicka stands as a defender of individual rights in this argument. The most compelling defenders of a group right to culture that subordinates individual rights are Moshe Halbertal and Avishai Margalit when they argue that a "right to culture" obligates democratic states to support cultural groups that violate basic individual rights. As they put it:

> Protecting cultures out of the human right to culture may take the
> form of an obligation to support cultures that flout the rights of
> the individual in a liberal society.[42]

Halbertal and Margalit do not contest any of the rights that I have defended as democratic. Instead their argument tries to justify subordinating all individual rights but one (a right to exit) to a group right to culture. They argue that a democracy must *as a matter of obligation* protect cultures even at the expense of protecting the basic rights of persons.

Since Halbertal and Margalit present the strongest case in favor of elevating claims of cultural groups into group rights that take precedence over basic individual rights, it is worth looking more carefully at their central arguments. They argue that democracies not only may but *must* support cultures in their midst that violate the rights of women to be treated as the civic equals of men. To their credit, in support of their argument Halbertal and Margalit offer an example that presents a formidable challenge to it, direct state subsidies of the schools of Ultra-Orthodox Jewish groups in Israel and state enforcement of Orthodox Judaism's marital, inheritance, and other family laws that discriminate against women. Halbertal and Margalit would be among the first to recognize that many Ultra-Orthodox and Orthodox Jewish groups in Israel discriminate against women in their schooling, family law, and many other practices, discrimination that the state actively sponsors, subsidizes, and enforces.

How do they defend these state-supported discriminations? They argue that the democratic state may protect one and only one basic right against claims of cultural groups: the right of individuals to exit cultural groups. This, and only this individual right is inalienable on their argument. Every other right of individuals becomes subordinate to the cultural group's right to culture. As we anticipated above, individual rights (with the exception of the right to exit) become subordinated to the group right to culture. Because of the group right to culture, the state becomes obligated to support this right and therefore to subordinate individuals to the group right to culture, preserving only an individual right to exit the group.

What, we should ask, is the moral basis of the obligation of a democratic state to support cultural claims that flout individual rights? The implied basis, ironically enough, is a liberal argument from individual informed consent. When people fail to exit a group, they must be assumed to consent to its practices, including practices that deprive them of rights as basic as equal freedom or civic equality. Members of cultural groups are assumed to have consensually abrogated all of their other basic rights by not exiting a group that flouts these rights. One right—and one right only—is inalienable, for reasons Halbertal and Margalit do not provide.

What is the strongest defense of only one inalienable right of exit? The strongest defense would be that informed consent by individuals—as evidenced by the failure to exit a cultural group—justifies the violation by cultural groups of all individual rights except the right of exit. If consent justifies all rights violations, then it can follow that democratic states are obligated to support the rights violators, *provided the groups have the consent of all their members*. This proviso—consent to the group by all its members—is critical to arriving at the conclusion: All persons must have a truly effective right to exit their cultural group for the group to have a right to violate their rights. A formal right to exit alone, as Ayelet Shachar shows, "throws upon the already beleaguered individual the responsibility to either miraculously transform the legal-institutional conditions that keep her vulnerable or to find the resources to leave her whole world behind."[43]

Can theorists of culture consistently defend the right to exit as the *only* inalienable right? If they cannot, then the right to culture is far more constrained by individual rights than Halbertal and Margalit claim it to be. The best basis for defending a right of exit is to ensure individual informed consent to a cultural group that violates basic rights. If this is the moral foundation for an inalienable right to exit, then it follows that a democratic society needs to defend the conditions that make a right to exit effective and not only a formal right. If the right to exit were merely formal (no guards at the gate), then it could hardly be defended as the one and only individual right.

Surely it cannot be enough for a democratic state to say that by law, anyone is able to exit any group (including the state itself). For informed consent to cultural group membership to be real, at minimum, states would need to ensure that all children receive an education that enables them to exercise informed consent about membership in any given cultural group, which means being exposed to alternatives and taught the skills of critical thinking about them. This is one of the strongest arguments for a child's right to an education that is not exclusively controlled by a single cultural group. If the education of children is exclusively controlled by a single cultural group that aims to make their entire upbringing as encompassed by one group as possible, then it surely cannot be said that their democracy has afforded them an effective right later in life to exit this cultural group.[44] If informed consent by members is the justification for state subsidies of cultural groups, then the democratic state, at minimum, needs to ensure that children are educated to understand and then actually have viable alternatives to remaining within even the most encompassing cultural communities.

Informed consent is a rigorous standard and probably not a viable one for membership in many cultural groups. That doesn't mean that membership in these groups is unjustified, but it does mean that violation of individual rights by groups cannot be justified on the basis of informed consent. The absence of internal dissent or exit from a cultural group that systematically violates the basic rights of its members—with state support—certainly cannot be taken as a sign of informed consent. When a state cedes to dominant members of a group the political authority to control the schooling of children, marital, and family law, it denies the effective right of exit to the most vulnerable members of the group. The more encompassing a group is that flouts basic rights, the less effective is the freedom of its most vulnerable members to leave it.

Informed consent therefore cannot be inferred from the failure of vulnerable individuals to leave more encompassing cultural groups, or democratic societies themselves, which often fail to secure the civic equality, equal freedom, and other basic rights of their most vulnerable citizens. Vulnerable citizens who remain within democratic societies or cultural groups within democracies cannot be said to consent to the denial of their basic rights by the group. This is an important reason why the denial of basic rights is not justified simply because people remain within a democracy or within a rights-violating cultural group that claims consent by its members to alienating the rights that otherwise would be the obligation of that democratic society to protect.

It is both a mistake and a sign of disrespect to infer the consent of individuals from their failure to leave a group that denies them their basic rights. To see why, we need only consider what happened to a group of Orthodox and Conservative Jewish women who peacefully marched to the Western Wall in Jerusalem in 1989, holding a Torah. They were determined to pray there as men freely do, only without the male leadership or approval that the Orthodox rabbinate, with the force of law behind it, requires. The "Women of the Wall" were violently attacked by defenders of the Orthodox Jewish establishment in Israel. The reaction to their peaceful march in support of their basic liberty shows what uncommon courage it takes to dissent from cultural group practices that are supported by the state.

When dissent takes uncommon courage, its absence cannot be considered consent. The Women of the Wall risked their own safety in publicly demonstrating against state-sanctioned discrimination. The failure to exercise internal dissent or to exit a discriminatory group cannot be taken as consent when dissent carries with it such risks, and exiting the group entails great sacrifice of oneself and the welfare of one's family. Many vulnerable individuals—such as the "Women of the Wall" and Julia Martinez—reasonably would rather improve their position within their culture than give up their cultural membership.

The claim that someone's overriding interest is to subordinate herself to others is not one that anyone can make authoritatively in democratic politics on behalf of another person.[45] To treat a woman as the civic equal of her male counterpart therefore means that she and only she must have the right to make this claim—or to deny it—authoritatively. But for a woman to have the authority to make this claim in her own voice, she must have the effective freedom of exiting a group that flouts her basic rights. There is no democratic obligation to support cultural authorities that make claims on behalf of other people while depriving them of the conditions of civic equality and equal freedom. Quite the contrary, there is a democratic obligation to deny group rights to cultures that are incompatible with civic equality.

To defend a right to exit from cultural groups is implicitly to acknowledge the value of individual informed consent and respect for persons. We cannot consistently acknowledge this value and then subordinate individuals to cultural groups that deprive them of the necessary conditions for making the right to exit effective. For any authority to know that any person wants to be subordinated within a cultural group, every person must have the basic freedom and opportunity to decide the kind of life she wants to live within the range that a democratic society can make possible to all of its members.[46] Democratic states may regretfully tolerate oppression of individuals by a cultural group when political intervention would make matters worse, but a pragmatic argument of this contingent, contextual type is completely different from recognizing an obligation on the part of a democratic state to support cultural groups at the expense of violating the basic rights of some of their members.

At least as troubling are the ways in which group rights of this sort can threaten the basic rights of outsiders to the group. Supposedly self-contained cultural groups adversely affect the rights of people who are not members (and cannot become members) of the group. The internal dynamic of these cultural groups is rarely if ever conducive to democratic justice for outsiders to the groups. Even if the claims to political authority of the Ultra-Orthodox Jewish community in Israel could be justified to all of its own members, its effects on nonmembers would still need to be taken into account. The politics of cultural minorities rarely can be isolated from a broader politics, which often profoundly affects the basic rights of others, as the politics of Ultra-Orthodox Israelis affects Palestinians, Israeli Arabs, and non-Orthodox Israeli Jews.

Cultural groups within democratic societies are an interdependent part of the larger society and world. Most depend heavily on governmental support for education, commerce, police protection, national security, and more. Their own politics, in turn, affects the civic equality and freedom of both children and outsiders to the group. Even quite segregated groups influence the larger politics of democratic societies and are also often very dependent on the larger society to support their distinctive cultures. This is not an argument against the political influence or the dependency of cultural minorities on a larger society. Quite the contrary, it is an argument for recognizing that cul-

tural minority groups are influential and interdependent parts of democratic politics and therefore an argument for not treating their political claims as if they significantly affected only the members of a single
group.

DELIBERATING ABOUT DIFFERENCES
AND DEFENDING CIVIC EQUALITY

Does opposition to cultural group practices by outsiders show disrespect for the people who willingly engage in those practices? Richard
Shweder charges critics of unfamiliar cultural group practices, especially liberal feminists who criticize female genital mutilation (FGM),
with disrespecting the people who defend and engage in these practices. He charges liberal feminists with having a "moral yuck response"
to all the various kinds of surgeries that he says are tellingly lumped
together under the label of FGM.[47] According to Shweder, this critical
response of liberal feminists flies in the face of the very respect for
persons that allegedly informs a liberal defense of individual rights.[48]

Since not all cultural practices are morally equivalent, the critique
needs to be evaluated as it is specifically directed to critics of FGM.
Either to criticize or to praise all foreign cultural practices would be
untenable. Even if not all female genital surgeries, as Shweder emphasizes, are appropriately called mutilations, at least two kinds of surgeries performed on adolescent girls are appropriately so called. Infibulation and clitoridectomy inflict irreversible injury, and they are
performed on adolescent girls without informed consent. Infibulation
entails excision of the clitoris and labia minora (the totality of the
external genitalia), followed by paring and stitching of the labia ma-
jora. Clitoridectomy entails removal of the clitoris. Both kinds of surgeries, even if performed in the safest and least painful way possible,
which they are often not, are likely to cause substantial pain later in
life and (in all likelihood) irreversibly decrease a woman's capacity for
sexual pleasure. A sympathetic analyst of the data reports: "From the
available evidence we can say that clitoridectomy is mainly associated
with an increased risk of bleeding and infection, whereas the complications of infibulation are both more dangerous and more frequent,

and include serious bleeding, infections, urinary problems, and complications of labor, delivery, and infertility."[49]

The incidence of these surgeries is greatest in countries such as Sudan, Somalia, Egypt, Ethiopia, and Kenya, where access to reliable data is limited, making good scientific studies scarce. There is a lot we do not know, but what the most reliable reports recognize is that these surgeries on adolescent girls are undertaken not for reasons of health or because they are religiously prescribed (Islam does not prescribe the surgery and non-Islamic groups also engage in it) but rather, because the surgeries are "thought to be crucial to the definition of a beautiful feminine body, the marriageability of daughters, the balance of sexual desire between the sexes, or the sense of value and identity that comes from following the traditions of the group."[50] Whatever the historical origins of the surgeries, many women today still accept them, and many other women, including some members of the very same cultures, oppose the practices as harmful, inhumane, and manifestations of sexual discrimination against women.

When parents who support these surgeries immigrate with their children to a society in which the surgery is illegal and widely considered appalling, the question arises: Does opposition to legalizing these surgeries in democratic contexts by outsiders to the immigrant cultures express disrespect for the parents or the adolescent girls who support them? It must be possible to express respect for people while opposing the legalization of some of their preferred cultural practices. Were this impossible, democratic citizens could not oppose some of their own cultural practices without disrespecting their friends and fellow citizens who defend these very same practices. Public disagreement of this sort is central to democratic politics and consistent with mutual respect among citizens.[51]

Opposition to an oppressive cultural practice may even show more respect for vulnerable persons than indifference to how they are treated within their culture.[52] Considering how dangerous dissent often is for vulnerable people, opposition by outsiders may help open the door to internal dissent by giving potential dissenters powerful allies to their cause. It takes extraordinarily uncommon courage (and probably also foresight) on the part of adolescent girls to oppose clitoridectomy or infibulation in the face of education and socialization to the contrary, especially if they have been led to believe that deviations from cultural norms lead to ostracism from the culture. Under such circumstances, outside allies may make internal opposition a bit easier.

Even when many vulnerable members of a culture do not ally with external critics, outside criticism of oppressive practices can demonstrate respect for the potential of persons to live together as civic equals rather than in a way that subordinates the freedom of some individuals (in this case women) to others (men). The women who want to be treated as civic equals also see that they have an option outside the group if they cannot change its cultural practices. This option increases their freedom to identify as they wish rather than as the dominant members of a cultural group insist. External criticism can make the right of individuals to exit more effective than it otherwise would be. Criticism of civic inequality and unequal freedom is also a first step toward vindicating these basic rights.

External criticism is not without serious risks. One risk is getting the issues wrong, and another is being correct but counterproductive. The risk of misdirected criticism is of course ever present, but something particularly troubling occurs when critics accept similarly problematic practices in their own cultures that they subject to brutal criticism when practiced by others. Misdirected criticism of this sort is often difficult to identify because of disagreements about what constitutes a similarly problematic practice. A now classic controversy that illustrates this risk is the "Affair of the Scarf" in France. In 1989, three Muslim adolescent girls went to their local public high school in Creil wearing chadors. French public schools are secular by law and centuries-long tradition. The relevant law in this controversy dated back to 1937 and prohibited the wearing of religious symbols in government-run schools. Yet the law was honored in the breach when "inconspicuous" religious symbols were permitted; crucifixes and yarmulkes were treated as inconspicuous but chadors were not. Even if chadors are more conspicuous in this cultural context, does this justify prohibiting them and not crucifixes and yarmulkes?

While some citizens wanted to prohibit chadors as a protest against the immigration of Muslims into France, many liberals protested the sexist symbolism of the chador, as undermining of the gender equality that public schools should (and presumably could) teach all students.

Liberals were acrimoniously divided between prohibiting the chador and permitting it on grounds that religious symbolism differs in social context. The willingness of Muslim girls and their parents to be educated in public schools itself could be taken as a sign of cultural change, as would be the willingness of the schools to educate the girls wearing the chadors as the equals of chadorless girls and boys. I refer here to this controversy, which still goes on in France, not to resolve it but rather to illustrate how hard it can be to draw the appropriate comparisons between different cultural practices in a fair-minded way. Democratic deliberation over such controversies should prominently include the people whose cultural practices are being criticized and threatened with exclusion. In the absence of culturally impartial spectators to adjudicate such controversies, the presence of people who represent all the relevant cultural differences is particularly important.[53]

When engaging in criticism of foreign cultures, we can also easily underestimate the risk of being counterproductive. Some critics who argued for excluding the chadors from French public schools assumed that the Muslim girls would then come to school without them rather than be subject by their parents to more sexist schooling. Even when critics intend to be respectful, their criticism may be viewed by those who are its targets as precisely the reverse of respectful—as demeaning them and their culture. The greater the cultural distance between the critics and those whose cultural preferences they are opposing, the greater the risk of this conflict between the intended and the perceived message.

Anne Fadiman tells a tragic and poignantly true story of such a disconnect in *The Spirit Catches You and You Fall Down*.[54] An emigrant family of Hmong from Laos, who did not speak English, tried to care for their epileptic child, Lia Lee, according to their own cultural understandings, which conflicted at almost every critical turn with what the American doctors thought would be medically best for their child.

When the parents' understandings collide with the physicians' prescriptions, Lia's medical condition deteriorates. Both the parents and the doctors are well intentioned. The doctors are far from perfect in their medical prescriptions and even more fallible in their assessment of what would enable Lia's life to improve, all things considered. Still, the doctors are competent by any reasonable standards, and they are dedicated beyond the call of duty. They treat Lia at no profit and considerable emotional distress to themselves. The Lees are extraordinarily loving parents and also do everything in their power to help Lia. In stark contrast to and conflict with the doctors, however, they believe—among other things—that epilepsy is not a disease but a divine inspiration. The parents and the doctors devote extraordinary time and care to trying to help Lia. Both often make matters worse because there is so little trust—or the basis for developing it—between them. At issue is the very notion of what it would mean to help Lia. Their views are not complementary but conflicting, and it is hard even to conceive of how they could be made sufficiently complementary in the short run to overcome the many misunderstandings that resulted in tragedy. (The doctors could have depended more on a translator, but translation alone would not have been enough to bridge the cultural divide.)

This kind of tragedy may be inevitable under circumstances in which the communication between cultures is so poor. (Lia dies after a series of traumatic episodes.) From a long train of oppressive experiences before the Lees immigrated to the United States, they learned the advantages of being fiercely independent and not trusting others. They held firm to a religion that views epilepsy as a kind of divine spirit, a common view across many cultures until quite recently in human history. In summary, we see that the deepest cultural commitments of the parents and the doctors had little overlap, and the difficulty of communicating across this cultural divide is about as great as it gets in democracies today. When confronted with extreme cultural conflicts, as between viewing epilepsy as a disease versus as a divine spirit, the opposing cultural perspectives may have appeared encompassing of the individuals who held them. Yet even in this context, the cultures turn out not to be all-encompassing. The Lees and the doctors learn a lot from one another, and both change quite dramatically as the narrative progresses but not enough to bridge what becomes a tragic divide.

When critics have had no close relationship with the people whose cultural practices they are opposing, criticism is almost bound to be resented. In Lia's case, she desperately needed lifesaving medical treatment that her parents could administer in a way that they could understand and accept. The only way to avoid tragic misunderstanding would have been through far greater mutual understanding than was possible by a strictly professional relationship or by people insisting upon their basic rights. Suppose that mainstream critics of Hmong medical practices are scientifically correct in their criticisms. They are also exercising a right to free speech in criticizing the Hmong medical practices. But as Fadiman's account of Lia vividly illustrates, such criticisms turn out to be sorely inadequate to what is at stake—and often even beside the point of how to help well-intentioned people like Lia's parents cope with her disease. Stories of cultural conflict situated within a single democratic society raise the question of whether it is possible to oppose cultural practices that are foreign to your own while respecting (and not harming) people who are just as committed to engaging in those practices as you are to opposing them.

Is there any way of expressing respect across cultural divides while opposing cultural practices that one reasonably thinks violate the civic equality or equal freedom of individuals? One potentially productive way is illustrated by the reaction of a group of Seattle doctors, who in 1996 were confronted with some recent Somali immigrant parents requesting that the doctors perform clitoridectomies on their adolescent daughters. The doctors declined to perform clitoridectomies, but they did not leave their response at that. When the parents made clear their resolve to find some other way of initiating their daughters into their culture, the doctors deliberated with the parents and daughters, consulted with their hospital's board, and arrived at an alternative to clitoridectomy. They proposed to perform a kind of female circumcision—one that does not entail removing any clitoral tissue—on the adolescent daughters with the informed consent of both the parents and daughters. (Notice that the doctors treated informed consent not as a sufficient standard, but as a necessary one.)

The counterproposal was that the surgeon would make a small incision on the clitoral hood under anesthesia. The operation was proposed only with the knowledge that it could be performed as safely as the standard American male circumcision and probably less painfully. The proposal was explicitly recommended as a way of accommodating a group of Somali immigrant parents and their daughters while avoiding the physically impairing kinds of genital surgeries—such as infibulation and clitoridectomy—that have painful after-effects and that the parents otherwise wanted to have performed on their daughters, if necessary, outside the country.

Many people who accept the legality of male circumcision in the United States opposed the Seattle proposal as vehemently as they oppose clitoridectomy and infibulation. They therefore threatened to drag the Seattle hospital into court if it proceeded with the proposal.[55] The opponents to the proposal suggested that even the small incision could be seen as a way of symbolizing the subordination of women in Somali and American culture. One problem with this argument is that so can many kinds of cosmetic surgeries that are legally performed on adolescent American girls with their parents' approval be seen as symbolizing the subordination of women in more mainstream American culture as well as subjecting adolescent girls to the pain and dangers of surgery.[56] The opponents of the Seattle proposal accept the legality of these kinds of cosmetic surgeries; they do not threaten to bring hospitals, doctors, or parents to court who routinely perform these mainstream surgeries. Moreover, the proposed surgery probably symbolized something quite different to the individuals who are most directly affected by it. To oppose legalization of an otherwise safe and harmless cosmetic surgery on symbolic grounds alone is a weak position for a defender of free and equal personhood to take.

The female circumcision that was proposed by the Seattle hospital would have been safer and less painful than many cosmetic surgeries. More important, like male circumcision, but unlike infibulation and clitoridectomy, the surgery cannot credibly be considered a violation of a basic right, since it is not painful and does nothing to impair sexual functioning. If it is reasonable to think that adolescent girls can consent to belly button, tongue, nose, and ear rings, it is no less reasonable to think they can consent to this surgery. And there is no more reason to think that consent is a sufficient standard by which to judge its justification. The lack of physical impairment is another necessary condition.

The right to oppose cultural practices that violate basic rights is as fundamental as any right within a democracy. Indeed, this right may even be considered an (unenforceable) obligation of citizens. But when citizens selectively oppose unfamiliar cultural practices that are as compatible with free and equal personhood as other familiar cultural practices (whose legality is well-entrenched), they reinforce the unfortunate tendency of democratic governments to limit the basic liberties of members of cultural minorities more than those of members of mainstream cultures. This tendency also exacerbates civic inequality.

One way that democratic societies can help counteract this common tendency is to create more forums—modeled on the most successful institutional review boards in hospitals—with professional and lay representatives of minority and majority cultures on them who deliberate with one another about controversial cases. Such deliberation encourages individuals with different cultural perspectives to exchange their views, expand their understandings, and therefore arrive at a more broadly informed collective decision. Deliberation does not promise agreement; but even continuing disagreement is good for a democratic society to the extent that it reflects more mutual understanding than would otherwise exist and affords citizens a chance to demonstrate their mutual respect across cultural divides as they continue to disagree, as free people invariably will.[57]

Deliberative forums are also valuable when their members search for significant points of convergence between different cultural perspectives on what cultural practices are and are not legally defensible. The practice of economizing on our moral disagreements is possible, it is worth emphasizing, only if two complementary conditions hold. The first, which theorists of culture often overlook, is that cultural group identities do not completely encompass individual identities. The second, often overlooked by liberals, is that the protection of civic equality and equal liberty and opportunity does not completely encompass democratic politics. A conception of democratic politics must leave moral room for reasonable disagreement and for treating controversies that are within the realm of reasonable disagreement differently from those that threaten basic human rights.

The many practices subsumed under the term FGM provide an important case in point for distinguishing among different cultural practices, both theoretically and practically speaking. From any perspective that defends human rights, the legalization of infibulation and clitoridectomy should be opposed on grounds that these surgeries impose irreversible physical harm on girls. At the same time, and for completely consistent reasons, the legalization of the surgery proposed by the Seattle hospital can be defended, even if (like male circumcision and an assortment of body piercing) it is not recommended by some who defend its legality. The risk of disrespect in opposing valued cultural practices can be avoided—or at least lessened—when democratic societies, and the citizens who support them, demonstrate a willingness to accommodate controversial practices of minority cultures on the same terms as they accommodate comparable practices of more mainstream cultures that do not violate human rights.

To accommodate a cultural practice—such as violence in American popular culture today—is of course not the same as recommending it. Yet the distinction between accommodation and recommendation is commonly neglected when unfamiliar cultural practices are under consideration. It therefore is useful to remind ourselves of the many familiar cultural practices to which we have a "yuck" response and make explicit standards for seeking legal recourse in the name of protecting individual rights. We then should use the same standards for both familiar and unfamiliar cultural practices. If we do, we are likely to recognize the importance both of defending basic individual rights against some cultural practices that violate human rights and accommodating some "yucky" cultural practices that do not violate human rights, although they still may offend our moral or aesthetic sensibilities.

Although it may be difficult to draw the line between a human rights violation and a merely offensive cultural practice, the refusal to draw a line leaves democracies with two unjustifiable alternatives: ban all cultural practices that offend a majority in the name of rights (or majority rule), or permit all cultural practices at the expense of rights (and majority rule). It is far more defensible for democratic societies to recognize the need to protect human rights, give scope to objectionable behavior that does not violate human rights, and encourage deliberation, especially at the disputed margins (as in the Seattle circumcision case) among a diversity of citizens and their accountable representatives.

The Seattle hospital controversy also helps to illustrate, in microcosm, the importance of a diverse cultural presence in decision-making in democracies. There is an ongoing debate about whether it is at all important for members of disadvantaged groups to be represented by individuals who share their group identity when they could just as well be substantively represented by individuals who defend their interests and share their values but not their group identity.[58] Substantive representation is good as far as it goes, but it often does not go far enough in understanding situations—such as the Seattle controversy—in which members of disadvantaged groups have reason to be suspicious that their perspectives—including their cultural particularities—are unlikely to receive equal consideration and fair treatment unless they themselves (or representatives of their group) are actually present at the deliberations. The need for a politics of presence is particularly acute when fair consideration of cultural particularity would otherwise be unlikely and therefore unequal liberty or opportunity is likely to result for members of the group.

Because the presence of members of the group cannot guarantee equal consideration and their absence does not preclude a fair outcome, the claims for inclusive deliberation are necessarily contingent and probabilistic. Contingent and probabilistic grounds are no less important to invoke in support of a scheme of democratic representation, especially if that scheme is also consistent with the *expression* of civic equality. One way of *expressing* the civic equality of individuals is to include members of disadvantaged cultural minorities in decision-making bodies so that when diverse cultural claims like those of the Somali parents are considered, they are more likely to receive equal consideration. Equal consideration, however, does not mean that all cultural claims are considered of equal merit. Quite the contrary, equal consideration means that cultural claims are considered as much on their merits as possible rather than on the basis of who happens to be making the claims or how familiar or strange those claims may strike us by virtue of our particular cultural prejudices.

CULTURAL SURVIVAL

"Indisputably . . .," Charles Taylor writes, "more and more societies today are turning out to be multicultural, in the sense of including more than one cultural community that wants to survive."[59] Do all the

cultural communities that want to survive in contemporary democracies have a group right to survive? If so, then some basic human rights
would take a back seat to the survival of some cultures. Taylor defends
cultural survival, but not at the price of violating basic human rights.[60]
Before deciding whether cultural survival should take a back seat to
basic human rights, however, we need to know what cultural survival
is.

The idea of cultural survival is surprisingly hard to pin down,
given the central role it plays in many political arguments on behalf of
cultural groups. What do defenders of political support for cultural
survival mean by the survival of a culture? They must not mean survival of the totality of a culture, since there is no reason to think that
the status quo of a culture is worthy of political support in its entirety.
Even if we assume for the sake of argument that cultures are discrete
wholes, we have no reason to conclude that preserving the whole of a
culture would be morally good or even aesthetically valuable. The alternative of designating essential parts that must be preserved is even
more daunting. Which parts of a culture are essential to preserve for
the sake of its survival?

Cultures are continually changing by virtue of the creative interpretations and actions of people who identify with them and their
interactions with other people and cultures. Since a culture does not
completely encompass the identity of its members, cultural change
cannot be equated with an objectionable coercive alteration of the
identities of individuals. If cultural survival is to be treated as a moral
value in democratic politics to be weighed against protection of human rights, it must be something other than the conservation of existing cultural practices. What could that something of moral value be?

Suppose that cultural survival means the survival of the persons
who now identify with a culture. Then the value of cultural survival is
another way of expressing a right of personal survival while highlight-
ing the greater vulnerability of cultural minorities. Democratic societies should protect people against greater risks of disease and death as
a result of more vulnerable cultural identities. If cultural survival
means that the people who identify with disadvantaged cultures have a
right to life every bit as important as the right of members of more
dominant cultures, then democrats can readily defend cultural sur-

vival. But cultural survival on this understanding does not call for any special group rights. Instead, it is a shorthand for defending the human rights of members of disadvantaged cultures; it says that no person should be denied an equally effective right to life because of cultural group identities that are not merely a matter of choice and do not threaten anyone else's human rights. Unfortunately, this is rarely what cultural survival means when political claims are made on its behalf. Nor can the survival of a culture be meaningfully equated with the survival of individual persons since they may not carry on the culture.

Cultural survival is almost always intended to mean something more or other than the survival of the persons who identify with a culture. Cultural survival often refers to the secure continuation over time of a "people"—such as the Catalan, Basques, Québécois, Maori, or French—who identify with a culture. Survival in this second sense differs from the first sense because it refers not to protecting the life of any particular persons but rather to continuing the "life" of a collectivity. Suppose that all the individuals who today identify with a specific culture are thriving but over time their children and children's children assimilate into another culture, thereby causing the demise of the parents' culture over time. What has happened is inconsistent with cultural survival, even though no individual lives have been threatened or basic rights violated, because a distinctive cultural group has ceased to exist even though there was never any unjustified threat to the survival of its members. (For Nazi or Stalinist cultures, for example, one might hope that this would happen. For the many other cultures that instantiate positive values, their demise might be fervently regretted even if no individual was harmed in the process. The loss of a Yiddish culture is to be regretted in its own right; the injustices that accompanied that loss are more than regrettable.)

The survival of a culturally-specific people rather than the survival of persons captures what most defenders of a right of cultural survival mean by the term. Honoring a right of cultural survival calls for perpetuating a group associated with a particular culture, even if its members and their progeny would otherwise freely choose to identify with another culture over time. This understanding of cultural survival immediately raises the question: How can we know whether the same particular cultural group actually is surviving over time? The most common way of answering this question is to assume that when some particular features of a culture—such as its language—survive, it remains the same culture. When Taylor defends the democratic support of a groups right to cultural survival, his aim is to ensure the survival over time of certain central features of a cultural group such as the Québécois, most obviously its language, rather than simply the survival of the living persons who identify with the group at any given time. (Without living persons who identify with the culture the culture would not survive, but their survival is not enough.)

The question then arises as to whether and why cultural survival, so understood, should be democratically supported. One answer is that cultures instantiate positive values—such as the aesthetic value of the French language—and democratic support for these values is good, provided it does not violate basic rights. If state support of a culture does not violate basic rights, then democratic citizens may legitimately support its survival over time just as they may legitimately enlist state support to preserve valuable artistic creations over time.

The objective value instantiated in some cultural practices is not the only, or even primary, defense of democratic support for cultural survival. The primary defense is the valued identification of individuals with cultures and the assurance that their cultural identity has as great a chance as anyone else's to be perpetuated over time by a community with which they are connected. If only members of dominant cultures are so assured, is this not unfair? The opportunity to live in a way that helps assure the perpetuation of one's cultural community over time can reasonably count as a valued opportunity for a democratic society to secure for its members. If this is a valuable opportunity, then this argument helps account for the criticism of some liberals for defending the cultural neutrality of the state and therefore opposing democratic support of minority cultures. These liberals are accused of unfairly favoring the ongoing operations of democracies in dominant languages and customs without due regard for the value that members of minority cultures legitimately place on ensuring that *their* cultures have an equal chance of enduring over time.

The worry of many liberal critics of state support for cultural survival is that it may violate such human rights as basic as freedom of speech and religion. How can a democratic state that protects basic rights also ensure to all citizens that their favored cultures have an equal chance of survival over time? Such a blanket assurance is not possible. Democratic citizens must be free to criticize or simply ignore inherited cultural practices and therefore to adopt new practices that may lead to the demise of a culture with which some people identify. When a culture appears threatened with extinction because not enough people value it enough to keep it alive by means of their own civic freedoms, political attempts to prevent its extinction can easily become tyrannical. Governments may overreach in their aim to secure the survival of a culture, for example, by forbidding citizens to learn or speak anything other than the favored language or forbid them to worship in ways that threaten the favored culture. A democratic state can easily become tyrannical in many small but significant ways out of an overarching concern for cultural preservation.

The same concern to resist tyranny, however, pushes in precisely the opposite direction when a culture is threatened as a consequence of injustices committed against its members. A democratic state then may be obligated to support the culture in order to help overcome the injustices inflicted on its members. One of these injustices is the culture's undue demise. Among the worst injustices committed against individuals has been, and continues to be, the threatened extermination of entire groups of people because of their cultural identities. Democratic states have an obligation to counteract the threat of cultural extinction when it comes as a byproduct of injustice against a group. Cultural survival at the expense of individual rights is then at issue. The most straightforward way of defending cultural survival of this sort is to defend human rights. Because a culture can cease to exist as a consequence of systematic injustices committed against the people who identify with it, the people who identify with that culture may have a group right for the culture to survive. Far from threatening human rights, this group right is derivative of human rights to equal freedom and civic equality.

Cultural survival in and of itself is therefore not a human right, since the ultimate beneficiaries and claimants of human rights must be persons, and the price of enabling some cultures to survive may be violating human rights. Once we heed this warning about not subordinating the well-being of individuals to groups, we must also recognize that cultural survival still may be an important derivative right in certain circumstances. Fighting the legacy of historical injustices against members of disadvantaged groups may mean supporting their culture or honoring their political rights as a group to support their own culture to the extent that it is threatened with extinction as a consequence of injustices. In the case of many aboriginal groups, such as the Inuit in Canada and the Pueblo in the United States, the injustices are legion; they include a long legacy of violence, theft, treaty violation and unilateral nullification by the more powerful group.[61] Among the consequences of these injustices are threats to the self-governing capacities of these groups, which in turn threaten their ability to support their own cultural preferences in legitimate political ways.

Historical injustices committed against members of aboriginal groups remain relevant to the case for honoring their (nonabsolute) sovereignty and their ability to sustain their culture consistent with their respecting the human rights of their members. Therefore the cause of fighting injustice may be well served, for example, by honoring treaties that give aboriginal groups rights of self-government, which in turn give them more power than they otherwise would have to support the culture of their collective choice. But fighting injustice is not well served by elevating culture in itself—something that is neither conscious nor sentient—above sentient and conscious persons who may legitimately use their freedom to support cultural practices other than the ones they inherited. Attributing a group right of survival to cultures, independently of human rights, is a recipe for tyranny and injustice. Whenever a culture is threatened because of injustices committed against individuals, the injustices themselves should be addressed. One way of addressing injustices committed against people because of their cultural identities is to provide public support for their preferred cultural institutions. To address injustices in this way, however, does not entail creating a group right of cultural survival.[62]

Democratic governments can justifiably defend the survival of many cultures out of fairness to their citizens and their valued cultural identities and attachments, as long as this defense does not elevate a group right to survival above the basic rights of individuals. Because the precise content of basic rights is subject to reasonable disagreement, room exists for reasonable dispute about when governmental measures that aid a culture do and do not violate basic rights. Does a signage law in Quebec that requires French to be the dominant language on commercial signs but permits other languages to be used violate a basic right of free expression? There are justifiable limits on the exercise of free speech, and this law (one can acknowledge with or without agreeing with it) does not prevent people from expressing themselves publicly in any language. An earlier law forbid the use of any language other than French in commercial signage. Did that law violate a basic right of free speech? Were the basic rights of Orthodox Jewish citizens of Quebec infringed, for example, when they were legally prohibited from posting and therefore viewing public signs with the word "kosher" in Hebrew as well as in French. Judgment calls need to be made on matters of basic rights over which people may reasonably disagree.

Reasonable disagreement is no excuse for abdicating our judgment on these issues. The stakes are far from trivial, and what is beyond reasonable judgment (I think) is that all individuals have a basic right to arrive at judgments about the basic rights of individuals and express these judgments publicly in a peaceful way. Justifying attempts to impose judgments is a far more difficult matter. A democratic perspective emphasizes that the moral claims of contemporary cultures to survival depend in no small part on their respect for basic human rights and because of reasonable disagreement, that defense itself often needs to be subject to democratic deliberation.[63] Cases where people reasonably disagree about whether a basic human right is at stake are prime candidates for ongoing democratic deliberation.

To summarize: Cultural groups cannot encompass the identities of individuals who are creative subjects and not just objects of socialization. Basic human rights are instruments to protect and respect individuals as creative subjects or agents. Democratic states, therefore, should give priority to basic rights over the claims of cultural groups that are incompatible with those rights, whether the group be called a nation, a culture, or the state itself. When a democratic state fails to do so, it should be subject to the same constraint as any cultural group in its midst. Powerful groups should be required either to constrain themselves or to be constrained by respect for human rights, just as the authority of the democratic state should constrain itself or be constrained to the extent that it is institutionally feasible to do so. (Institutional feasibility will depend on whether any other effective institution can be trusted to enforce human rights.) Respect for persons and the corresponding obligations on political authorities (limits to their sovereignty) are central to a democratic perspective.

ONE OR MANY CULTURES OF HUMAN RIGHTS?

Defenders of human rights are often accused of unjustifiably privileging a particular culture—the culture of human rights—over all others. Some cultural critics say that there are no external standards by which to judge any culture but the standards of another culture.[64] Democrats are thought to defend human rights in a viciously circular way because there is nothing other than particular cultures from which to defend them. Human rights seem to lose any special critical standing vis-à-vis oppressive cultural practices. Oppression, like beauty, is in the eyes of the beholding culture.

Is there a response that gives human rights standing beyond a particular culture of human rights? Critics of oppressive cultural practices need not claim to stand above all cultures. They can admit that their identities are partly constituted by particular cultural predispositions, which may include a commitment to human rights and opposition to practices that violate those rights. A democratic identity does not stand outside all cultures, looking down in criticism from a cultural nowhere land. Democrats, like everyone else, stand inside cultures, but they do not therefore stand inside only one single comprehensive culture. They stand inside many different cultures, as varied as Pueblo, Navajo, Hindu, Muslim, Buddhist, Catalan, Chinese, Québécois, Anglophone Canadian, Russian, Czech, and American.

Because some members of all cultures can support a defense of human rights, it is misleading to say that a defense represents just another particularistic and comprehensive culture. The rights culture is not a culture in the strict sense of the term. A rights culture does not have, nor does it claim to have, the substantive features and advantages possessed by a culture. A culture of rights does not aim to be comprehensive in its reach over people's lives. It is not distinguished by a common language, distinctive literary and artistic traditions, national music, or particular customs, dress, ceremonies, and holidays. It does not provide a secure sense of *cultural* belonging to its members. A culture of rights, if one insists on calling it that, is far more limited in scope and far more open to alternative contents than the more comprehensive cultures that theorists of culture describe and defend.

No single comprehensive culture of human rights exists, nor should any single culture comprehensively characterized by human rights aspire to exist. The aspiration of human rights is to be part of many diverse cultures. There are in fact many interacting and evolving cultures throughout the world that defend human rights, although all (regrettably) do so imperfectly. The many cultures that contribute to American democracy are not the same as those that contribute to Indian democracy, which in turn are different from those that contribute to the democracies of Canada, South Africa, Australia, Sweden, Japan, or the Netherlands, although substantial overlap also occurs as a consequence of the interaction and evolution of cultures the world over. All democratic governments are aided by various cultural defenses of human rights and impeded by cultural obstacles to those defenses. The term "culture" here, however, does not designate a comprehensive self-contained culture; it designates an ordinary language sense of culture as including socially transmitted beliefs and patterns of behavior. All multicultural democracies contain cultures that accept and reject various human rights. Most undemocratic countries also contain such cultures, even though those human rights that are necessary for democratic governance are more roundly rejected by their reigning political powers.

Reducing a defense of rights to a single comprehensive rights culture is therefore misleading. The reduction echoes an equally misleading critique of the Universal Declaration of Human Rights for being ethnocentrically Western.[65] This charge is recurrent but it is also belied by the cultural identities of the Declaration's framers, the many state constitutions that adopt human rights provisions and the hundreds of human rights organizations with memberships that span the world. The drafting of the Universal Declaration of Human Rights was heavily influenced by Latin American socialists as well as by the Soviet Union to include social and economic as well as civil and political rights. It cannot accurately be called ethnocentric in the content it gives to human rights, let alone in the origins of its framers.[66] The constitutions of at least twenty-six countries with widely varying cultural communities recognize the Universal Declaration as a standard by which their citizens may judge their own government's action regarding human rights.

Human rights doctrine is multicultural. So is its rejection. The dominant authorities of many cultural groups reject human rights, if not comprehensively, then sometimes quite close to it. The Taliban and Khmer Rouge are striking examples. When their rejection of human rights is put into terrifying and terrorizing practice, revealing their willingness to engage in massive slaughtering of innocent people, often on the basis of their "incorrect" cultural identities, we often witness a multicultural alliance against such practices among communities that span many cultural groups. The alliance is not equally representative of all cultural groups or nationalities, for reasons that have as much to do with their politics as their culture.

The rampant violation of the practice of human rights also illustrates what calling human rights universal cannot mean. It cannot mean that human rights are universally accepted or even close to it. Calling human rights universal means that rights should apply not parochially to a few groups but to all persons, variously but similarly considered as civic equals, dignified beings, free and equal persons, or simply human agents who should be able to live a decent life, regardless of their cultural membership. These are among the many bases on which to defend human rights, which resonate within many cultural communities.[67] The fact that the dominant forces in many nations, including many democracies, reject some human rights makes their multiple bases all the more important to defend.

Although human rights are not universally defended, groups that defend human rights against their governments abound in almost every country. The most careful and detailed analysis to date of the Universal Declaration concludes that "at the end of the twentieth century there is not a single nation, culture, or people that is not in one way or another enmeshed in human rights regimes."[68] Being enmeshed in human rights, however, does not entail anything close to universal acceptance within the group. Just as critiques of human rights vary, so do the defenses. They do not define a single comprehensive culture called "the rights culture" any more than opposition to them defines a single "antirights culture." The United States government and many American citizens, for example, have been both staunch defenders and equally staunch opponents of some human rights that are widely considered basic.

It is probably true that there is increasingly widespread support for a defense of human rights in many diverse democratic societies and even among many nondemocratic societies (which is not to say that human rights are unanimously supported by all societies, let alone all cultures, that our world contains). There can be increasing support for human rights without damaging cultural diversity because identifying as a person who respects human rights does not encompass the entirety of anyone's cultural identity or the entirety of any particular culture. This is one reason why democracies that respect human rights can be culturally very different from one another.

Cultures include far more than what human rights contribute to them—ways of greeting, eating, reading, writing, speaking, singing, dancing, painting, building, celebrating, and mourning, to mention just a few behavior patterns that are much broader than the political morality of human rights. Human rights therefore leave undetermined a large part of every group that identifies itself with human rights. Moreover, human rights do not ask people to identify as "comprehensive liberals" throughout their lives, since human rights do not encompass the entirety of moral identity.[69] Human rights are part of political morality, which is a subset of total morality. Human rights make demands upon every cultural group when entering into politics, and these demands typically take precedence when they conflict with the goals of the group. Precedence in politics is part of what basic rights mean, which is why they are both critical and controversial.

Democratic standards are shared by particular cultures that can defend human rights in their own way. All particular cultures that defend human rights may be called rights cultures. The ability to defend human rights is important to democratic societies because human rights are necessary to make claims in democratic politics without fear of reprisal or unfair treatment. The protection of human rights applies to members of groups that make illiberal and undemocratic claims in democratic politics. These groups depend on respect for their human rights by the larger democracy as much if not more so than do members of diverse democratic groups who are themselves committed to human rights.

Because human rights can find footing within diverse cultures and within democratic politics itself, it is misleading to identify a defense of human rights with a single comprehensive rights culture. A defense of human rights is a defense of many cultures and of democratic politics itself because democracy depends on respecting the civic equality, equal liberty, and basic opportunity of all persons to make good on its moral promise. Some theorists of culture, as we have seen, defend a far more minimal understanding of the rights upon which democracies depend, but even they defend human rights, for example, the right of all persons to exit any cultural identity group.[70] They defend human rights as politically enforceable constraints on cultures. Since there is no reason to privilege any particular set of human rights on its face, substantive arguments for and against alternative understandings of human rights are all we mortals with imperfect empirical knowledge and ethical understanding have to go on. Democratic deliberation across cultures about the content of human rights is one way of furthering our understanding.

To summarize: Cultures consist, among other things, of ideas, and among those ideas are ethical defenses of human rights. The multiple moral footings that basic rights can find in many cultures offer a practical advantage in democratic politics. Many cultures can defend basic human rights on multiple moral grounds—human agency, dignity, mutual respect, civic equality, free and equal personhood, and related ideals—which find their inspiration in diverse traditions of thought, religious and nonreligious, Western and non-Western, deontological and consequentialist. The ideals overlap, but a democratic perspective need not choose one among the many traditions that provide grounding for human rights. It can draw upon many cultural traditions that help us better understand the multiple sources, meanings, and interpretations of human rights. More democratic deliberation among cultures can help develop and spread that understanding.

Democrats can consistently criticize group rights that flout human rights. So, too, can theorists of culture like Taylor and Kymlicka, who defend only those group rights that are compatible with human rights. They, too, include civic equality, equal liberty, and basic opportunity among basic human rights. Theorists of culture therefore can also be rights-defending democrats. Many admittedly are, and for good reason. Only with basic rights—or their equivalent—can democracy be an ethical political ideal and its citizens be free to identify culturally as they see fit rather than as an oppressive group has determined.

CHAPTER TWO
The Value of Voluntary Groups

> "To be free, to live as one likes, includes associating on one's own terms, which means engaging in voluntary relationships of all sorts. . . ."
> —George Kateb, "The Value of Association," in *Freedom of Association*

> "Freedom of association . . . plainly presupposes a freedom not to associate."
> —Justice William Brennan, writing for the majority in *Roberts v United States Jaycees*, 468 US 609, 623 (1984)

In order to express our many different identities as individuals, we must be free to associate with one another. Referring to voluntary associations, de Tocqueville wrote that "Nothing deserves more attention."[1] A short list of voluntary groups in the United States illustrates a small portion of their diversity and influence on democracy: Amnesty International and the American Legion, B'nai B'rith and the Boy Scouts, Girl Scouts and the Grange, Hadassah and the Jaycees, Knights of Columbus and the Ku Klux Klan, the League of Women Voters and the Lions, the Free-Masons and the National Association for the Advancement of Colored People, The National Organization for Women and the National Rifle Association, the Odd Fellows and the Optimists, Parent-Teachers Associations and the Red Cross.

With freedom of association, individuals join with others to express social parts of their identities, to pursue instrumental aims, and to offer mutual support, which can aid or impede the legitimate aims of outsiders to the group. Equal freedom of association is necessary for equal citizenship because voluntary groups both manifest the freedom of individuals and also enable individuals to influence the democratic process as otherwise only rich or otherwise powerful people could realistically hope to do on their own. Civic equality therefore entails having the equal freedom to associate in voluntary groups.

Like other equal freedoms, associational freedom implies its own principled limit. The freedom to associate as I see fit must be compatible with the equal freedom of other individuals to associate as they see fit. Voluntary groups that discriminate against categories of individuals threaten the conditions of *equal* freedom of association. People who want to join voluntary groups but are prevented from doing so by prejudice—against their race, religion, ethnicity, gender, or sexual orientation, for example—do not enjoy equal freedom of association. Since being a civic equal entails enjoying equal freedom of association, people who are excluded from voluntary associations out of prejudice are treated as less than the civic equals of their fellow citizens.

There is another side to discriminatory exclusion that presents an even greater challenge to democratic justice. Some individuals express parts of their identities by joining discriminatory groups and defending their discrimination. Part of free expression in a democracy consists of the freedom to defend ideas that are antithetical to democracy, and some voluntary associations exist partly or even largely in order to express such ideas. Freedom of association entails some substantial freedom to exclude people; yet to enjoy equal freedom of association, individuals must also be free from discrimination. This tension within free association poses a considerable challenge in every existing democracy, where prejudice still prevails. Some individuals express their identities by becoming members of voluntary groups that discriminate, whereas other individuals are blocked from expressing their identities by being excluded from these very same groups.

In this chapter, I consider how democracies can deal with this tension within the ideal of voluntary association as it operates in actual contexts, focusing on two landmark cases: *Roberts v United States Jaycess* (the informal name used by the nation-wide civic association, the Junior Chamber of Congress), and *Boy Scouts v Dale*. Both cases feature a voluntary group that discriminates against individuals (women in the *Jaycees* and gay men in *Dale*) because of their group identity. These individuals are denied equal membership in the group and equal freedom of identity expression. Far from being a random or isolated phenomenon, the exclusion of women and gay men from equal membership in these groups reflects two common kinds of discrimination. It therefore cannot be said that their exclusion is counterbalanced by the exclusion of men and heterosexuals from a similarly influential set of voluntary associations.

How can a democracy best cope with the conflict between two logical entailments of free association: the freedom to form an exclusive group and the freedom not to be excluded from a group on discriminatory grounds? To answer this question, I first consider the value of voluntary association (section 1, "Valuing Voluntary Associations"). I then examine the strongest case for preventing a voluntary group from discriminating (section 2, "Identification by Inclusion") and the strongest case for permitting a voluntary group to discriminate (section 3, "Expression by Exclusion").

My analysis leads to recommendations that respect equal liberty and civic equality: When voluntary groups are permitted to discriminate as part of their members' right to free expression, they should receive no state support beyond toleration of their free expression. In order for democratic societies to support free and equal citizenship as a matter of public policy, governments must not actively support discriminatory associations. Some line needs to be drawn between toleration and active support. Like the line between night and day, the line between toleration and support is not always clear and self-evident. There are hard cases, like dawn and dusk, where democratic deliberation is most critical. Without some line drawn between toleration and support, democratic governments will either entirely fail to tolerate any voluntary associations that are not themselves democratic (even if they do no injustice) or entirely fail to oppose the many common kinds of discrimination practiced by voluntary associations that serve to undermine equal liberty and civic equality. When a reasonable line is drawn between toleration and state support, a democratic government distinguishes between exclusions that do and do not undermine civic equality and between exclusions that it can and cannot tolerate consistently with its basic principles. One of its basic principles is freedom of expression, and the same freedom of expression that per-

mits some associations to discriminate also calls upon those who oppose discrimination to speak out against it. Section 4, "Public Pressure
and State Support," therefore considers the importance of public pressure against those discriminatory voluntary groups that democratic
states decide (whether rightly or wrongly) to tolerate.

A neglected dimension of free identity expression through voluntary association is the freedom not to associate. Membership in formal
associations has significantly decreased over the past several decades in
the United States and many other democracies.[2] Even participation in
league bowling in the United States—in which far more Americans
participate than congressional elections—decreased by over 40 percent
between 1980 and 1993. At the same time, however, the total number
of bowlers increased by 10 percent. "Bowling alone" has become a
metaphor for disassociation, yet we need to keep in mind that non-
league bowlers do not bowl alone but with friends. Section 5, "Should
Democracies Discourage Bowling Alone?" asks what democrats should
make of the widespread decline in membership in conventional voluntary groups. Not all decreases in membership are equally troubling.
This is because democracies have no moral interest—beyond respect
for expressive freedom itself—in encouraging discriminatory associations. While democratic justice tolerates the expression of discriminatory ideas and therefore associations that express those ideas, it does
not justify encouraging their activities on the assumption that associations per se—even discriminatory association—are good for democracy. To pursue their promise of free and equal citizenship, democracies need fewer associations that discriminate and more associations
that enable people to express their identities consistently with a public
commitment to treating all law-abiding individuals as civic equals.

Before discussing the value of voluntary associations per se, it is
important to clear up a common misunderstanding. When speaking
about free identity expression and its connection to voluntary association, I am not implying that individuals form their identities entirely—
or even primarily—by their own voluntary actions. Individual identities are partly the product of involuntary socialization and education
by others, and even adult identities are constrained within social contexts not of their own choosing. Under the best of social circumstances, identity formation and expression would be socially influenced

and even constrained. Some constraints are clearly desirable, such as socializing children not to lash out against others in random acts of violence. These constraints are consistent with the equal freedom of individuals to identify themselves over time in a multiplicity of ways. But even after recognizing the social constraints on identity formation, equal freedom of association remains an important part of what it means to be a free person.

VALUING VOLUNTARY ASSOCIATIONS

Valuing individual freedom entails valuing free identity expression and freedom of association.[3] In living their lives, free individuals choose whether or not to identify with a vast array of voluntary groups. Since living the life of a free person, as put forth by theorists of choice, means identifying as one likes, voluntary associations are valuable insofar as they support the freedom of individuals to identify in many different ways by entering and exiting groups and speaking out within them. This value of voluntary associations—as a manifestation of free identity expression—does not depend on anyone being free from some complex combination of social and genetic determination. Instead, it depends on individuals being free within social and genetic limits to identify as they themselves see fit *rather than as government—or any other powerful agent in society—determines for them.*

To live their own lives, free individuals must be able to decide whether or not to identify with groups whose membership is not conscripted. For this basic value to be realized, voluntary associations must be protected by law. Like all lawful freedoms, freedom of association has limits. The value of free association is part of a larger whole of democratic justice. It therefore follows that a right of free association ends where injustice to others begins. This is why a legal right to free association, to be consistent with democratic justice, will not be equally conducive to the formation of every kind of voluntary association. Compared to groups such as the 4-H, the American Association of University Women, Amnesty International, and the NAACP, for example, groups like the KKK and the Michigan Militia should find more of their preferred activities—especially (but not only) those that threaten the lives of other people—restricted by law. A democratic view of voluntary association accepts the limits of "do no injustice" and therefore favors some identities and associations over others: those that are consistent with democratic justice.

Associational freedom within the limits of "do no injustice" is obviously not a morally neutral principle, but it still supports a remarkably wide range of voluntary associations, some internally democratic, others undemocratic, some liberal, others conservative and radical, some secular, others religious, and so on. Freedom of identity expression for individuals depends on voluntary groups being free not to model themselves on the organizational principles and philosophy of a democratic government. To the extent that their membership is effectively free to enter and exit at will, voluntary groups may be internally undemocratic and dedicated to sectarian purposes—as anathema to democracy as the advocacy of monarchy and discrimination—that a democratic government itself cannot legitimately pursue.

Democratic governments therefore can consistently tolerate voluntary associations that themselves reject democratic values, as long as they do no injustice to individuals, but they cannot consistently tolerate the infliction of injustice by groups any more than by individuals. As long as voluntary groups are not permitted to inflict injustice on others, even groups with pernicious ideologies may be tolerated. When a group crosses the line into inflicting injustice can be difficult to determine and subject to reasonable disagreement, but crossing the line—as best as it is determined with the aid of democratic deliberation—signals the point at which their activities no longer may be tolerated. The critical point for a democratic society to make clear is that it is committed to accommodating associations that would not be chosen by individuals who identify comprehensively as democrats.[4] Voluntary associations are constrained but not governed by democratic values. "Associate freely but do no injustice" therefore expresses a democratic view of the value and limits of voluntary association: freedom within just limits.

Voluntary and nonvoluntary associations are both indispensable parts of individual lives and democratic societies. The fundamental difference is that families, democracies, and other nonvoluntary associations cannot assume consent of either entry or exit on the part of their members, whereas voluntary associations can (to the extent that they are truly voluntary). An association is voluntary to the extent that its members are effectively free to exit after having also freely entered. Voluntary associations therefore may be more or less voluntary with respect to various of their members. When "do no injustice" is effectively applied by a democratic government to voluntary associations, it ensures that freedom of association is consistent with democratic justice. In other words, the value of free association should not be compromised by injustice.

Free individuals, George Kateb writes, tolerate "being regulated only with deep constitutional regret."[5] Deep regret, however, does not rule out regulation in avoidance of injustice. The regret of permitting injustice—serious harm to others—should be far greater than the regret of restricting the kind of freedom that inflicts injustice. Free association within the limits of legitimate law does not rule out regulation of associations. Instead it suggests that voluntary associations can be valuable even if they are not themselves instrumental means of combating injustice and even if they do not conceive of themselves as serving a public cause, such as educating their members in civic virtue. By virtue of being voluntary, associations permit their members to live the lives of free people, expressing their identities in part through their associations. This freedom itself is extremely valuable in any democracy that aspires to respect individuals as free and equal persons.

There are other values of voluntary associations. Like cultural groups, discussed in chapter 1, voluntary groups are also valuable for providing many people with a sense of social belonging. The sense of belonging that voluntary associations can provide is not politically authoritative. The lack of official political endorsement is a virtue from the perspective of individual freedom. Freely associating people can choose to create, sustain, or alter their identities without political authorization or even acknowledgment. Public recognition of identities by a multiplicity of associations need not be either politically authoritative or comprehensive. Public recognition can be as pluralistic as the variety of voluntary groups that populate our world: churches, synagogues, and mosques; colleges, universities, and museums; sports leagues, literary societies, sororal and fraternal orders, environmental groups, national and international charitable organizations, self-help groups, parent-teacher associations, residential associations, professional associations, and expressive organizations of almost every conceivable ideological stripe. In light of the sheer diversity of voluntary identity groups, the value of free identity expression cannot possibly depend upon political recognition and endorsement of identity, which by its very nature would limit the free association to those groups that are approved and not just tolerated by democratic governments.

What constraints are consistent with valuing an association as voluntary? A common usage of the term voluntary draws upon a thin conception of voluntariness. An association is voluntary to the extent that people are not coerced into joining or prevented from leaving.[6] Religious groups, for example, are considered voluntary associations even if people feel compelled by their own conscience or a divine presence to join and not to leave. Internal compulsion to join is compatible with an association's being voluntary as long as the compulsion is not created by the association or other social agents (for example, by indoctrination from birth or brainwashing). A religious group whose members feel compelled by conscience to remain together still counts as voluntary as long as the group has not prevented members from leaving, for example, by depriving them of all their property. A voluntary group also presupposes that its members have not been socialized in ways that block their capacity to appreciate viable alternatives. Since associations can be more or less voluntary, the more effective the freedom of exit afforded by the group and society to members, the more voluntary a group can be considered. A democratic view relies on democratic governments to create the conditions under which individuals are effectively free to exit any association that is valued as voluntary.

What are the conditions under which members of an association are effectively free to exit?[7] The value of voluntary associations, as we have just seen, does not depend on their being either psychologically or morally easy for members to exit. This is because freedom of association includes the freedom to join groups that elicit great psychological and moral commitment over time. "Membership in voluntary associations is formative," as Nancy Rosenblum writes, "sometimes powerfully so . . ."[8] The formative power of voluntary groups is reflected in the greater commitment many members have to remaining within the group than they had to joining it in the first place. The greater the member's commitment, the more psychologically difficult exiting the association may be. But psychological difficulty is compatible with ease of exiting if one decides to do so. Religious associations, for example, often elicit strong psychological and moral commitment, but they can be considered voluntary from a political perspective as long as exiting them is compatible with a person's realistically looking forward to living a decent life (in nonreligious terms) outside the group.

What freedom of association entails is not psychological or moral distance from one's membership in a voluntary group but one's effective ability to exit it and still live a decent life. A democratic government that values individual freedom must therefore try to secure a social context within which voluntary associations afford their members an effective freedom to exit. The conditions of freedom of exit are those that permit individuals to exit any association without sacrificing the opportunity to live a decent life if they decide to exit.

An actual case that arose in Canada, *Hofer v Hofer*, helps illustrate one plausible boundary condition of free exit in a democracy. Several members of the Hutterite Church colony in Canada renounced the church's beliefs and were therefore expelled from the colony. Just as a condition of entering the church colony was giving up all private property, so too was a condition of expulsion leaving all personal property with the church colony. The case illustrates why a formal right to exit an association is not enough for the association to be considered voluntary. The Canadian Supreme Court majority upheld the authority of the Hutterite Church colony to deprive its members of all their property when they exited, even the shirts on their backs. The dissenting opinion by Justice Pigeon was notable for its defense of an effective right to exit, not just a formal one.[9] Since the value of voluntary groups lies in the effective freedom to form, and re-form, one's identity, only an effective right to exit voluntary groups is consistent with valuing them so greatly as to defend a right to free association.

To be free over time, individuals must have an effective right to exit voluntary associations when they decide to do so. This moral claim is frequently confused with the very different and false empirical claim that individuals can change their commitments over time simply by wishing these commitments were otherwise. (The false claim is what gives "wishful thinking" its negative connotation.) For an association to be voluntary, people need not be able simply as a matter of will power to wish away their commitments and make them otherwise. Rather, they must be publicly free—not just formally but effectively free—to exit *if* they decide to do so. And they must be capable of making the decision, which brainwashed people are not. If an effective right to exit is absent, for example because the penalty for leaving is exorbitantly high, as in the case of the Hutterites, associations do not support the value of free identity expression. They may be valuable for other reasons, as democracies themselves are valuable even if most of their citizens are not effectively free to exit. But democracies should not be considered voluntary associations any more than birth families should be so considered. The barriers to leaving the League of Women Voters, the Odd Fellows, and the Optimists Club are low, and these associations are therefore voluntary even if members develop deep commitments to staying.

Freedom to exit is necessary for voluntary associations but not sufficient. Trade unions that preside over union shops in which a company's workers must become union members unless they choose to leave the job are not voluntary associations. Trade union workers often have no real choice as to where to work. Even though they are free to leave a job, the lack of better alternatives renders union shops nonvoluntary groups. The example of union shops also warns us against assuming that associations must be voluntary to be valuable or justified.[10] The value of voluntary associations—identifying as one sees fit—is significant and long neglected, but it is not therefore the only value that is served by associations. Associations serve instrumental values too numerous to mention, most of which are fully consistent with the value of free identity formation.

IDENTIFICATION BY INCLUSION

Voluntary associations are an antidote to atomistic individualism that is completely consistent with a free society. When a democracy safeguards a right of free association, it recognizes that individual freedom does not entail atomism. Voluntary groups show that mutual identification and communal support are common among individuals who have the legal freedom to remain apart. Voluntary associations also can be fully consistent with democratic justice even if justice is beside their point. A voluntary group that is oblivious to matters of justice may nonetheless provide mutual support among people, which is one among many reasons for democrats to value voluntary associations.

When voluntary associations exclude categories of people on discriminatory grounds, however, they present a serious problem of political morality. Discriminatory exclusion of groups of individuals from a voluntary group or subordination within the group threatens injustice. Group exclusions are often based on false or statistical stereotyping. False stereotyping imposes inaccurate generalizations on members of a group. Women, for example, are still often considered less fit for the professions and the commercial world than men. Statistical stereotyping is another form of discrimination against individual members of a group, which operates by assuming that all individual members of the group share a statistically common identity. Individual woman applicants for a job are assumed to want to take time off to raise children without any knowledge of their actual intentions. In similar ways, job applicants are discriminated against on the basis of their race, ethnicity, or religion based on false or statistical stereotyping.

When individuals are excluded from voluntary associations on the basis of such stereotyping (or unabashed discriminatory prejudice), the proper response may be difficult to determine, since voluntary association presupposes the freedom to exclude. One response—taking away the freedom to associate and forcing all associations to include anyone who wants to join—would be worse than the discrimination itself, as it would deny freedom of association almost completely. The other unacceptable extreme would permit all voluntary associations to exclude would-be members on any grounds, no matter how great the injustice of their discrimination or how small the burden that a non-discrimination law would place on the association's pursuit of its primary purposes. Associational freedom cannot permit all exclusions and still be equal. The democratic value of freedom to exclude presupposes that individuals will be treated as civic equals with equal liberty to live as they like.[11] (Equal liberty is shorthand for an equal set of basic liberties.[12]) Suppose a conflict arises between the freedom to form an exclusive association and the freedom to join one without discrimination, and the exclusion is to the detriment of less advantaged individuals. Democrats can draw upon a "principle of equal advantage [for all persons] in adjusting the complete system of freedom."[13] Mandating nondiscrimination can be justified when it serves the cause of civic equality and equal liberty.

A historic example can help illustrate how important it has been for democracies to mandate inclusion by some associations that once were considered voluntary. Before 1932, the Executive Committee of the Democratic party of Texas excluded black citizens from voting in Democratic state primaries on grounds that it was a voluntary association. No one was forced to join the party, and everyone who joined was free to exit, but blacks were excluded. Writing for the majority in *Nixon v Condon*, Justice Cardozo did not deny the voluntariness of membership in the Democratic party of Texas, nor did he deny that the party served some valuable "private" purposes, such as the camaraderie and mutual support of its members. What Justice Cardozo denied was that "a political party is *merely* a voluntary association."[14] The political party distributes a public good, he argued, and therefore it is subject to legal regulation of its membership. Moreover, because discriminatory exclusion from a primary election clearly expresses the civic inequality of the excluded citizens, the case for equal freedom and identification as a civic equal by inclusion was compelling.

The court's conclusion in *Nixon v Condon* is now largely taken for granted, but it was not at the time, and the reasoning behind the state's opening up a blocked entry is very instructive for how we approach what appear to be harder cases today. Why does discriminatory exclusion from primary elections threaten the civic equality of the excluded? Not because excluded individuals would necessarily gain any clear advantage for themselves by being included, but rather because the exclusion itself *publicly expresses* the idea that they are not the civic equals of those who are included. A general lesson to be learned from the reasoning behind *Nixon v Condon* is that discriminatory exclusion is harmful when it *publicly expresses* the civic inequality of the excluded even in the absence of any other showing that it *causes* the civic inequality in question. A court or legislature need not document harmful consequences to individual persons to establish a connection between a blocked entry and an actionable threat to civic equality of members of a group. The blocked entry is bad enough if it expresses civic inequality, especially in the context of a society where the excluded group is negatively stereotyped and therefore excluded from associations that provide public goods or services. A voluntary association that serves public purposes may justifiably be regulated even if it also serves private purposes for its members.

Opening up blocked entries can therefore be justified even when a voluntary association does not directly harm individuals by its exclusion, because the standing of citizens as civic equals should be *expressed* as well as supported by associations that distribute public goods and services. The excluded individuals may not stand to gain much, if anything, *directly as individuals* from being included as equals, and yet the case for inclusion may be strong, as *Nixon v Condon* demonstrates. Many voluntary associations are a source of public goods (such as commercial contacts) as well as private goods (such as camaraderie). Whereas discriminatory exclusion from private goods (such as friendship and love) is not the public's business, discriminatory exclusion from public goods is. The freedom to associate by exclusion therefore cannot be absolute if civic equality is a basic right.

Exclusions by voluntary associations are particularly problematic when they exclude individuals through no fault of their own and when the exclusionary basis—whether it be gender, race, class, religion, sexual orientation, or ethnicity—is a general source of civic inequality and therefore injustice. This is why an assessment of exclusion from voluntary associations needs to be contextual.[15] When exclusions from large voluntary associations target disadvantaged individuals as members of negatively stereotyped groups, the exclusions often publicly express and thereby exacerbate the civic inequality of these individuals. Public expression that is unofficial may be no less detrimental to the cause of democratic justice. Government becomes complicit in prejudicial exclusion when it fails to place justifiable limits on discriminatory associations.

This problem of discriminatory exclusion from voluntary associations—and its politically-based resolution—was first confronted in a serious way in the United States with regard to African Americans. Exclusions from a wide array of voluntary associations prejudicially limited their freedom and gave added expression to their civic inequality. When de Tocqueville wrote that nothing deserves more attention than associational life in democracy, he was not referring to discriminatory exclusions. Many of his fans who focus on the subject have neglected this problem. Yet discriminatory exclusion must be addressed in order to understand and evaluate the contribution of voluntary groups today (as in de Tocqueville's time). Many prominent voluntary associations in the United States have been discriminatory for most of their history, and not only against black Americans, for whom the issue of opening up blocked entries has been most effectively addressed even if not fully implemented.

Beginning in the civil rights era, states have passed laws that prohibit discrimination on many grounds—color, creed, religion, disability, national origin, gender, and sexual orientation—by any "place of public accommodation" where "goods, services, facilities, privileges, advantages or accommodations are extended, offered, sold, or otherwise made available to the public."[16] These antidiscrimination laws have been invoked to open up prejudicially blocked entries into many voluntary associations, but not without resistance. A reasonable basis of resistance is the consideration of associational freedom. Associational freedom, which supports freedom of identification, pulls in both directions: it favors the freedom of individuals to exclude so as to identify as they wish, and it also favors the freedom of individuals to join an association so as to identify as they wish. The issue of identification by exclusion and inclusion is therefore still highly unsettled. When and why should discriminatory exclusions from voluntary associations be regulated by the law?

Although voluntary associations would not be voluntary if they were forced to include anyone who wanted to join them, not all exclusions are equally defensible on grounds of associational freedom or consistent with the basic principles of democratic justice. The landmark case of *Roberts v Jaycees* illustrates how prohibiting discrimination can increase freedom of association for large numbers of people. In the early 1980s, two local chapters of the Jaycees called upon the Minnesota Department of Human Rights to invoke the state's Human Rights Act in support of their decision to admit women as full members, against the dictates of the Jaycees' national charter. The Human Rights Act made it "an unfair discriminatory practice . . . [t]o deny any per-

son the full and equal enjoyment of the goods, services, facilities, privileges, advantages, and accommodations of a place of public accommodation because of race, color, creed, religion, disability, national
origin or sex."[17] The United States Supreme Court upheld Minnesota's decision to force the Jaycees to admit women as full members.

Because not all exclusions are equally defensible, associational
freedom may legitimately be constrained in the name of "eliminating
discrimination, and assuring . . . citizens equal access to publicly available goods and services."[18] A democratic state has a compelling interest in opening up prejudicially blocked entries to some voluntary associations, as Justice Brennan argued, because of the "serious social and
personal harms" that accompany "discrimination based on archaic and
overbroad assumptions about the relative needs and capacities of the
sexes [that] force individuals to labor under stereotypical notions that
often bear no relationship to their actual abilities."[19]

Excluding individuals from equal access to public goods out of
prejudice, passed along through false social stereotypes, violates their
equal freedom and opportunity. Because discriminatory exclusion from
an association like the Jaycees harms women in this way, the burden
should not be on them to establish that they were denied jobs down
the road because of this discriminatory exclusion. A burden of proof
of this sort would effectively be a presumption protecting prejudice.
Putting the burden of proof on the excluded would further limit their
equal freedom. One value of individual freedom, as we have seen, is
the freedom to identify as one sees fit rather than as others prejudicially presume and impose. The freedom of women to identify si-
multaneously as women and professionals would remain unequal to
that of men as long as associations distributing public goods, such as
commercial contacts, prejudicially exclude women or relegate them to
second-class membership.

Three features of discriminatory exclusion create a strong case for
public intervention to open up prejudicially blocked entries to voluntary associations. (The absence of these features creates a correspondingly strong case against public intervention.)

- First, the exclusion must be discriminatory, based on false or statistical stereotyping. (Exclusion of dangerous felons from an association, for example, would not express a false or statistical stereo-

type, since every dangerous felon is dangerous. But exclusion of women from a commercial association because they are uninterested or unsuited for commerce is discriminatory.)

- Second, the discriminatory exclusion occurs in a public realm and is connected to the distribution of a public good. (Discriminatory exclusion from an intimate relationship, for example, would fail to satisfy this condition. A realm of privacy is preserved by this safeguard.)

- Third, the voluntary association is not primarily defined by its dedication to an expressive purpose—such as an advocacy group for male supremacy—that makes its discrimination against a group an important part of its advocacy and therefore its freedom of expression. (Expressive freedom for advocacy groups is preserved by this safeguard without letting all voluntary groups, regardless of whether they are primarily advocacy groups, invoke expressive freedom as a pretext for discrimination.)

Deliberative disagreements about the balancing of basic liberties are an inherent part of the democratic search for fair terms of social cooperation.[20] In order that there be a fair democratic search, however, individuals must be treated as civic equals. When discriminatory exclusion limits equal freedom or otherwise impedes the civic equality of individuals, a strong case can be made for a democratic government to oppose the discrimination and open the entry.

Roberts v Jaycees illustrates how the three features of discriminatory exclusion enumerated above can create a strong case for opening up a prejudicially blocked entry. First, exclusion of women as a group from full membership in the Jaycees bore no relevant relationship to the capacities of individual women to engage in the world of solicitation and management, nor did the Jaycees claim that it did. The exclusion was therefore discriminatory against women. Second, by their own stated purposes, the Jaycees aimed to provide and promote, as public goods, the skills of "solicitation and management." Third, the Jaycees—again by its own stated purposes—was not primarily an expressive association dedicated to advocating the exclusion or subordination of women.[21] The case for opening up the blocked entry to equal membership for women was therefore strong.

Roberts serves to show that the public realm extends beyond political institutions to all associations that distribute public goods and services and therefore implicates the equal freedom, opportunity, and civic equality of individuals. "It is hardly surprising," as Judith Shklar wrote about the extension of the public realm beyond narrowly political to work-related associations, "that the middle-class feminists who came to resent being excluded from the world of gainful employment should have been quite aware of the intimate bond between earning and citizenship."[22] What *Roberts* helps to establish is that earning and citizenship are linked not only by the way employers treat individuals but also by the way associations that distribute public goods and services do.

But *Roberts* also raises the question: How broadly should we construe the realm of public goods and services? Some theorists of choice claim that the *Roberts* decision construed the public realm too broadly. Rosenblum presents the strongest case against mandating the inclusion of women into the Jaycees, although her case turns out to be equivocal in its conclusion. Legally mandating nondiscrimination, according to Rosenblum, is justified only if a voluntary association is the *exclusive* purveyor of advantage or privilege, and therefore *the* general source of the publicly available good in question.[23] This standard sets the threshold much higher than it has been for commercial enterprises, no one of which is typically the exclusive purveyor of the public good. Also troubling is this standard's neglect of how discriminatory exclusions from voluntary associations both deny equal freedom and exacerbate civic inequality, even in situations where it is possible for women and disadvantaged minorities to create alternative associations for themselves. A democratic government can reasonably consider equal freedom and civic equality threatened by voluntary associations that distribute public goods and services and discriminate in their membership policies, even if they are not monopolists.

Second-class membership in an association, as Rosenblum rightly emphasizes, does not always express or entail second-class citizenship. Moral psychology is too complex to assume that people who are treated as second-class members in some private associations are therefore also treated as second-class citizens in society more generally. Moreover, "freedom of association is no stamp of public approval of the internal life of an association in a liberal democracy. If it were, the fundamental principle of toleration would be meaningless."[24] It is important to add that the principle of toleration remains meaningful when democratic governments require associations that provide public goods and services not to discriminate. Toleration would not be defensible were it an unqualified license to discriminate.

Second-class membership in discriminatory associations often does express second-class citizenship—a combination of unequal freedom and civic inequality—in societies that have a long history of discrimination against the groups whose members are relegated to second-class membership. This is why Rosenblum recognizes that: "Viewed in the light of the interplay in American ideology among earning, moral improvement, and public standing, women's second-class membership in the Jaycees could be taken as a mark of second-class citizenship."[25] Moreover, positive changes in women's civic standing have followed extended enforcement of antidiscrimination laws in the twentieth century. Although the sociology and politics here are far too complex to supply a single definitive account of the causes of greater civic equality for women over time, it is eminently reasonable to count the extension of antidiscrimination laws in the past half-century as a major consequential factor.[26]

Democratic governments have been a primary source of antidiscrimination laws. Since democratic decision making is itself a basic freedom, there is good reason to uphold legislative protections of nondiscrimination in light of reasonable disagreements about the precise conditions of equal freedom and civic equality.[27] What is at stake in such legislation is nothing less than the equal freedom of women and members of negatively stereotyped minorities to identify in as many valuable ways as their more privileged counterparts are able to by entering and exiting voluntary associations on terms of civic equality rather than being excluded by discrimination.

EXPRESSION BY EXCLUSION

Many people express their own identities by excluding others from their associations. Sometimes exclusion from voluntary associations is morally benign. If a bowling league rejects people like me who are severely strike-challenged, there is no invidious discrimination to be found in its preference to recruit better bowlers. Or if the Objectivist Society excludes you because you don't subscribe to its libertarian philosophy, that, too, is a perfectly justifiable form of exclusion. The society's primary purpose is to express a message that your membership could undermine. Freedom of expression operates in important ways through voluntary association.

Not all exclusions from voluntary associations, however, are so morally benign. Not even all exclusions from expressive associations are morally benign. Associational freedom, as we have seen, pulls in two different, often incompatible, directions. It affords individuals both the freedom to form an exclusive group and the freedom to join an exclusive group. When associational freedom is used to form an exclusive group and some people who want to join that group are prejudicially excluded on discriminatory grounds, their freedom of identity expression is constrained. They may still be able to form their own group, but if the group excluding them is as prominent as the Jaycees and Boy Scouts are in the United States, no new group that is open to them may be a real substitute for the freedom of identity expression that is denied them. First, the costs of forming an equally prominent group may be prohibitively high, and this is especially likely to be the case for members of disadvantaged groups. Second, the exclusion itself limits the free identity expression of the excluded and may make it more difficult for the excluded, if they are already negatively stereotyped in society, to achieve the standing of civic equals.

Discriminatory exclusions limit more than the freedom of expression of the excluded. They also constrain members of the exclusionary group who are not themselves prejudiced. The national leadership of the Boy Scouts now stands publicly opposed to admitting gay boys and men as Scouts. Members of the Boy Scouts today who would otherwise have no brief against associating with gay Scouts are constrained by their membership as Boy Scouts to associate on a discriminatory basis. Heterosexual men are still significantly freer than excluded gay men, since the choice of identifying as a gay Boy Scout is simply not an option. The discriminatory membership policy therefore leaves heterosexuals and homosexuals with unequal freedom.

Why not simply outlaw discriminatory associations? Because expressive freedom includes the freedom to join together with others in a voluntary association that discriminates. Why not simply allow all discriminatory associations to exclude people as they see fit? Because equal freedom, opportunity, and civic equality would be undermined in the absence of any limits on the freedom of expressive groups to exclude people on discriminatory grounds. Clearly, then, we need to consider how best to adjudicate between competing values.

The controversy over excluding gay men from the Boy Scouts illustrates both the need for such adjudication and its difficulty. What is at stake for free identity formation? When an expressive group identifies itself by prejudicially excluding individuals, it limits the expressive freedom of these individuals and may also threaten their civic equality. The Boy Scouts officially excludes openly gay boys and men. Dale's sexual identity became public when he exercised his freedom to associate as copresident of the Rutgers University Lesbian/Gay Alliance. Only then did the Boy Scouts expel him, and not on the basis of anything Dale had done as a Scout but rather on the basis of who Dale publicly acknowledged himself to be: a gay man.

The exclusion of Dale from the Boy Scouts illustrates a forced choice of associational freedom that members of some negatively stereotyped groups routinely face as long as prejudice against them continues. The forced choice as it applies to gay Boy Scouts goes as follows: As long as gay boys and men were not socially free to admit their sexual identity to others, they were socially free to identify as Boy Scouts. When Dale was an Eagle Scout, he did not acknowledge his homosexuality to others or even to himself. Only when he felt free to recognize his homosexual identity and also acknowledge it in public was he deprived of the freedom to identify as a Boy Scout.

This forced choice between identifying as gay and as a Boy Scout can be generalized to other discriminatory exclusions from voluntary associations. If members of a negatively stereotyped group are willing *and* able to "pass"—neither identify nor be identified with the excluded group—then they thereby become freer to join some discriminatory groups. The prejudice thereby shows itself to be just that: it depends on nothing more than an exclusion based on ascriptive identity. (What the Boy Scouts knew about Dale when they decided to expel him was that he was admittedly homosexual. They knew—and still know—nothing more about his sexual behavior than they knew about the sexual behavior of Scouts who identify as heterosexual.) Of course, many members of ascriptive groups who are targets of discrimination—most women and African Americans, for example—do not even have a forced choice. They have no choice at all if they cannot pass. For people who can pass, however, prejudicially blocked entries to voluntary associations present a classic forced choice: give up one or the other of your preferred identities, and in either case, you lose a valued and valuable part of your freedom of identity expression.

Discriminatory exclusions from voluntary associations, like the exclusion of Dale from the Boy Scouts after he publicly acknowledged his sexual orientation, deny equal freedom to excluded individuals both to identify and to associate as they see fit. Such individuals can be included only if they succeed in passing for someone they are not. Often the negative stereotype is intended to deny that the excluded individuals, precisely because of their identity, deserve the equal civic standing that democracies owe individuals who have done nothing that justifies denying them their equal freedom or civic equality. Discriminatory exclusions implicitly deny that the excluded individuals merit standing as equal citizens. Sometimes the exclusion is based on an explicit denial that members of the excluded group deserve to be treated as civic equals, which makes the exclusion even more problematic.

The Boy Scouts of America today officially claim that being openly gay is inconsistent with being "morally straight" or "clean." According to Scout doctrine, as interpreted by its national leadership, living a "clean" life for a man means keeping not only "his body and mind fit and clean" but also keeping his "community clean."[28] It appears to follow that a gay man makes his community dirty simply by acknowledging his homosexuality. The identification itself is apparently considered sufficient for the person to disqualify as a civic equal, and the association claims an expression freedom to stand up for excluding gay boys and men as unclean individuals.

When discrimination against some people is part of an expressive association's freely chosen message, then there is something to be said, on democratic grounds, for the freedom to discriminate. But there is nothing to be said for a democratic state's active support of such freedom, beyond simply tolerating it. Support by subsidizing the Boy Scouts, whether by giving it public space or tax subsidies, would be a way of underwriting discrimination, and this surely goes against basic democratic principles.

What has happened in the case of *Boy Scouts v Dale* is the following. While the New Jersey Supreme Court upheld the state's antidiscrimination law, a majority of the United States Supreme Court shielded the Boy Scouts from the same law on grounds of associational freedom of expression.[29] The four dissenting justices, however, argued that if *being* openly gay—but *doing* nothing to violate the explicit policy of an association—is sufficient ground for exclusion, then the majority's decision "is tantamount to [imposing] a constitutionally prescribed symbol of inferiority" on openly gay men.[30]

What makes the Boy Scouts case both difficult and troubling is that free identity expression is centrally at stake on both sides. The decision makers therefore cannot escape ranking the competing values of free expressive association and freedom from discrimination. Both the majority and minority downplay their ranking and focus only on the freedom that they are championing, making their case seem simpler than it is. We need to remind ourselves, especially in controversial cases like this one, that a system of equal freedom requires trade-offs between competing liberties. To be in keeping with the principle of civic equality, the trade-offs would aim to equalize liberty among individuals regardless of their ascriptive identities.

Comparing the value of competing liberties is not a science, however, and we should both expect and respect reasonable disagreements over how hard cases are best legally resolved.[31] Nonetheless, all sides should be able to recognize the competing freedoms that are at stake and the fact that the freedom of an association as prominent as the Scouts to exclude people on discriminatory grounds entails limiting the free expression of those who are excluded. A democratic commitment to making trade-offs between competing liberties so that they equally advantage all individuals, regardless of their ascriptive identities, would argue in favor of inclusion of gay boys and men in this case.

When this ranking of the competing freedoms is reversed, as it was by the court majority, and the Boy Scouts are granted the freedom to discriminate, it becomes critical that courts also insist that democratic governments not associate themselves with the Boy Scouts' message or otherwise offer any special support to the Scouts. The freedom to express and act upon discriminatory views can be defended only if democratic governments do nothing either to endorse or support such views or to give the public appearance (to a reasonable person) of endorsing or supporting such views.

When the Boy Scouts were granted the constitutional freedom as an expressive association to exclude gay boys and men, the court did not take this important extra step to insist that democratic governments and public officials not support the Scouts' expressive message. The special support of the Boy Scouts by public schools and local governments clearly violates the principle of nondiscrimination by democratic governments as long as the Boy Scouts insists on discriminating against gay boys and men. The freedom to express discriminatory viewpoints must not be entangled with official acts of democratic governments, such as giving special status to the Boy Scouts that is not available to other associations to use public property (including schools) for their meetings. If close associations like these continue between local governments and Boy Scout troops, a democratic state becomes a complicit (and powerful) agent in imposing symbols of inferiority on individuals because of their sexual orientation.

Only if public officials and institutions clearly dissociate themselves from discriminatory exclusion can a case like *Boy Scouts v Dale* justifiably affirm the legal freedom of an expressive association to exclude people on such grounds. Disassociation requires public schools and other official organizations to stop allying themselves with the Boy Scouts, as they often have been allied in the past. When this requirement is not honored by state agencies—either because they are sympathetic to the prejudice or do not recognize the mistake of official complicity—another question arises: What public pressures may aid a democracy in moving in the direction of equal freedom for all individuals to identify as they see fit when official agents of government and law fail to do enough to move a democracy in this direction?

PUBLIC PRESSURE AND STATE SUPPORT

Theorists of choice who begin with a presumption against governmental regulation make no presumption against public pressure to
change discriminatory membership policies of voluntary associations.
What pressure is both legitimate and supportive of civic equality and
free identity expression?

"Vigorous competition" among voluntary associations, Richard
Epstein writes, serves the cause of democratic justice. Individuals "who
are offended by the Boy Scouts or the Jaycees can go elsewhere."[32] A
critical problem obscured by this claim, however, is that discrimination by associations like the Boy Scouts and Jaycees is often not
merely offensive. Discrimination can be an additional obstacle in the
way of achieving equal freedom and civic equality for members of
negatively stereotyped minorities, which is another reason why the
dissenters in *Dale* had such a strong case.

Even if the individuals who are offended by the Boy Scouts can
exit and go elsewhere, discriminatory exclusion by an expressive association still publicly matters when it expresses negative stereotyping
and therefore denies the equal freedom of the excluded to identify
publicly as they see fit. It is therefore misleading to claim that "vigorous competition keeps these organizations in line, so there is no
public reason to second-guess their policies."[33] Alternatives do matter:
The presence of the robust association of the Girl Scouts protects the
Boy Scouts against succumbing to the kind of discrimination that
would deny girls their standing as future civic equals. But the claim
that there is no public reason to second-guess discriminatory policies
of voluntary groups unduly narrows the notion of public reason. Setting aside the issue of forced inclusion, there are surely public reasons
that justify noncoercive public action on the part of citizens, such as
public criticism of discriminatory groups and advocacy of nondiscrimination.

When freedom of expression is used by associations in discriminatory ways to exclude members of negatively stereotyped groups, it
subordinates something of public value: the equal freedom of the excluded to identify as they see fit. Unless effective countervailing pres-

sures are brought to bear, it is very misleading to claim that competition by itself will resolve the problem that the court majority in *Dale* did not permit the state legislature (or state supreme court) to resolve by legal sanction.

Competition alone cannot be counted upon to protect equal freedom for members of negatively stereotyped groups. Enforcing nondiscrimination is therefore not a more problematic role for government than tolerating discrimination. The preferred alternative for theorists of choice, public pressure, also has serious dangers. Public pressure may more often operate in the direction of discrimination than nondiscrimination and in democratically and legally unaccountable ways. As John Stuart Mill and Alexis de Tocqueville both warned, tyranny often operates through the pressure of an amorphous (but nonetheless real) public opinion. Moreover, the tyranny of majority opinion is often even harder to resist than a bad law because it is so elusive and ultimately unaccountable.

In the wake of the *Dale* decision, many nongovernmental groups across the country withdrew funding from the Boy Scouts and discontinued their subsidies of meeting space and campground facilities. Two dozen United Way chapters reduced or eliminated their funding. Private companies as varied as Chase Manhattan Bank and Levi-Strauss cut their contributions and ties. Religious groups, including bishops of the Episcopal Church, the Unitarian-Universalist Association, Reform Jewish leaders, and the United Methodist Church, condemned antigay policy and in many cases cut off their support for local Scout chapters. "It may be that the Scouts won the battle but end up losing the war," one town manager said after his school district joined other organizations in ending their official support and subsidies in the wake of the Court decision.[34] So far the Scouts still discriminate against gay boys and men, and no nondiscriminatory youth organization has come close to the Scouts in membership or social status.

The best we can defensibly say about public pressure is that it is of great value when it pushes associations in the direction of nondiscrimination and democratic justice. What we cannot conclude is that public pressure is generally to be preferred to legislative and judicial decision making. The Boy Scouts still exclude gays. Although two dozen United Way charity chapters reduced or eliminated their funding, over a thousand chapters did not. Most major companies continue to fund the Scouts. The Roman Catholic and Mormon Churches actively defend the discrimination on the basis of their sincere moral objections to homosexuality. Public pressure in the *Dale* case at best pushes in opposing directions and at worst reinforces the unequal freedom of openly gay men. Although public pressure can play a role in moving discriminatory associations in the direction of democratic justice, its role is undependable and certainly no substitute for legislative and legal action. No procedure—not majority rule or interest group politics—is a substitute for standing up for just principles.

We still may offer two cheers for public pressure on discriminatory associations in the direction of nondiscrimination. First, the pressure represents the freedom of citizens to associate voluntarily in opposition to what other voluntary associations are doing. Second, the pressure pushes in the direction of equal freedom simply by challenging the public sensibility of discriminatory exclusions. Among the Boy Scouts' most prominent critics are the Girl Scouts, which does not discriminate on grounds of sexual orientation. As the director of the Florida Girl Scouts declared in a public debate that resulted in ending a public subsidy to the Boy Scouts: "Even men can be Girl Scouts."[35]

As long as the Boy Scouts are permitted to exclude gay men and all women, may democratic governments legitimately subsidize the association? This is a critical question; since democratic governments often subsidize voluntary associations. Charitable and nonprofit associations in the United States, for example, are heavily subsidized by tax law with tax exemptions and other indirect subsidies. (The subsidies are often more direct in other democracies.) Surely a democratic state should not give special privileges to discriminatory associations, but may it justifiably support all voluntary expressive associations regardless of their discriminatory or nondiscriminatory membership policies?

When a public park is open to all speakers, public access to all speakers does not express support for discrimination; it expresses equal access to an open public forum whose purpose is free expression. But when public schools give discriminatory associations access to their classrooms during after-school hours, they may be sending quite a different message because of the school context: It is permissible to teach young children to discriminate among one another in a public school setting, as long as it is after hours. Public schools thereby help perpetuate negative stereotypes that are inimical to an nondiscriminatory education for democratic citizenship.[36]

The more freedom that expressive associations have to discriminate, the less state support they should receive beyond the support of legal toleration. A democratic state committed to equal freedom, opportunity, and civic equality should refrain from supporting discriminatory groups through public funding, interest-free loans, publicly subsidized space, and the like. These kinds of support are positive incentives to associations, and positive incentives are precisely what a democratic state should not give to discriminatory associations. A discriminatory association need not be considered charitable and therefore privileged by tax exemption. There is good legal precedent in the United States for refusing tax exemption to a discriminatory associations that distribute a public good such as higher education. Bob Jones University was not considered charitable after it insisted on discriminating against African Americans.

Individuals should be free to express their identities, and this freedom often means that they will express prejudices in expressive associations that discriminate. It does not follow, however, that discriminatory associations have any right to state support for their discriminatory expression. Toleration of discrimination in the form of free expression does not entail or imply subsidization. As we have seen, state support for discrimination is incompatible with the equal freedom of individuals to identify in public as they see fit as long as they do not harm others in so doing. When states go beyond tolerating discriminatory associations to actively supporting them, such as through tax subsidies, they stack the social deck in favor of discrimination and thereby make it far more difficult for public pressures against discrimination to succeed.

SHOULD DEMOCRACIES DISCOURAGE BOWLING ALONE?

Although as we have discussed freedom of association is central to free identity expression, by its very nature it also leaves people free not to join groups. Bowling alone has come to signify the choice not to join formal voluntary associations, and the tendency toward bowling alone has led many observers to issue a clarion call for democratic governments to take active steps to encourage more associations of all kinds rather than simply leaving people free to choose whether or not, and how, to associate together. How should democracies react to the choices that many individuals increasingly make not to join formal voluntary associations?

Social scientists present evidence to suggest that the choice to associate in voluntary groups leads people to identify not only with each other but also with people like those within the association, and this identification produces the social good of reciprocity, which is the generalized form of mutual aid.[37] Reciprocity is a social good that is capable of producing two kinds of benefits: to individuals directly and to democracy directly (and thereby to individuals indirectly). Identification with others through association, the evidence suggests, supports various kinds of mutual aid that most people need to live healthy, happy, safe, and secure lives. Identification through association also supports the mutual aid that democracies need in order to establish a sound degree of trust among citizens and also between citizens and government.

Conversely, the decline in association decreases mutual identification among people, which in turn leads to a decline in reciprocity and therefore to less healthy, happy, safe, and secure lives and a less secure democracy. Social problems that have been correlated with disassociation include:

- Higher levels of distrust of other people that make it harder to solve collective action problems, which require coordinated efforts among large numbers of individuals;

- Higher crime rates that not only harm individuals but also further increase social distrust and decrease (actual and perceived) quality of life in neighborhoods;

- Less civic and political participation, which creates a far lower capacity of any individual to change society for the better.[38]

The evidence for these causal connections is probabilistic and reasonably contested but still worth taking very seriously, since it is the best available evidence for assessing how democratic governments should react to the decline in membership in face-to-face voluntary associations. Also worth taking seriously is the fact that these generally good effects of associations are dampened by those voluntary associations that perpetuate discrimination, cultivate distrust, and/or teach hatred between "them" and "us."

Because the freedom to engage in or disengage from groups is a basic liberty, a logical entailment of free association, democratic governments have a basic obligation to tolerate both engagement and disengagement. This toleration extends both to bowling alone and to those voluntary associations that do no injustice but also do not support the instrumental goods—mutual trust, security, and civic participation—that often flow from mutual engagement. Democratic governments, as we have seen, have an obligation to regulate voluntary associations so that they do no injustice. This is because associative freedom should operate within the limits of laws that protect people from being harmed by others. What is more, the same basic freedom of expression that permits some discriminatory associations to exist also permits people to join together in using their own expressive freedom to pressure those associations to cease discriminating.

Democratic governments need not support all voluntary groups in order to encourage individuals to associate. Toleration, legal regulation, and public pressure are among the means that democrats can use to support free association while opposing discriminatory groups. Opposition to discriminatory groups is made far less effective, however, when democratic governments subsidize voluntary associations regardless of whether they engage in discriminatory practices that are inimical to the value and conditions of free and equal citizenship. Yet this is precisely what most existing democratic governments do with regard to voluntary associations: they subsidize them indiscriminately, which means that they subsidize a vast array of discriminatory associations, including those that preach and therefore practice discrimination, distrust, and even hatred of people who are ascriptively unlike themselves.

The strongest argument in favor of democratic governments subsidizing all voluntary associations, regardless of whether they discriminate, is the general evidence that voluntary associations *as a whole* aid individuals and society as a whole. Yet this argument does not justify governmental aid to discriminatory associations if it is possible—as it is—for governments to subsidize only nondiscriminatory associations or else none at all. An underappreciated fact about the three decades from 1960 to 1990, when more Americans were bowling alone (with friends) and fewer in leagues, was that Americans were also becoming more tolerant by virtually all available measures, attitudinal and be-havioral.[39] Greater toleration and more equal freedom for individuals, regardless of their race, gender, ethnicity, disability, or sexual orienta-tion, are basic public goods. These goods can be squandered by state subsidizes to discriminatory associations. It is self-undermining of de-mocracy in Israel and Palestine, for example, when the states provide enormous subsidies to associations that teach discrimination, distrust, and hatred among members of different religious and ethnic groups, including those that support violence and terrorism. There may be no viable political alternatives at the moment, but we should not there-fore confuse political tragedy with precepts of democratic justice.

If more involvement in discriminatory associations cultivates in-tolerance of people associated with out-groups, then subsidizing dis-criminatory associations threatens a loss in liberty for members of the out-groups. Fewer state subsidies to discriminatory associations can produce a gain in liberty for the less advantaged. This gain in liberty is a basic democratic good, which discriminatory community is not.[40] Those who defend basic liberty can also say something more about the way in which a democratic government can encourage association without supporting invidious discrimination. A democratic govern-ment has a legitimate option to subsidize only nondiscriminatory as-sociations on grounds that the government must not identify itself with discrimination.

There is no necessary trade-off between increased toleration and decreased voluntary association. Freedom, as we have just seen, is a means to mutual identification through association, not a substitute for community, as the debate between liberals (defending individual freedom) and communitarians (defending community) sometimes mis-leadingly suggested. Associating in groups is a way of both manifest-ing our freedom and using it to further many social goods, ranging from camaraderie to security to economic opportunity. The value of voluntary communities is now far more widely recognized than ever before as a means by which individuals can freely express their identities and also further democratic justice. Those voluntary associations that are good from a public perspective, as discriminatory associations are not, may justifiably be subsidized by democratic governments, for example, with tax exemptions as charitable institutions.

It is one thing for a democratic state to tolerate those voluntary associations that express discriminatory ideas through discriminatory membership policies but that do not distribute public goods. It is quite another thing for a state to subsidize such associations. Toleration goes along with freedom of expression, which extends even to insidious points of view, but toleration does not imply state support.

By not subsidizing discriminatory associations, democratic governments can discourage discrimination without discouraging associations that are compatible with democratic justice. When democratic governments go a step further and subsidize nondiscriminatory associations, they support the public goods that flow from voluntary association. Democratic justice leaves broad latitude for citizens and their accountable representatives to decide what kinds and levels of subsidy make sense, distributed among nondiscriminatory associations.

CHAPTER THREE

Identification by Ascription

"Identity depends to some large degree on how others see and identify you."
—Hazel Rose Markus, Claude M. Steele, and Dorothy
M. Steele, "Colorblindness as a Barrier to Inclusion:
Assimilation and Nonimmigrant Minorities," *Daedalus*
129:4, Fall 2000, p. 248.

*"If I were able to hear and speak, I wouldn't be deaf anymore.
That means my identity would be gone, and I'd be completely
different person, and I don't want that."*
—Jason Lamberton, a junior at Gallaudet University who
uses American Sign Language, responding to a
reporter's question about whether he would want a
cochlear implant if it could enable him to hear. (*The
NewsHour with Jim Lehrer*, Februray 19, 2001,
transcript.)

What distinguishes ascriptive identity groups is that they organize
around characteristics that are largely beyond people's ability to
choose, such as race, gender, class, physical handicap, ethnicity, sexual
orientation, age, and nationality. The nominal basis of an organized
ascriptive group is an involuntary characteristic such as gender or race,
but the organized group itself may be voluntary for those who join it.
The ascriptive group may also have its own culture, as does the signing deaf community in the United States, which they signify by using
the capital "D" to indicate that they are not only deaf by birth but also
members of a signing culture. The Sons of Poland, Italy, Norway, and
so on combine on the basis of culture, voluntary choice of member-

ship, and several ascriptive bases of identity (gender and nationality or ethnicity). Some primarily ascriptive associations, such as the National Association for the Advancement of Colored People (NAACP), are open to individuals who do not share the ascriptive characteristic, while many others are not. Ascriptive identity groups may also overlap with religious identity, but this chapter concentrates on those issues of identity group politics that are most closely associated with the ascriptive nature of the identity.

Like cultural, voluntary, and religious groups, groups that organize around ascriptive identities are ethically as well as descriptively diverse, as the Ku Klux Klan (KKK) and the NAACP (both explicitly organized around color) illustrate. Their inclusiveness also varies: the NAACP includes whites, while the KKK excludes blacks, although in both cases their members choose to join and are free to exit. This freedom of choice coexists alongside the absence of freedom in how people with certain ascriptive characteristics are viewed by others, since color, gender, class, physical handicap, ethnicity, sexual orientation, age, and nationality are often socially stereotyped characteristics of individuals over which they have far from complete control. It is this absence of freedom in how other people view ascriptive identifications that raises the most critical issues about ascriptive groups.

Identification by ascriptive association can contribute to negative social stereotyping or combat it, depending on (among other things) the context. Whether an ascriptive association aids or impedes the free expression of identity is only one important dimension on which these associations range. Many ascriptive associations, like the National Association of the Deaf (NAD), offer their members mutual support and access to cultural options that they would otherwise not find in the larger society. (The NAD identifies as a "group of deaf people who share a language—American Sign Language—and a culture."[1]) When such support does not come at the expense of hatred or hostility toward nonmembers, it is all to the better. Many ascriptive associations, like the NAACP, NAD, and The National Organization for Women (NOW), fight injustices that are associated with ascription, and this is the social role that raises the most interesting set of questions about these groups.

Ascriptive groups are also often straightforwardly strategic and self-interested and in this sense no different from any other interest group. The story of how the almost extinct Pequot Indian tribe managed to create a billion dollar gambling business in Connecticut (what has been called the "revenge of the Pequots"[2]) raises a basic conceptual question about ascriptive identity groups, addressed in section 1, "Interest Groups by Another Name": Are they interest groups by another name? Section 2, "Can Ascriptive Groups Be Justice-friendly," poses a basic ethical challenge to ascriptive groups: Are they bad for democracy because people should relate to one another as human beings rather than on the basis of ascriptive characteristics? To respond on grounds of democratic justice, we need to distinguish between ascriptive groups that are justice-friendly and those that are not, where justice-friendliness is associated with support for civic equality, equal liberty, and opportunity for all persons. Section 3, "Bearing Burdens of Representation," examines how organized ascriptive groups, such as the NAACP, NOW, or NAD, can bear the burdens of being seen as representing an entire nominal group—all black, all women, or all deaf Americans. Section 4, "The Special Obligation View," evaluates a commonly articulated view that members of disadvantaged groups— middle-class African Americans are a prominent example—have special obligations to their ascriptive identity group. Although the obligations are not thought to be legally binding, their public articulation is intended to place special moral burdens on the most advantaged members of disadvantaged groups. I call the special obligation view into question, and in the concluding section 5, "The Identification View," propose an alternative to it, which is consistent with the pursuit of democratic justice. The identification view, if more widely articulated and adopted, would also help further more justice-friendly democracies in which citizens live better lives by identifying with and aiding less advantaged others.

INTEREST GROUPS BY ANOTHER NAME?

Erik Erikson wrote of the "identity possibilities of an age," and in our age many identities appear to be available, and the choices seem to be increasing by the year. In 2001, the San Francisco city government

revised its health care benefits to cover the cost of sex change operations for city employees, reinforcing the view that: "People are limited
by, but they are not prisoners of, their genes, their physiognomies, and
their histories in settling on their own identities." As David Laitin
notes: "And if powerful social forces motivate identity exploration—as
they seem to do in our age—it is the constructivist face of identity
that seems the more real."[3] The social construction of identity is most
evident when identities are "constructed and reconstructed as social
opportunities change."[4]

One of the conventional wisdoms these days about identity is that
it is socially constructed. To say this, however, is not to say much
more than that genes and physiognomies do not determine our social
identities. Almost everything else that informs our social identities—
such as race[5], gender (as distinct from biological sex),[6] ethnicity,[7] and
nationality[8]—can be called social constructions.[9] To say that racial,
gender, ethnic, and national identities are social constructions, as
Laitin recognizes, is not to say that they are any easier to change than
our genetic inheritance or physiognomy. Most African Americans,
women, and deaf people cannot "pass" for white, men, or hearing
individuals; they can reinterpret their ascriptive identities but it is difficult if not impossible to give them up. For some people, ethnic and
national identities connected to a native language may be easier to
change by a decision to speak a second language and give up certain
customary ways of acting, but even an ethnic or national identity can
be difficult to alter except by generational change.

Yet some people do decide to assert, retain, or change their ascriptive identities quite deliberately and strategically. Ascriptive identity
groups, therefore, also strategically change over time through individual choices that are themselves strategically interest-driven. Are ascriptive identity groups therefore a subset of interest groups, which
can be adequately understood by a rational choice theory of politics?
A rational choice theory posits that people identify according to what
best satisfies their interests, and what best satisfies their interests depends in turn on the payoffs people (consciously or subconsciously)
perceive from the alternate identities that are available to them. In any
given social context, people choose the available identity that they
perceive will best serve their interests.

It is important to note that interest cannot be identity-driven on a strict rational choice theory because if it were, the notion of "rational choice" would be viciously circular. If interest explains the choice of identity, then identity cannot explain the choice of interest. On a rational choice theory, ascriptive identity is one among many tools in the arsenal of an interest-driven politics. Instead of letting theory override evidence, we should be open to the possibility that people's interests and understanding of their interests are as identity-driven as their identities are interest-driven. Neither interest nor identity can be assumed to have causal priority. Conceptually and empirically, the idea of a dynamic interaction between interest and identity makes more sense.

Changes in ascriptive identity are often interest-driven, and ascriptive groups generally do pursue their interests in identity politics. But the opposite causal path also operates powerfully in democratic politics. Ascriptive identities *inform* people's interests. People cannot make sense of their interests completely apart from their particular identities. Being a woman has had a formative influence on my identity, not the only formative influence, to be sure, but an important one. Being black, deaf, homosexual, bisexual, and so on has a formative influence on other people's identities. Many dimensions of identity help shape a sense of what our interests are, and our interests in turn help shape how we interpret, seek to preserve, or revise parts of our identity. Because identity often informs interest, identity cannot be reduced to interest. As the example of gender identity suggests, interests do not always, or even generally, precede identity in a way that would permit an observer to explain people's behavior by their prior interests without knowing their identities. If this is the case, as I will show by pursuing an example friendly to the idea of interest driving identity, ascriptive identity has an important independent role to play in democratic politics. Conceptually, this means that we cannot reduce ascriptive identity to interest, or ascriptive identity groups to interest groups, without losing some significant explanatory power of how ascriptive identity groups operate in democratic politics.

It would be hard to find a better example of how ascriptive identity is used strategically, in keeping with a rational choice model, than the conversion of Skip Hayward to a Pequot Indian in the mid-1970s.[10]

Skip was born in 1947 to a Navy seaman whose mother and grand-mother were active in the Daughters of the American Revolution. Skip's maternal grandmother was the last person to have been brought up as a Pequot Indian on the tribal reservation in Connecticut. Skip was at most one-sixteenth Indian on his mother's side. He was edu-cated as a white American boy in public schools in Rhode Island and Connecticut. He occasionally visited his grandmother on the then im-poverished Pequot reservation. After she died, state law would have turned the Pequot property into a state park had Skip not strategically seized the opportunity to identify as a Pequot, move with other family members to the reservation land, and enlist the aid of a superlawyer, Tom Tureen, to fight for more land and state aid for the tribe. Tureen had helped the Passamaquoddies and Penobscots win back 300,000 acres (plus $1.5 million a year for 15 years) from Maine, and he was enlisted by Skip to do something similar for the Pequots, who now consisted mainly of Skip and those members of his family he could recruit to join the suit. The new Pequots had a similar legal basis to reclaim tribal land from Connecticut, which they did, along with an exemption from the state's gambling laws available only to Native American tribal reservations on the basis of their tribal sovereignty. In short, Skip struck it rich by choosing to become a Pequot in his mid-20s. He also thereby rebuilt what would have otherwise been an extinct Pequot reservation around a billion dollar a year gambling business, the Foxwoods Resort Casino.

Skip's choice of an ascriptive identity was apparently as interest-driven as possible. He would not have adopted a Pequot identity had it not been for the economic interest that this identity permitted him to pursue. Rational choice theory can also explain how people pursue noneconomic interests by means of ascriptive identity politics. The NAACP and NOW, for example, pursue their organizational interest of furthering civic equality for African Americans and women, respec-tively. These and other ascriptive associations find their interest-based niche in democratic politics, as do any other associations. If we forget for a moment about the content of their aims, these associations look no different from any other on the rational choice view. When indi-viduals support an ascriptive association because of their own identi-fication with a subordinated group in society, they further their own interests at the same time as they support the group's cause. From the perspective of rational choice theory, when individuals support just causes—such as civic equality—on the basis of their ascriptive identity, their support for a justice-friendly identity group is just one among many manifestations of the universal pursuit of self-interest.

It does not follow, however, that ascriptive identity politics is reducible to interest-group politics, which in turn is reducible to the universal pursuit of self-interest by individuals. Moreover, a rational choice theorist like Laitin can accept that this does not follow, since his own account of the relationship between identity and interest actually gives an independent role to ascriptive identity in driving interest-group politics. Why give any independent role to ascriptive identity? There are two reasons. The first is that individuals cannot simply choose their ascriptive identities from a limitless smorgasbord of possibilities. Ascriptive identity choice is always limited, and often very much so. Skip could not have chosen to be a Daughter of the American Revolution had this ascriptive identity been in his economic interest. The range of ascriptive identities open to individuals therefore helps explain how interest-group politics works rather being explained by it. The second and less obvious reason why ascriptive identity politics cannot be reduced to interest-group politics is even more basic to understanding the importance of identity politics: ascriptive identities inform people's sense of their interests, and they do so in an interactive way. Many people who are born and raised as Native Americans identify their interests as remaining on their tribal lands and preserving their tribal language and customs. These interests cannot be explained apart from a prior identity. But it is also the case that interests in turn can influence how people understand their identity, as Skip's example also illustrates. Having found that they could build a thriving casino business on the Pequot reservation, the Hayward family contributed powerfully to a revision of what Pequot identity means today.

Rational choice theory does not set out to demonstrate—nor can it demonstrate—that human behavior is reducible to the pursuit of any determinate kind of self-interest. What it sets out, instead, is a goal-oriented view of human action into which all human behavior can be fit, whatever its content. This is the basis on which rational choice may lead to the assumption that when people support ascriptive identity groups, they must do so out of self-interest.[11] But must they? Not if self-interest is a falsifiable assumption and joining out of identification with others or commitment to a cause (with which one identifies) is therefore not assimilated to self-interest. The self-interest assumption, to the credit of any rational choice theory worthy of discussion, is in principle falsifiable. Some people may act out of commitment to or identification with others, or both, when they support ascriptive identity groups. When blacks who can "pass" or women who are extremely privileged contribute to groups like the NAACP and NOW, we cannot simply assume they are acting out of self-interest (in any determinate sense of the term). Any perspective that gives determinate content to what counts as an individual interest cannot assimilate all ascriptive identity politics to Skip Hayward's adoption of a Pequot identity for the sake of striking it rich.

Even Hayward's story, which is a model of how ascriptive identity can be used to pursue interest-based politics, shows how we also need to attend to the independent causal role played by ascriptive identity in interest-group politics. The Pequot land claims were based on the Indian Nonintercourse Act of 1790, which cannot be explained without taking into account the separate ascriptive group identity of Native Americans. Claims of partial sovereignty for Native Americans as separate identity groups were the legal basis for the gambling exemption that permitted Hayward to build the Foxwoods Resort Casino on Pequot land. Considerations of ascriptive identity also are necessary to explain why Skip and his family and not every other ordinary American were permitted by law to lay claim to the Pequot reservation. These and other identity-driven features of the "revenge of the Pequots" challenge the one-sided claim that interest governs identity with a far more defensible view that identity and interest interact in democratic politics. Democratic politics is *both* interest *and* identity driven in ways that depend on particular historical, cultural, and political circumstances, and the identity-driven direction has been neglected by conventional political science.

Had the Pequots never existed in the United States, Skip Hayward could never have succeeded as he did in pursuing fortunes for himself and his extended family. (This is only one among many examples that can help fuel the moral critics of identity politics, to whom I turn in the next section. Here I consider only the conceptual foundation for giving independent consideration to the role of identity in democratic politics.) The rich history of the Pequot and other Native American groups, along with their near extermination by New World settlers, forms an ongoing historical legacy without which the "revenge of the Pequots" could not have occurred. Had the Pequot or surrounding non-Pequot groups created a different politics and culture (suppose that commercial gambling had become generally legal or a thoroughly unappealing activity in the larger society), there also would be no revenge of the Pequot story to be told. Together these considerations show that identity group politics cannot be reduced to interest politics any more than interest politics can be reduced to identity politics. The two interact, in often fascinating and frustrating ways, in democratic politics.[12]

The interaction between identity and interest in democratic politics makes it futile to ask in general, "Which came first, the interest or the identity?" Like the classic unanswerable question, "Which came first, the chicken or the egg?", if forced to answer, we can only say, both and neither. As we have seen, even in the extreme case of someone who adopts an ascriptive identity that he had never before seriously considered as his group identity in order to make a living, the identity plays a causally important and independent role in shaping how the living is pursued. Had Native Americans not existed as major ascriptive identity groups in American politics, Hayward would not have been able to rely upon his remote association with the Pequots to pursue his interest. Had there been no living to be made by these means, the Pequot tribe would no longer exist today; it would have become extinct. Identity change that is driven by economic interest is common in democratic politics, but so is interest change that is driven by identity. Ascriptive identity group politics is an important phenomenon precisely because ascriptive identities exert powerful influences in their interaction with interests in democratic politics.

CAN ASCRIPTIVE GROUPS BE JUSTICE-FRIENDLY?

Inequality based on ascriptive identity is a regrettable fact of life that democratic justice attempts to ameliorate. Does democracy need ascriptive groups to move in the direction of democratic justice? Having shown why ascriptive identity is conceptually important, we now need to assess its ethical importance in democracy. Two different views of ascriptive groups are common. One view is symmetrically critical of all ascriptive identity groups for perpetuating the idea that morally arbitrary features of individuals are morally relevant when they are not. The other view is asymmetrically supportive of ascriptive groups, supportive of some but critical of others, depending on their politics. One attraction of the symmetrical view is that it appears to be nonpartisan, indifferent to the role that particular identity groups play in democratic politics, since its primary concern is the way ascriptive identity groups as a whole perpetuate the political importance of ascriptive identity and thereby threaten democratic justice. By contrast, the asymmetrical view appears more partisan because it assesses particular identity groups on the basis of their political aims: whether they further civic equality and other components of democratic justice.

This contrasting appearance is misleading. The asymmetry view judges particular ascriptive groups by their contributions to democratic justice, and the symmetry view judges ascriptive identity groups as a whole (rather than case-by-case) by this very same standard. The two views differ in how they use the same standard—democratic justice—to guide their judgments.

Both the symmetry and asymmetry views are critical of the many ascriptive groups that stand for the proposition that some people are unequal because of their ascriptive identity. But the symmetry view also emphasizes how all ascriptive identity groups exacerbate the ongoing problem of injustice by perpetuating the idea that ascriptive identity is politically relevant. No one need deny the persistence of injustices attached to ascriptive identities, but advocates of the symmetry view argue that ascriptive identity groups should not be necessary to fight against injustice. They are right in this regard: People who believe in democratic justice should be willing to join together for a just cause, regardless of their ascriptive identity. It is even *unfair* to expect mainly the victims of injustice to organize against it. This expectation, coupled with the persistence of powerful discriminatory associations, help perpetuate the very injustices that justice-friendly ascriptive groups are fighting against.

The symmetry view need not be oblivious to the difference between pernicious and progressive ascriptive groups. It does not deny that some ascriptive groups (such as the NAACP) have done a great deal of good in a democracy that still suffers from legacies of injustice based on ascriptive identities, while others (like the KKK) have done a great deal of harm. But has the time not come for fair-minded people to recognize that ascriptive groups are generally counterproductive to the cause of democratic justice? There are two different arguments bound up in this question, both of which are worth pursuing. One argument is that ascriptive identity politics violates the very terms of democratic justice by publicly expressing the idea that people should identify with their own kind for the sake of fighting against injustice. A second argument adds that justice-friendly ascriptive groups instrumentally harm the cause of democratic justice by discouraging participation in just causes by a broader range of people, outsiders to the identity group in question. Ascriptive identity politics both expresses an inegalitarian view of people divided by their group identities and also actually discourages people from pursuing broad egalitarian goals by focusing on the particular needs of particular identity groups rather than on the more universal cause of egalitarian justice.[13]

The symmetry view is correct in suggesting that the presence of ascriptive identity politics is a sign of the absence of democratic justice. Justice-friendly ascriptive identity groups express the idea that organizing on the basis of ascriptive identity is a legitimate means of pursuing democratic justice. Where the symmetry view goes astray is in arguing that ascriptive identity groups therefore should be treated as a general hindrance to an ongoing effort in pursuit of democratic justice.

When we discussed voluntary associations in chapter 2, we uncovered a reason to be skeptical of a blanket critique of ascriptive identity groups. Some ascriptive identity group such as the NAACP and NOW are voluntary associations that struggle against the injustices that still afflict individuals because of their race, gender, or other ascriptive identity. These ascriptive identity groups enlist the power of association, which is far greater than that of dissociated individuals, to mobilize support against various social injustices. But do they thereby offer an effective response to the expressive and instrumental arguments against organizing on the basis of ascriptive identity? After all, other nonascriptive voluntary associations such as American Civil Liberties Union and Amnesty International fight against injustice without any attempt to organize on the basis of ascriptive identity.

The asymmetry view meets the symmetry view on its own ground when it defends the expressive value of subordinated people publicly standing up for their own rights. Uncommonly courageous or famous individuals like Rosa Parks and Jackie Robinson may be able to do this on their own, but most members of subordinated groups cannot act alone to further democratic justice. A central feature of subordination based on ascriptive identity is being treated as someone whose ability to speak and act publicly is less than that of individuals associated with more dominant groups. When those who speak up on behalf of ascriptive identity groups are members of the subordinated group themselves—when African Americans and women speak for themselves—they express precisely the opposite of the stereotypical view of their ascriptive identity group. When the stereotypical view is false, they help to convey its falseness publicly. When the stereotypical view has some truth in it because of past discrimination, they help to make it false. Ascriptive identity groups therefore give public expression to the dignity of individuals whose ascriptive identities have been negatively stereotyped. They voice a variant of Rabbi Hillel's maxim: "If we are not for ourselves, then who will be for us?"

Defenders of the symmetry view can respond: "If you are only for yourselves, then who are you?" If ascriptive groups stand up only for themselves, then they express, even if unintentionally, the idea of each group for itself, no one for us all. Moreover, if each group is only for itself, then how can justice-friendly ascriptive groups claim to be furthering the cause of democratic justice, which requires cross-racial, cross-gender, cross-ethnic (and so on) coalitions? Solidarity on purely ascriptive lines even among the unjustly subordinated therefore threatens to be counterproductive to the very cause of democratic justice that it adopts as its own.

An asymmetry view, also taken at its strongest, accepts these refined arguments of the symmetry view and adds some refinements of its own. An ascriptive group that is only for itself expresses less than the ideal of democratic justice. The ideal is that all people, regardless of their ascriptive identities, are civic equals. Organization along purely ascriptive lines, even among the unjustly subordinated, also may spell danger down the road for democratic justice because cross-ascriptive coalitions are necessary means to achieving democratic justice. The asymmetry view accepts both these refinements, and adds that many ascriptive groups such as the NAACP and NOW have never been only for themselves. Justice-friendly ascriptive groups often join coalitions for democratic justice. Some, like the NAACP, are also inclusive of others in their own organization and all join cross-ascriptive coalitions.

Justice-friendly ascriptive groups encourage subordinated individuals to organize and stand up for themselves. They are inclusive of others in their organization; and they also join in coalitions that pursue the general cause of democratic justice. By this synthesis, the expressive value of ascriptive identity groups supplements their instrumental value in fighting for democratic justice. If the NAACP had not played an effective role in the struggle for civic equality, then its organizational expression of solidarity among black Americans would not have sufficed to make it a justice-friendly ascriptive group. But its use of identity exemplifies how identity informs interest and aids its pursuit: "black Americans in the pre-*Brown* period understood that their fate depended in large measure upon their own efforts to achieve liberation."[14]

Even if black Americans in the pre-*Brown* period correctly understood that their fate depended in large measure upon their own efforts, the question still arises as to whether justice-friendly ascriptive identity groups are valuable in the post-*Brown* era. The civil rights struggles in the United States established the historical importance of the asymmetry view, but the post-*Brown* period may be significantly different. We need to ask whether ascriptive groups are outmoded in the post-*Brown* era. The NAACP is a good test case because if the asymmetry view is outmoded with regard to a justice-friendly group like the NAACP, then it is likely to be so more generally in contemporary democracies. Among ascriptively-based injustices in democracies, few have been more persistent than those flowing from slavery and racial discrimination in the United States. The role of the NAACP in the post-*Brown* period is therefore a test case for assessing whether the asymmetry view is outdated. Have justice-friendly ascriptive groups like the NAACP become an obstacle to achieving democratic justice?

Let's begin with a lesson learned in the wake of the Supreme Court's decision in *Brown*, when local school districts were expected by law to desegregate their schools. What happened in the town of Milford, Delaware, is revealing of why just laws alone do not make justice-friendly ascriptive groups unnecessary. The school board of Milford belatedly desegregated the white high school but did so in a token fashion. Facing threats of violence by the local white community, the school board shut the school down. Bryant Bowles, founder of the National Association for the Advancement of White People (NAAWP), organized a mass rally to support "segregation as it has always been in Delaware."[15] Standing before a crowd and holding up his three-year-old daughter, Bowles asked: "Do you think I'll ever let my little girl go to school with Negroes? I certainly will not!"[16] At a second rally, he told his all-white audience that "The Negro will never be satisfied until he moves into the front bedroom of the white man's home, and when he tries that a lot of gunpowder will burn."[17] The Milford school was subsequently boycotted, as the NAAWP recommended.

The NAACP fought back, largely unaided by President Eisenhower, who said he was duty-bound to obey *Brown* but refused to endorse it.[18] What he had written to the daughter of Booker T. Washington turned into a self-fulfilling negative prophecy: "We cannot do it [improve race relations] by cold lawmaking, but must make these changes by appealing to reason, by prayer, and by constantly working at it through our own efforts."[19] The efforts of most white Americans, who still make up the majority, left a lot to be desired. Many schools in the United States are still not desegregated by race, nor are they schools of civic equality. A history of resistance by whites to desegregation, white flight to white suburbs, and judicial invalidation of desegregation orders that cross city-suburban boundaries combine to support the continuing need for justice-friendly (predominantly) black groups to defend their civic equality in a society still characterized by democratic injustice on grounds of race and class combined.

Is the NAACP outmoded in the post-*Brown* era? Not as long as injustices persist like the ones that occurred during the presidential election of 2000. The NAACP was the first major organization to call public attention to major problems in the way voters who were poor and disproportionately African American were treated at the polls. As the Civil Rights Commission later reported:

- Many African Americans did not cast ballots because they were assigned to polling sites that did not have adequate resources to confirm voting eligibility status;

- Many Haitian Americans and Puerto Rican voters were not provided with language assistance when required and requested;

- Too few poll workers were adequately trained and too few funds were committed to voter education activities;

- Nonfelons were removed from voter registration rolls based upon unreliable information collected in connection with sweeping, state sponsored purge policies;

- Old and defective election equipment was found in poor precincts;

- Persons with disabilities faced accessibility difficulties at certain polling sites;

- Many Jewish and elderly voters received defective and complicated ballots that may have produced "overvotes" and "undervotes."[20]

All of these charges, if true, constitute injustices that accrue to individuals partly because of their ascriptive identities despite the spirit and letter of laws to the contrary.[21]

Both the symmetry and asymmetry views can agree that the ideal means of fighting these injustices would be widespread association on nonascriptive grounds. In the absence of the ideal means, the asymmetry view warns us against assuming that these injustices will be effectively addressed without the attention of justice-friendly ascriptive associations like the NAACP or NOW. And the symmetry view reminds us that even justice-friendly ascriptive associations are not always all to the good, since political solidarity on the basis of ascriptive characteristics may need to be overcome in order to fully realize democratic justice.

In sum, justice-friendly ascriptive associations at their best do important work that otherwise would not be done in their stead. When they are most successful, they express the civic equality of their members, they form coalitions with other justice-friendly associations, and governmental institutions follow up with decisions in the direction of democratic justice.[22] When they are least successful, they create new (or deeper) divisions among the disadvantaged and convey the dangerous impression that people need only band together on the basis of their ascriptive identities and not on the basis of their common humanity or a commitment to fighting injustice whoever its victims happen to be. Even if justice-friendly ascriptive groups could be superceded in an ideal democracy, democrats can consistently support them in nonideal democracies, after asking critical questions about their expressive and instrumental role in politics.

BEARING BURDENS OF REPRESENTATION

Justice-friendly ascriptive organizations play a legitimate role, often urgently needed, in representing disadvantaged people, but they also bear burdens of representation. Because nominal ascriptive groups like African Americans and women are so internally diverse, organizations like the NAACP and NOW cannot possibly represent all their apparent constituents. If these organized groups claim to do so, they misrepresent some individuals against their will. But even if the NAACP and NOW do not claim to represent all African Americans and women, critics suggest that their very success as prominent politically active identity groups may convey this misimpression to the detriment of members of the nominal ascriptive group who are not really represented by them.

The internal diversity of nominal ascriptive groups—African Americans, women, or deaf people, for example—is relevant to evaluating the representative role of organized ascriptive groups—the NAACP, NOW, or NAD. Internal diversity does not undermine the valuable role that organized ascriptive groups can play in representing people any more than the internal diversity of organized interest groups undermines their valuable representative role. Were it not for organized interest and identity groups in democratic politics, there would be far fewer effective mediators between individuals and government, and the formal mechanisms of democratic government would be the only means for individuals to make their voices heard. Identity groups are as legitimate a part of democratic politics as interest groups. They function politically as advocates and lobbyists for their members, just as interest groups do in democratic politics. The issues of representation that identity groups raise are best understood when their similarities to interest groups are also appreciated.

How do identity groups function like interest groups in representing people in democratic politics? Socially salient parts of people's identities—such as their color, gender, and physical disabilities—shape their interests, and their interests in turn shape their identities. The dynamic interaction between identity and interest need not be deterministic in any narrow sense: individuals identify themselves partly by how they are identified by other people and institutions but also partly by their own creative self-reflection. Social discrimination affects the identity of individuals, especially (but not only) children, supporting the idea that "Identity depends to some large degree on how others see and identify [individuals]."[23] But individuals who share the same ascriptive identity based on color, gender, or deafness also differ, often quite strikingly, in their interpretations of that identity, supporting the idea that identity depends to some large degree on how individuals view themselves. The two-way interaction between how individuals are identified and identify themselves is the backdrop for the burdens of representation borne by organized ascriptive groups.

The first and foremost burden of representation is a negative one, avoidance of injustice. Justice-friendly ascriptive groups do not seek goods for their group by inflicting injustices on other disadvantaged groups or individuals. The injunction "do no injustice" is important for organized identity groups to keep in mind—or to be reminded of—insofar as identification with a group may reduce the tendency of group members to sympathize with people outside the group and correspondingly increase their willingness to inflict injustices on outsiders. (Precisely the opposite phenomenon can occur if identity groups adopt the "do no injustice" injunction as their own: identification with a justice-friendly group may increase the willingness of members to support other justice-friendly groups.) Not only the practical force but the moral force of the injunction also increases to the extent that organized identity groups can be assured that their members will not themselves be mistreated as a consequence of their desisting from doing injustice to others.

Other burdens of representation apply to organized groups by virtue of their advocacy on behalf of the individuals who are nominally associated with them but do not accept their policies as representing their interests. Ascriptive associations often have no better alternative than to take positions that disadvantage or at least displease some of the people nominally associated with them. When NOW champions equal rights for working women and emphasizes that "every mother is a working mother," its mission, if successful, may further marginalize women who have no children and who do not work outside the home. When the NAACP defends affirmative action, it does not represent those African Americans who oppose affirmative action and are not themselves benefited by it. When NAD gives priority to supporting deaf individuals who sign and are part of a Deaf culture, it does not represent those deaf individuals who choose to speak English or who do not identify with Deaf culture. It is no solution to this problem to point out that these organized groups sometimes claim to represent the interests of all nominally associated individuals even in the face of adamant, well-reasoned opposition from members of the nominal group. The problem is only exacerbated, not resolved by claims of universal representation in the face of reasonable dissent from the organized group's policies.

The problem would be no better resolved by imposing a moral expectation of neutrality on organized ascriptive groups vis-à-vis the interests or views of the entire nominal group from which they draw their membership. Organized ascriptive groups serve the valuable political purpose of advocacy by *not* being neutral with respect to the interests or views of everyone ascriptively identified with their group. Far from seeking to be neutral, they should try to justify their positions to those individuals who disagree with the group's positions and cannot completely dissociate themselves from the group because of their nominal ascriptive association with it. What might be called internal justification is the effort to justify the association's positions and priorities to those who share the same ascriptive identity.

By doing their best to fulfill the demands of internal justification, organized ascriptive groups recognize a burden of representation to those individuals who are associated involuntarily with the group. Engaging in a process of internal justification supplements rather than supplants the first "do no injustice" principle. It demonstrates respect for the diversity of the nominal ascriptive group and is also likely to be conducive to more justifiable decisions by large ascriptive organizations that represent groups that are more diverse than their policies can reflect. When internally justifying its policies, an ascriptive association also takes into account whether or not other organized groups are available to be advocates for those members of its nominal group that its policies least support.

NAD's evolving position on cochlear implants for children provides an example of how a process of internal justification can operate for the better, even after some serious missteps by an ascriptive association. When cochlear implants were first approved by the medical community as effective devices to help deaf children hear, NAD opposed their legalization and offered many reasons for doing so, including the uncertainty of their results, the impossibility of consent by children to a risky operation, and the ability of deaf children to live fulfilling lives by being integrated into the Deaf (signing) culture. The impossibility of consent by children, however, does not favor one side or the other on the issue of cochlear implants. Nor does the claim that the operation is risky. The critical question concerning risk is how the benefits compare with the risks. Moreover, the ability of deaf children to live fulfilling lives without cochlear implants tells us nothing about whether they can live equally or more fulfilling lives with them.

NAD could not justifiably ignore the fact that over ninety percent of deaf children are born to hearing parents who do not sign and often want to have access to cochlear implants for their children so that their children can live fulfilling lives outside of a signing culture and within the parents' culture. As evidence mounted that the cochlear implant enables deaf children to process sound and thereby to develop language on the basis of speech, it became clearer that NAD could no longer credibly justify its opposition to legalizing cochlear implants either to deaf children or their hearing parents. Public criticism of NAD also increased, and it reconsidered its original policy. To its credit and consistently with a principle of "do no injustice" and a process of internal justification, NAD developed a more justifiable policy statement on cochlear implants, which it stands by today.

NAD now recognizes the right of parents to obtain cochlear implants for deaf children, and it offers reasons for legalization that are consistent with its support of Deaf culture. In light of the legalization of cochlear implants, NAD's priority of supporting Deaf culture is all more justified. Now that deaf children of hearing parents are able to function as hearing individuals, Deaf individuals (who are part of a signing culture) would be more marginalized in the absence of a powerful organized advocate, which the NAD is. Deaf children also have powerful organized advocates in the medical community if they or their parents want cochlear implants for them. This means that NAD's priority in representing members of the Deaf culture does not leave a large part of its nominal ascriptive group without organized advocates. NAD's advocacy gives public expression to the dignity of Deaf individuals and their capacity to live full lives in a vibrant Deaf culture. In so doing, NAD does not deny the difficulties of being deaf in a hearing world, but it speaks on behalf of individuals who can take pride in being Deaf.

It's worth pausing for a moment to ask: What sense does it make to take pride in an involuntary identity? An ascriptive association's claim to express the dignity of individuals on the basis of their ascriptive identity would be unjustifiable if taking pride in an involuntary identity is senseless. The key to its making sense is recognizing that the appropriate object of pride is not the ascriptive identity in itself but rather the identity's manifestation of dignified, self-respecting personhood, the personhood of someone who has overcome social obstacles because of an ascriptive identity.

When individuals take such pride in part of their identity, it becomes a constitutive part of who they are. When asked whether he would choose to hear and speak by using a cochlear implant if the technology were perfected, a 20-year old junior at Gallaudet University who communicates by ASL responded in a way consistent with this analysis: "Would it be easier? Yeah. I'm not going to lie, it would. But if I were able to hear and speak, I wouldn't be deaf anymore. That means my identity would be gone, and I'd be a completely different person, and I don't want that."[24] That is something that many hearing and speaking persons find hard to comprehend, which helps explain why associations like NAD serve important educational roles as well as advocacy roles in democratic politics. By reconciling its support of Deaf culture with the legalization of cochlear implants, NAD publicly recognizes the internal diversity within its ascriptive group without giving up its own (non-neutral) priority of supporting Deaf culture and taking pride in it.[25]

The fewer alternative means of representation available to disadvantaged individuals, the more powerful an ascriptive association is relative to its nominal members and the more vulnerable they are in relation to the larger society. By these standards, NAD is justified in giving priority to defending the interests of Deaf individuals who sign and identify with a Deaf culture: they have the fewest alternative means of representation and are among the most vulnerable individuals. Because all deaf children, including those whose parents choose cochlear implants for them, are also very vulnerable, NAD also bears a burden of justification to these children (which is typically exercised through their parents even though the children's interests are what count above all else). The justification NAD can offer today for giving priority to representing the needs of the signing community is reinforced by the fact that a powerful medical community lobbies on behalf of the use of cochlear implants but not on behalf of Deaf individuals who sign. NAD is therefore not leaving a large part of its ascriptive identity group without effective organized advocates.

Ascriptive associations face competing reasonable demands from their members. Deliberation about competing alternatives is both a respectful and a potentially productive means of internal justification. Deliberation not only expresses respect for the diverse perspectives of members but also increases the opportunities for the association to improve its own understanding of the merits and demerits of competing alternatives. Deliberative processes of internal justification cannot guarantee good results, but they can offer a better chance of justifiable results than nondeliberative alternatives, which do not take opposing points of view seriously. The willingness to take opposing points of view seriously also offers mutual respect along the way to diverse members of an ascriptive identity group.

NAD's position shifted over time from one that would have done an injustice to some deaf children (had cochlear implants not been available to them) to one that does no injustice and gives reasons for the association's priorities to a wider range of ascriptively-identified individuals. This example is just one of many that show how both ascriptive organizations and the individuals identified with them can benefit by their engaging in a deliberative process of internal justification. Giving reasons opens an association up to counterargument, but, as the NAD example illustrates, the potential benefits of this practice are considerable and likely to outweigh the costs. There is also the consideration of expressing mutual respect among all those individuals who are ascriptively identified with an association. In the NAD case, the criticisms directed at its original position on cochlear implants helped to move the association in a more justifiable direction. The potential benefits of internal justification similarly apply to all ascriptive associations that advocate on behalf of individuals whose interests are otherwise underrepresented in democratic politics.

THE SPECIAL OBLIGATION VIEW

Just as many people depend on the support of justice-friendly ascriptive associations, so, too, do these associations depend on the support of many people in contributing to their causes. Yet individuals can benefit from the actions of justice-friendly ascriptive associations without doing anything to support them. This is a version of the classic free-rider problem, and it raises the question of whether individuals who benefit from a social good have a moral obligation to contribute to its production. The question is made more difficult to answer when it is directed at individuals who are not themselves among the most advantaged in society.

The free-rider problem is thought to arise in relationship to justice-friendly ascriptive associations as follows. Although a justice-friendly ascriptive association needs the support of individuals to be effective in pursuing just causes, no single individual needs to support the association to reap the benefits of its advocacy. If the NAACP succeeds in overcoming the negative stereotyping and elevating the social standing of African Americans, African Americans generally benefit, and not only those who contributed to the NAACP's efforts. When NOW succeeds in its advocacy of equal pay for equal work, women who are not members benefit without doing their "fair share" to support the organization. When NAD effectively advocates for the deaf, individuals also benefit who did not support NAD.

Whenever the political efforts of a justice-friendly ascriptive association are directed at improving the life prospects of members of a disadvantaged ascriptive group, the benefits of its advocacy accrue to ascriptively identified individuals whether or not they contributed to the cause. Since these causes are typically costly to pursue, the question arises as to whether all potential beneficiaries are morally (even if not legally) obligated to contribute their fair share to the cause. The fair share of more advantaged members of the group is presumed to be greater than that of less advantaged members of the group. Therefore middle-class African Americans are often said to be specially obligated to contribute to the NAACP and similar black causes. I call this the special obligation view.

The question of special obligation is important even if an affirmative answer does not force anyone to contribute to any cause against his will. Publicly criticizing people for not contributing is a serious statement in itself. Such criticism—especially when it is prevalent and public—often places enormous moral pressure on the people to whom it is directed and by implication reduces the moral pressure on the people to whom it is not directed.

When the pressure of moral suasion is justified, it can be welcomed as a way of socializing people to think about how they should live their lives and whether or not they should contribute to just causes. Public life in democracies includes practices of moral suasion. Moral suasion can change how people live their lives. It also distributes praise and blame in ways that affect people's reputations. Few people are entirely indifferent to the praise or blame that is directed toward them. By the end of our lives and while we are thinking about our lives in the process of living, whether we are honored or dishonored may matter more than money and other material goods, which can be achieved by more single-mindedly pursuing our self-interest.

A lot is at stake, therefore, in how we answer the question of whether relatively advantaged members of disadvantaged ascriptive groups have a special obligation to contribute more to achieving justice for their group. To answer this question in the affirmative is to support the special obligation view.[26] The special obligation view criticizes individuals who benefit from the efforts of justice-friendly ascriptive associations because of their identity but who do nothing to support them although they can afford to do so. These individuals are criticized for being free-riders on those who sacrifice to produce a good from which other members of the ascriptive group benefit.

In their own defense, the alleged free-riders can say several different things, depending on their own perspective on their identities. They can say that they are not obligated to contribute to a voluntary association that represents an identity that is not of their own choosing. It is unfair to impose an obligation on them that is not imposed on people whose ascriptive identities, by the distribution of the natural lottery, happen to be different and also more advantaged by society. The fact that the obligation is not imposed by law but by public opinion may make it less onerous but no less insulting or even less harmful to their reputations.

The alleged free-riders may not wish to distance themselves in any way from their ascriptive identities, but they can still claim that they are not beneficiaries of the particular causes (associated with their identities) that they do not support. Simply because those causes are pursued in the name of their ascriptive identity surely does not mean that all members of the ascriptive group benefit from them or value the benefits enough to contribute to them. It is unfair to assume that African Americans, for example, benefit from every cause that bears the imprint of their ascriptive identity. People should not be forced to distance themselves from an ascriptive identity in order to escape criticism for not contributing to every cause associated with their identity. African Americans may identify as such without identifying with every cause—even every just cause—that is pursued in their name. The same can be said about women, deaf individuals, gays and lesbians, and every other ascriptive identity group vis-à-vis justice-friendly associations that act in their name.

These replies are hard-hitting, but they have yet to hit at the heart of what is wrong with the special obligation view as it is publicly invoked in criticism of relatively advantaged members of disadvantaged groups. The special obligation view focuses attention on the moral obligations of those (more advantaged) people who are ascriptively identified with a disadvantaged group. By so doing, it averts public attention from the far greater moral obligations of advantaged people who are not identified with disadvantaged groups. There is no good reason why obligations to fight injustice should be placed first and foremost at the feet of members of disadvantaged groups. In the context of nonideal democracies, there is good reason to support ascriptive associations in their struggles against ascriptively-associated injustices. But there is no good reason to think that this support should come—*as a matter of special moral obligation*—primarily from people of the particular ascriptive identity that is still unfairly disadvantaged in society.

It adds insult to injury to single out middle-class African Americans for criticism for not contributing to the NAACP. It is irrelevant in this context that the injuries inflicted on unemployed African Americans are greater. The very focus on obligations according to ascriptive identity is problematic. At best, it distracts attention away from the general obligations of all individuals, regardless of their ascriptive identity, to help combat injustice in the world, if and when they can do so without undue cost to their own lives. If such general obligations do not exist, then the view that saddles African Americans and members of other disadvantaged ascriptive groups with special obligations is without any credible foundation. Surely it is not the case that only those who suffer injustice are obliged to struggle against it and to contribute to that struggle.

At issue in the special obligation view, taken at its strongest, is therefore not whether there are any general obligations but whether members of ascriptive groups have any special obligations. Assuming everyone has a general obligation to combat injustice, this obligation would be distributed among individuals as their abilities and advantages permit. (If such a general obligation is indefensible, then the view that attributes special obligations to members of ascriptive groups cannot find any credible moral foundation.)

Advocates of the special obligation view can argue that they accept the idea that all people have a general obligation to combat injustice to the extent that it does not impose undue hardship on their lives. It is not an insult, they can then argue, to say that middle-class women and African Americans, for example, should act out of a special sense of obligation to more disadvantaged members of their group *when more advantaged outsiders to the group fail to live up to their greater obligations*. This special obligation view then explicitly accepts the fundamental premise about moral obligation in an unjust world: All people—*regardless of their particular ascriptive identities*—have a general obligation to do what they can against injustice without undue sacrifice. (The proviso "without undue sacrifice" recognizes that bringing about greater justice is not the only thing that makes people's lives go well. Enjoying basic liberties and opportunities is also important.) How, then, does the special obligation view end up attributing *special* obligations to members of ascriptive identity groups?

The special obligation attributed to relatively advantaged members of ascriptive groups becomes a subset of the general obligation when people who are not members of disadvantaged ascriptive groups do not live up to their general obligations. The special obligation attributed to middle-class African Americans and women, for example, turns out to be a consequence of the failure on the part of more advantaged white male Americans to live up to their general obligation to combat injustice. In a social context in which most white men, for example, do not stand up against gender and racial injustice, more support from women and African Americans is needed than would otherwise be the case. But to say that more support by members of disadvantaged groups is needed is not to say that their obligations should be considered greater. Recall that the general principle is that all people—*regardless of their particular ascriptive identities*—have an obligation to do what they can against injustice without undue sacrifice.

In a context where white men are not doing their fair share, women and blacks need to do more if injustice is to be effectively combated. There is no insult lurking in this empirical observation. But this observation turns to insult when middle-class African Americans are criticized for not sacrificing for the greater good of the group. Considering that other middle-class Americans are not expected to subordinate their interests to the cause of combating injustice, this criticism is unfair. The same criticism is not unfair, however, relative to the perspective of other African Americans who voluntarily contribute to the cause at some sacrifice to their self-interest.[27] Fairness depends on who the comparison group is, which helps explain why criticizing more advantaged members of an ascriptive group for being free riders has the greatest credibility when it comes from less advantaged members of the group. Even then, however, there is a response, which draws on the fact that it is not primarily members of the group who have the greatest capacity—and therefore the general obligation—to combat injustices against the group. Doing one's fair share is indeterminate when many better-off people do less and many worse-off people do more, but the general principle directs its criticism first and foremost at those who are most advantaged in relation to what they contribute to just causes.

More advantaged women and African Americans are capable of doing more than less advantaged women and African Americans without undue sacrifice to their own lives. It follows from the general principle of obligation that more advantaged women and blacks have greater obligations than less advantaged women and blacks. What does not follow, however, is that they therefore have a special (greater) obligation than they would otherwise have if white men and others were doing their fair share. It also does not follow that their obligations should be the focus of social criticism, which is what happens when it is said that blacks and women have a special obligation to combat injustice (compared with nonblack men). The problem with the special obligation view is that ascriptive identity takes on a morally relevant role in attributing greater obligations to members of disadvantaged groups than the general principle of obligation supports, even in a nonideal world.

There are good reasons to criticize the special obligation view, even if one accepts the general principle that all people have an obligation to do what they can against injustice without undue sacrifice. It is one thing to recognize that in a context where social injustices are still attached to ascriptive identities, the power to combat them increases proportionately with the support of the most advantaged members of the affected groups. It is quite another to attribute special obligations to African Americans, women, deaf individuals, gays and lesbians, and members of other disadvantaged ascriptive groups.

In his introduction to *Notes of a Native Son*, James Baldwin expressed the need to accept his inheritance, which was limiting, in order to claim his birthright, which was vast: "My inheritance was particular, specifically limited and limiting, my birthright was vast, connecting me to all that lives, and to everyone, forever. But one cannot claim the birthright without accepting the inheritance."[28] Accepting the inheritance for African Americans and members of other disadvantaged ascriptive groups may mean putting up with a widespread sense that they have special obligations to their own group, above and beyond what other people have to that group, or indeed to anyone. This sense, however, is seriously limited and limiting. The moral criticism that flows from it can be the cause of justified resentment, which democrats can ill afford to ignore.

The serious problem that motivates the special obligation view is that too few people do too little to support just causes. The response to this problem, however, should not saddle members of disadvantaged ascriptive groups with special obligations, adding insult to injury. The insult, moreover, is a form of injury. It is a moral mistake to pose the problem of furthering democratic justice as one primarily internal to disadvantaged ascriptive groups and thereby to attribute special obligations to members of disadvantaged groups.

THE IDENTIFICATION VIEW

An ideal theory of justice says that when people associate for political purposes, they should do so on the basis of a general moral commitment to oppose injustice.[29] They should not associate for political purposes on the basis of their identification with particular others. But in a society still characterized by nonrandomly distributed injustices, it is an error of practical judgment to *assume* that people *will* associate together primarily on the basis of a moral commitment, regardless of their ascriptive identities. To assume this is to ignore reality, not to build a better world on the basis of it. An ideal theory is no substitute for a set of moral considerations about how best to move closer to the ideal in a nonideal world.

I began with a premise shared by the general principle of obligation: The problem of injustice is a problem to be addressed by everyone, and it is therefore a mistake to focus on special obligations borne by members of disadvantaged ascriptive groups. Everyone is afflicted by injustice, even though members of disadvantaged groups suffer more from the affliction. The affliction is a moral blight on democracy, and therefore on everyone's life within it. The moral blight is especially great on the lives of people who materially benefit from injustice but do nothing to combat it. People live worse not better lives from a moral perspective when they live amidst injustice. These thoughts have pushed me in the direction of developing an alternative to the obligation view, which I call the identification view.

The identification view diverges from the special obligation view in its assumptions about what contributes to people's sense of living a satisfying life. In the special obligation view, individuals who contribute to just causes do so at the expense of their lives going as well as they can. The picture is typically of people's subordinating their own interests to a just social cause out of obligation. Morality stands apart from their interests in living the best life they can; it insists that they subordinate their own interests and inclinations to it, since it is a higher cause. Moral people act out of an obligation to do what is just, but this obligation, which is affirmed by their rational faculties, is separate from what they feel or sense makes their lives go well (and what therefore actually makes their lives go well by their own sensibilities). It is in this phenomenology, which may forever be subject to philosophical dispute, that the identification view paints a different picture from the special obligation view.

In the identification view, individuals perceive that their own interests are bound up with living in a more just society, and they therefore think that contributing without undue sacrifice to making society more just will improve their own lives.[30] People who identify their interests with living in a more just society try to decrease social injustice as part of their own interests in living well and in making their lives go better. We can perceive it to be in our own interest to contribute to fighting injustice insofar as we identify with other people and therefore with a society that treats other people justly, as we wish to be treated ourselves. (The thought is not that we will be treated worse if they are, but rather that because we identify with them, our own interest is bound up with their being treated as we think they—like we—should be.) Our interests are therefore bound up with our identification with other people, and our identification with other people makes us want to contribute to making our society more just (without undue sacrifice).

For the identification view maximally to serve the cause of justice, identification must not be based exclusively on ascriptive identity. But identification can still further justice when it is partly based on ascriptive identities that are sources of injustice that need to be corrected by society. Humanity itself is an ascriptive identity, identification with which can serve the cause of justice. Identification with other people also can be based on a shared interest in democratic justice. The distinctiveness of the identification view depends not on the basis of identification, which can vary (with varying effects for social justice). It depends rather on how people perceive their contributions to combating injustice in relation to their interest in living a good life: Are those contributions in competition with their own interests (the obligation view) or are they a constitutive part of it (the identification view)?

Both the special obligation and the identification views capture an ideal type of a moral individual: the moral individual who subordinates her interests to her moral obligations, and the moral individual who acts morally because she identifies the success of her life with the achievement of justice in her society. Each view also captures a way that every person may occasionally perceive her relationship to her society when she acts morally, depending on whether or not she needs to sacrifice very valuable personal projects and attachments in order to act morally. When she needs to sacrifice a very valuable personal project or attachment, she may perceive herself as acting (or failing to act) out of a sense of moral obligation to reduce social injustice. When her personal attachments and projects are compatible with combating injustice, she may perceive herself as leading a particularly satisfying life in which she can fulfill many of her own interests as a moral person.

The identification view fits well with a commitment to pursuing democratic justice, to treating all individuals as civic equals, and to encouraging people to identify with other people and with humanitarian causes so that they see their lives go well when they pursue just causes (without undue sacrifice to their other projects). The identification view does not resolve the conflict between a sense of obligation and a sense of one's life going well. Instead, it shows us that the conflict need not always arise for moral people who live in democracies where the demands of doing what is just need not be onerous if fairly distributed among persons.

Rather than resolve the problem of people feeling a conflict between their obligation and their inclination to live a good life, the identification view avoids the conflict whenever possible and does so in a morally nonutopian way. Many people who spend part of their lives contributing to just causes in their society—without inordinate sacrifice to their personal lives—perceive their lives as going better because of their contribution to making society more just. Part of their identity develops around their moral perspectives. Certainly many African Americans and white Americans alike who have contributed to combating injustice think of their own lives as going better because of their moral contributions to society, and not only (if at all) because they gained personal benefits from their contribution.

Contributing to justice-friendly ascriptive associations is one important way, although by no means the only way, of making one's life go better by combating injustice. Making official acts of democratic government more just often depends on the political activities of justice-friendly ascriptive associations. People who identify with and therefore contribute to justice-friendly ascriptive associations can also live better lives as a consequence. The identification view builds on this plausible phenomenology and offers an alternative to the idea that members of disadvantaged groups have special obligations to combat injustice. It does not resolve the conflict experienced by people who are divided between their moral obligations to further justice and their desire to live a good life. Instead, it offers a way of thinking about one's life—and encouraging other people to think about their lives— in which the conflict does not arise except in those instances where a just cause requires extraordinary sacrifices. The encouragement is probably best accomplished through the education of children, but the public culture of a democracy in which the identification view is commonly articulated and acted upon could make a difference.

The identification view paints a plausible picture of how we can live better lives by identifying with disadvantaged people and with just causes by viewing our own interests as furthered by our contributions to social justice. The view therefore applies to everyone, not only members of disadvantaged groups, and it also extends beyond any single democratic society, suggesting that people can live better lives by finding ways of aiding the least advantaged wherever they happen to live. It is plausible to conceive of our own interests as bound up with furthering justice in mundane, nonheroic ways by contributing to causes that we identify as our own because we conceive of our own interests as bound up with acting in ways that help rather than harm others. This kind of self-fulfillment is related to what John Stuart Mill identified as living the life of a progressive being by pursuing higher pleasures, some of which are justice-seeking.[31] There is no guarantee, of course, that people will conceive of their lives in this way, but education and socialization, political institutions and public culture, can encourage people to do so.

For anyone who defends the identification view, it is critical to recognize that the identification of individuals in groups extends far beyond ascriptive identity as a basis for justice-friendly association. People also live better lives when they contribute out of identification and moral commitment to justice-friendly associations that are not ascriptively-based. The Red Cross, Oxfam, United Nations Children's Fund (UNICEF), Amnesty International, Doctors without Borders, Habitat for Humanity, the American Civil Liberties Union, and the Salvation Army are only a few prominent examples of associations not based in an ascriptive identity that effectively call upon people to contribute out of identification with just causes. (Of course the causes of justice-friendly associations may not always be just, since fallibility is part of the human condition.)

The identification view offers a way of avoiding the free-rider problem. In minimally decent democracies, most people need not sacrifice themselves to further justice. They can live more fulfilling lives by contributing to justice-friendly associations of their choice, out of identification rather than obligation. Those just causes can be specifically connected with their ascriptive identity, but they need not be. This view recommends that we follow up on de Tocqueville's urging to pay more attention to the associational life of democratic societies. Not all associational life supports justice (many associations are indifferent to justice and others hostile to it), but the more associations that support just causes, the easier it is for diverse democratic citizens to identify with justice-friendly associations and live more fulfilling lives by contributing to just causes. It is implausible to picture contemporary democracies progressing toward greater justice without the aid of justice-friendly associations—including ascriptive associations with whom disadvantaged individuals identify in light of legacies of injustice based on race, gender, disability, sexual orientation, and so on.

Justice-friendly ascriptive associations have an advantage born out of injustice: an identity base on which to build their membership and identify with groups dedicated to combating injustice. Nonascriptive associations have an equally important advantage: the ability to build a membership that bridges ascriptive divisions and directly identifies with just causes. Both kinds of associations can aid democratic societies in moving in the direction of greater justice and aid the individuals who contribute to them in living better lives.

The identification view also can address the issue of exclusion. Democratic justice cannot leave anyone out of its reach. The poorest individuals, regardless of their ascriptive identities, are likely to be the least organized by associations and therefore the least represented by democratic politics. The identification view therefore calls upon people, out of identification with humanity and a commitment to justice, to find ways of organizing the poor or (if their organization is not possible) organizing on their behalf in democratic politics. Nonideal democracies need more associations composed of people who identify with the cause of justice for the least advantaged, regardless of their ascriptive identities.

Nonetheless, identification with justice-friendly ascriptive groups can be a means of both furthering justice and living a better life. Ascriptive associations that pursue democratic justice, however, have reason to be as open as possible to people who do not share a single ascriptive identity. The NAACP is a model in this regard, open as it has been from its inception to all individuals regardless of race who share the aim of combating racial discrimination. Ascriptive associations like NAD that provide mutual support for their members who could not readily receive such support elsewhere have reason to be more exclusive. In both instances, however, we have seen that ascriptive associations have an important moral place in nonideal democracies. Democratic societies need justice-friendly ascriptive associations with which individuals can affiliate and contribute in ways that improve their own lives, and those of others.

CHAPTER FOUR
Is Religious Identity Special?

> *"The private judgment of any person concerning a law enacted in political matters, for the public good, does not take away the obligation of that law, nor deserve a dispensation."*
> —John Locke, *A Letter Concerning Toleration*

> *"No person who is conscientiously scrupulous about the lawfulness of bearing arms shall be compelled to do so."*
> —New Hampshire Constitution of 1784 in F. N. Thorpe, *The Federal and State Constitutions, Colonial Charters and other Organic Laws of the States, Territories, and Colonies Now or Heretofore Forming the United States of America*

Long before anyone coined the term identity politics, groups organized around religious identities were powerful political forces, so powerful in the West as to give rise in the sixteenth century to the Wars of Religion, which serve as historical backdrop to democrats who defend the separation of church and state. With or without church-state separation, a range of religious identity groups are politically active in the politics of all contemporary democracies, and the legitimacy of their involvement remains a matter of considerable controversy. In response to the liberal call for a strict separation of religion and politics, many contemporary conservatives argue against strict separation on the grounds that it discriminates against religious citizens by preventing them from bringing their most fundamental commitments to bear on democratic politics. Separating religious identity from democratic politics would be tantamount, they argue, to disenfranchising religious citizens. Liberals respond that separation does not disenfranchise religious citizens; it simply separates their religious commitments from their political ones. Whatever one's assessment of separating church and state, separating religious from political commitments is not simple and not necessarily of a piece with separating church and state.

A sense that religious identity is special underlies both liberal and conservative perspectives on the relationships between religion and politics. Religion is clearly a central part of many people's identities. But what follows for democratic politics is by no means clear. Soon after his inauguration, President George W. Bush announced a "faith-based initiative," which recognizes the importance of religion in people's lives by permitting government funds to flow directly to church programs that provide welfare with religious requirements attached. As religious identity politics in the past might predict, the reaction to the initiative was not pretty. The Protestant evangelical leader Jerry Falwell called on the government not to support the "Muslim faith [which] teaches hate." Falwell's statement provoked a leader of the initiative, John DiIulio, Jr., to lash back at Protestant evangelical groups for failing to reach out beyond their own religious communities to help people who are in need, regardless of their faith.[1] What happened should not have surprised anyone familiar with the history of political competition among religious groups. When democratic governments authorize religious groups to compete for direct aid, they start to wed the rancorous realms of church and state. This particular union does not appear to have been made in heaven.

We should be suspicious of faith-based initiatives by government. There is good reason to strive for a political organization that keeps organized religion largely separate from everyday politics. Religious identity then becomes far less a matter of everyday *political* contention. But as the uproar over faith-based initiatives reveals, separation of church and state is not a settled issue in contemporary democracies. For some, religion's proven capacity to provoke violence and intolerance within politics calls for strict separation from politics, whereas for others the importance of religion in people's lives calls for its special treatment within politics.

A democratic settlement that aims to protect individual freedom of religion in exchange for protecting politics from the power of organized religion is what I call "two-way protection." Two-way protection has two parts: it aims both to secure the free exercise of religion for all individuals and to separate church and state. Compared with most other democracies, the United States and France have greater separation of church and state. In the United States the separation is based on the establishment clause of the First Amendment ("Congress shall make no law respecting an establishment of religion . . .").[2] In France, there is also a long tradition of separation stemming from the settlement after the French Revolution. Church-state separation in the United States and France, however, differs in significant ways that suggest the complexity of the issue.

Many other democracies, such as Israel and England, are committed to something closer to a model of one-way protection, which accepts the first part of two-way protection—protecting religious freedom—but rejects the second part—separating church and state. One-way protection authorizes a state to treat one or more religious group identities (usually the largest religious groups) as deserving of special recognition within democratic politics. State-recognized religions wield widely varying degrees and kinds of state power under different versions of one-way protection. In Israel, the Orthodox Jewish Rabbinate and religious authorities of Islam and Christianity officially dictate marriage, divorce, and many matters of family law, respectively, for all Israeli Jews, Muslims, and Christians. The Anglican Church in England exercises far less extensive state power; its role is far more symbolic although nonetheless real. Delegation to the most common organized religious groups of various political powers—often over publicly-funded education as well as family law—is another feature of one-way protection, illustrated by Israel, India, Canada, and Belgium. Less religious citizens are expected to use the state-run systems of education and family law.

The enduring power of religion over people's sense of identity can scarcely be doubted. Does it follow that religious identity should be treated as special in democratic politics? Religious identity is often said to be special because of the importance of publicly acknowledging religious truths (the subject of section 1, "Supporting Religious Truth"), or because of religion's exceptional contribution to the public good (the subject of section 2, "Religion for or Against the Public Good"), or because conscience constitutes the ultimate ethical force in the lives of believers (the subject of section 3, "Conscience and Ethical Identity: Secular and Religious").[3] I argue that although religious identity is not unique in any of these ways, the ultimate ethical commitments of nonreligious and religious people alike are special and should be treated as such by democratic governments. The ultimate ethical commitments of individuals are special in a way that democratic government should respect when it can do so without undermining its own legitimate authority to make laws. Democracies should treat the consciences of individuals—whether they are religious or secular—as deserving of respect when such respect is compatible with protecting the basic rights of individuals.

If democratic governments should respect conscience in some situations, as in the case of conscientious objection from bearing arms, then separation of religion and politics (the subject of section 4, "Strict Separation") cannot be absolute. Even if not absolute, separation of church and state is still extremely important (as section 5, "One-Way Protection," shows). Religious freedom cannot be adequately protected without significant separation of church and state. In countries like Israel that practice largely one-way protection, religious freedom is more threatened. If nothing better than one-way protection is feasible in Israel, we should at least recognize what is threatened by giving state power to religious establishments. One-way protection downplays some democratic freedoms to the point of denigrating them, threatens at the extreme to disestablish democracy, and even in less extreme forms does not afford equal protection for freedom of conscience, which is its primary justification. A moderate version of two-way protection protects church from state and state from church, and neither protection is absolute (as section 6, "Two-Way Protection," shows) because either protection taken to its extreme limits would undermine the other. Two-way protection at its best accommodates conscience but also recognizes that freedom of conscience can be justified only within the limits of nondiscriminatory laws and policies.

SUPPORTING RELIGIOUS TRUTH?

Should religious identity be treated as special because some religions are true, and therefore identities based on these truths should be specially honored in politics? The moment we ask any generic question about religious identity, we confront the diversity of religion itself. All religions cannot be true since some contradict others, and therefore all religious identities cannot be special for this reason. Americans alone believe in variations of virtually every major world faith, with variations of Christianity being the most numerous and most popular. Even within a single nominal religion, such as Judaism or Christianity, believers hold contradictory views, which therefore cannot all be true.

The more we expand our religious horizons to include the widest range of belief systems, the more apparent the logical contradictions in belief become. Hindus and Buddhists, for example, do not share belief in a Supreme Being with Jews, Christians, and Muslims. Jews and Muslims do not believe in the Trinity, the Immaculate Conception, or the Resurrection. Muslims do not believe that the Jews are the Chosen People. "Since variant religions maintain sharply divergent beliefs about the significance of the universe and the nature of human beings," as Kent Greenawalt writes, "no one can coherently claim that religion in general is true."[4] We need to add that even within a single religion, contradictory interpretations of a single sacred belief abound, and therefore we cannot coherently claim that a single major religion is simply true.

Since it is so obvious that not all religious beliefs can be true, perhaps some people treat religion in general as true because they believe that some religion is true but they cannot know for sure. Some people think they will know for sure on Judgment Day, but they realize they cannot expect believers in other religions to accept their view today. What they can expect is that other believers will join them in treating all religions as special for the truth value of some religion.

The stakes of believing in the truth of the right religion are thought to be so high that believers may accept a kind of Pascal's wager and treat religion in general as special. Their religion, at least, will therefore be treated as special along with all other religions, even though they do not really believe in the truth value of all religions. They just speak or act that way for the sake of a public policy that specially protects their own religion along with all others.

This way of supporting a public policy that treats religion as special for its truth value helps explain why people who make a political argument for religion's being special because it is true actually have a particular religion or subset of religions in mind. In the United States, the most vocal public defenders of state support for religious truths identify those truths with a subset of Christian beliefs. But when anyone says that Christianity is the true religion, they cannot possibly mean that all Christians hold true beliefs since even those who are widely counted as Christian conflict. They must mean that the right kind of Christianity is the true religion. At the same time, they may deny that fundamental beliefs in conflict with their own count as Christian, even though such beliefs are deeply rooted in Christian tradition and widely identified as Christian. A similar phenomenon is at work in other democracies where the true religion is identified not with Christianity but with Hinduism, Judaism, or Islam, each of which also has conflicting beliefs internal to its tradition.

To treat non-believers and believers as civic equals entails not treating religious beliefs per se as true and therefore special in democratic politics. A prominent conservative believer—Richard John Neuhaus—responds to those on "the religious new right" who want "to enter the political arena making public claims on the basis of private truths." The integrity of democratic politics (not religion), he argues, requires that citizens not use "private truths" to make political arguments. Neuhaus targets arguments that rely on divine revelation rather than public reason. If religions in general were treated as special for their truth value, then there would be no grounds for resisting the political use of religious truths based on revelation. Neuhaus argues that "Public decisions must be made by arguments that are public in character." The convergence with John Rawls' argument for the use of public reason in politics is all the more striking as Neuhaus continues: "A public argument is transubjective. It is not derived from sources of revelation or dispositions that are essentially private and arbitrary."[5] This argument is compatible with a large family of democratic theories that emphasize the importance of reciprocity in democratic politics. Laws that are mutually binding should be mutually justifiable—in other words, reciprocal. Laws should not rely on private truths for their public defense. Reciprocity is a basic democratic value that is incompatible with treating religious belief generally as special in politics because of its truth value.

Neuhaus goes further than Rawls. He criticizes religious revelation as having "no inherently normative . . . force."[6] Rather than deny the truth of revelation for political purposes, democrats argue that revelation by itself cannot justify a coercive law because it cannot reasonably expect the public assent of citizens who have not experienced it and do not share the religious faith of those who take its dictates on faith. If the politically relevant content of revelation can be defended by publicly accessible arguments, then that part of its content can be democratically deliberated by citizens of many religions. But then it is the argumentative force of a revelation, judged in nonrevelatory terms, that is doing the justificatory work for democratic purposes, not the revelation itself.

Moving beyond revelation, we need to ask: Are religiously based arguments particularly suspect (or particularly valuable) in democratic politics compared to secularly based arguments?[7] Since it is impossible to answer this question in the abstract, let me pose it about one of the most common lines of religious argument in American democracy. Many religious believers today would agree, on the basis of their faith combined with reason, that God created human beings as equals and therefore slavery, unequal suffrage, dire poverty, invidious discrimination, and unequal protections of the law are unjust. This common line of argument is no more or less worthy of public consideration because it is religiously based; it is no more or less mutually accessible on its face than its secular parallel that begins with the idea that human beings are ends in themselves and reaches the same conclusion. Both rely on rather comprehensive philosophies but are mutually accessible despite this reliance, and serve important ethical purposes in democratic societies that still fall far short of treating people as free and equal citizens.

The idea that God created human beings cannot be proven true or false by empirical and logical means. Neither can the Kantian idea of human beings as ends in themselves. The democratic ideal of free and equal citizenship cannot be so proved either. Rawls recommends the democratic ideal not for its firmer foundations but rather for its better fit within a publicly defensible conception of politics, its lack of necessary foundation in any comprehensive philosophy, and its overlap with all reasonable philosophies, where reasonable philosophies include religious ones.[8]

Many of the most fundamental beliefs held by reasonable philosophies are far from proven; they are subject to reasonable challenge. In political ethics, as in ethics more generally, "there are intelligent, generally reasonable, and in many ways admirable people who disagree with us on smaller and larger issues about ethics. Our ethical beliefs must be held together with the knowledge that there is a sense in which 'we could be wrong.'"[9] Even though we could be wrong, strongly held convictions about free speech and freedom of conscience are essential to public morality in a democratic society. Because no complete political morality is beyond reasonable doubt, and because acting ethically in politics calls for strong commitment in the face of injustice, secular and religious citizens often need what the philosopher Robert Adams calls "moral faith."

Not all moral faith is equally valuable from a democratic perspective. The moral faith of some religious believers flies in the face of the best available evidence and the most basic ethical precepts of democracy. Faith that one's calling is to martyr oneself by killing people who do not share one's religious identity threatens any society. The problem, however, is not the religious basis of this moral faith, since secular faiths such as Stalinism and Maoism have also inspired self-appointed vanguards to kill millions of innocent people. Nor is the problem faith per se but rather faiths that inspire some people, secular and religious alike, to treat other people as if their lives were not worth living, a perspective that is antithetical to any plausible conception of democratic justice.

Religious and secular faith in the idea that human beings are created as equals should be treated similarly by a democracy. Both kinds of faith are compatible with, indeed supportive of, democratic justice. Secularists may be less aware of how they, too, rely on moral faith to support some of their deepest commitments. The method of reflective equilibrium that Rawls describes relies on having some deep commitments that guide our politics, not dogmatically, and therefore is open to empirical, logical, and ethical challenge but held firmly enough to resist the paralysis of doubt to which most ethical ideas are unavoidably vulnerable.[10] Whether consciously or not, morally committed individuals may all rely on a kind of moral faith. The kind of moral faith I have in mind is one that unites religious and secular defenders of democratic justice: it is compatible with the best available evidence and logic and therefore it does not separate religious from secular democrats. It is what can be called reasonable moral faith.

To some secularists the very idea of faith smacks of irrationality, but reasonable moral faith is not irrational. Faith goes beyond reason, but reasonable faith is compatible with what the best methods of reasoning can deliver at any time. A purely empiricist position would yield no commitment to democratic justice or to treating people as civic equals, since evidence and logic alone are morally inconclusive. Empiricism alone is amoral, and amorality is as compatible with doing bad as it is with doing good in politics. By amoral lights, good and bad are indistinguishable.

Reasonable moral faith in politics can help motivate ethical action. To motivate political struggles against invidious discrimination and unequal protection of the laws, for example, citizens need some moral faith even as they recognize that their moral faith can be reasonably challenged.[11] As Adams puts it, "the virtue of faith involves holding to a mean between vices of credulity and incredulity."[12] Reasonable moral faith supplements evidence and logic. (If it contradicts evidence and logic, it does not count as reasonable.) It is compatible with doubt when it is reasonable to have doubt. Reasonable moral faith supports believing in something in order to act morally that reason's resources can only defend with uncertainty. Those who dismiss religiously based ideas in politics as dangerous because they are dependent on faith do a disservice to the nondogmatic ways in which moral faith can work when it works best.

Does a commitment to democratic justice require any kind of moral faith? The basic ideal of democratic justice—whether it be to treat all persons as moral agents or to respect all persons, human dignity, or free and equal citizenship—probably requires reasonable moral faith. None of these related ideals, or all of them taken together, is resistant to reasonable doubt. A distinctive feature of a commitment to democratic justice is that many different comprehensive philosophies can and do support it, but this is far from saying that there can be no reasonable doubt about it.[13] If the ideal of human equality cannot be proved and can be reasonably attacked, then both religious and secular defenders of the ideal may need to depend on reasonable moral faith to stand up for it in democratic politics. As the reasonable moral faith in some version of free and equal citizenship becomes more widely shared, it may be less apparently (but not less truly) a moral faith. Already there are prominent versions of almost every major religion and comprehensive philosophy that converge in supporting free and equal citizenship. But strands of antidemocratic faiths, both religious and secular, remain prominent, and they demonstrate the danger of reliance on faith alone for furthering democratic justice.

Since there are both religious and secular ways of defending democratic justice, democratic politics should not treat one or the other way as special. Democratic politics needs all the help citizens can give it to make the most mutually justifiable arguments that are available to them. Many mutually justifiable arguments are not beyond reasonable doubt. What democratic politics therefore needs are citizens willing and able to make such arguments at the same time as they hold some plausible premises—such as the capacity of all persons for moral agency—as a matter of reasonable moral faith. In many political controversies, nonbelievers can readily translate the arguments of believers into nonreligious terms, and vice versa. To the extent that the translation supports some mutually acceptable ideals of democratic citizenship, the diversity of arguments has public value beyond that of free speech alone.

The public arguments of Martin Luther King, Jr., against racial segregation exemplify the use of religious beliefs in a way that anyone committed to defending basic rights—on whatever reasonable basis—can understand and applaud.[14] Part of King's civic genius was his ability to move between religious and secular sources of the same political argument in the course of communicating to his fellow citizens, showing that the religious identities of believers can be a powerful public force in support of democratic justice. The same could be said for the secular identities of citizens, since secular reasons are simply nonreligious reasons that may or may not be publicly accessible or reciprocally defensible.[15]

In "Letter from Birmingham City Jail," King invokes a secular basis (moral law) and a religious basis (law of God) for rights. He also expresses a religious idea that the moral law is the law of God. He then elaborates on the religiously based argument in a way that converges with some secular moral thinking:

> An unjust law is a code that is out of harmony with the moral law. To put it in the terms of Saint Thomas Aquinas, an unjust law is a human law that is not rooted in eternal and natural law. Any law that uplifts human personality is just. Any law that degrades human personality is unjust. All segregation statutes are unjust because segregation distorts the soul and damages the personality.[16]

In the course of the same letter, King offers a democratic argument for equal protection and against majority tyranny that is freestanding from religious argument yet fully compatible with it:

> Unjust law is a code that the majority inflicts on a minority that is not binding on itself. This is difference made legal. . . . A just law is a code that a majority compels a minority to follow that it is willing to follow itself. This is sameness made legal. . . . An unjust law is a code inflicted on a minority which that minority had no part in enacting or creating because they did not have the unhampered right to vote.[17]

Would the letter have been as exemplary had King limited himself to only religious or nonreligious arguments instead of showing his fellow citizens that they can be consistently combined? King invoked the values of a constitutional democracy in a way that offered both religious and secular citizens convergent reasons for opposing racial (and other forms of) discrimination.[18]

At other times religious claims of truth stand directly opposed to a legitimate governmental function, and then the faith cannot justifiably be the basis of a governmental policy (although it can and should be tolerated as a profession of belief). The claim that "creation science" is the true science while evolution is false, for example, stands directly in the way of teaching children biological science and the scientific method as part of democratic education. Teaching the scientific method is as incompatible with teaching creationism as it is with teaching astrology as scientific truth. (It is also politically naïve to interpret the demand for equal time for creation science, as some of its defenders do, as a demand simply to subject its claims to critical scrutiny equal to that of evolution.)

Democratic governments must rule out faith as a *sufficient* basis for making mutually binding laws, but faith may still supplement otherwise good reasons for laws and public policies. Democratic governments therefore should not treat religious faith as special for either its truth value or its lack thereof.

RELIGION FOR OR AGAINST THE PUBLIC GOOD?

Many commentators on religious identity have argued that it is special by virtue of the contributions that believers make to the public good. Many others have argued precisely the reverse, that religious identity is especially threatening to the public good because it sows the seeds of divisiveness and distrust among citizens on the basis of one of the most ardent and uncompromising forms of particularity. Both the positive and negative views have strong proponents, reflecting the great diversity of religious identities and views within contemporary democracies.

The idea that believers make a special contribution to the public good by their regard for others is among the most common views about what makes religious identity in democracy special. De Tocqueville surmised that religious believers are public-regarding citizens because "a taste for the infinite . . . restrain[s] the excessive and exclusive taste for [one's own] well-being" that otherwise dominates democracies.[19] Many contemporary thinkers echo de Tocqueville in arguing that religious identity serves a special public purpose in market- and media-driven democracies by helping "to overcome the aggressive individualism that so threatens civil order."[20]

Some religious antidotes, however, are far more destructive than atomistic individualism. Regard for others can be dangerous to democracy when it supports an intolerant and aggressive kind of collectivism, often in the name of saving lost souls. Despite all hopes to the contrary, hatred and devastation are still spawned by those who believe beyond a shadow of a doubt that they will become immortal by vanquishing nonbelievers in the contemporary version of holy wars.

Classical liberals like Locke and de Tocqueville thought that religions should (and increasingly would) be "most careful to confine themselves to their proper sphere," which they identified as the "spiritual." De Tocqueville's ideal was the Christian Gospels that "deal only with the general relationship between man and God and between man and man. Beyond that, they teach nothing and do not oblige people to believe anything."[21] By contrast, religions that seek political power and try to meddle with laws and public policies spell danger to democracy. While many have done just that, others have just as strongly supported a tolerant and public-regarding spirit. Religious identity per se is therefore not good or bad for democracy. The record of religion as a public good is mixed at best.

Do religious associations contribute to the creation of social capital or a sense of reciprocity among citizens that is conducive to democratic justice? In the United States, a high proportion of philanthropy is religious in character. Many religious communities support friendships, volunteerism, and other forms of reciprocal behavior that help a democratic society work well—perhaps better than it otherwise would—for many of its members. This means that religious associations supply far more than religious goods. Witness:

> A typical week in the life of Pasadena Presbyterian Church included activities ranging from meeting of Alcoholic Anonymous, Overeaters Anonymous and Sex Anonymous, Project Angel—helping new mothers in need, an open shelter for adults and children including food, substance abuse recovery assistance, counseling and health screening, meals on wheels, friends in deed—providing groceries and clothes for needy people in the community, concerts, alternative gift market and many more.[22]

Religious associations provide important social support systems, especially in democracies with less extensive welfare states. Churches have also been the basis for social movements whose activities have brought about major changes in the direction of democratic justice. The African American church in the United States famously "functioned as the institutional center of the modern civil rights moment . . . [and] provided the movement with an organized mass base."[23]

There is no doubt that religious identities help create social capital, but there is equally no doubt that religious identity also does the reverse and is not unique in either regard. Charity work alone does not ensure that a religious organization on balance is promoting the public good. Charity work is often connected with teaching hatred, sustaining illiteracy of the recipients of support, and making assistance conditional on support for political activities, not always of a constructive sort.[24]

Moreover, religious identity is neither a necessary nor a sufficient condition for the creation of social capital through associational life. The mixed record of religious associations is typical of voluntary associations generally, as discussed in chapter 2. Almost half of the civic associations in the United States are church-related, but over 90 percent of Americans identify as believers.[25] It may be that strong religious identity creates social capital, whereas weak religious identity does not, but it surely is not the case that religious identity by itself suffices. It appears that "the social ties embodied in religious communities are at least as important as religious beliefs per se in accounting for volunteerism and philanthropy."[26]

Religious associations, however, are not unique in fostering volunteerism and philanthropy, even in a democracy that is overwhelmingly religious and relies more heavily than most on nongovernmental groups (often supported by the state) to carry out many social welfare functions.[27] The fact that most Americans identify themselves as believers means that religious identity per se is bound to be a very poor predictor of contribution to the public good. Being a member of a religious association is a better predictor than being religious, but religious associations themselves also vary greatly in their commitment and contribution to social welfare. There is a significant difference in social outreach beyond the religious community itself, even among Protestant religious associations: "[w]hereas the mainline churches participated in progressive social betterment programs during the first half of the twentieth century, evangelical churches focused more on individual piety."[28] Bringing the comparison up to date, Robert Wuthnow concludes that "mainline Protestant churches encourage civic engagement in the wider community, whereas evangelical churches apparently do not."[29] Synthesizing the available evidence, Putnam concurs that "both individually and congregationally, evangelicals are more likely to be involved in activities within their own religious community but are less likely to be involved in the broader community."[30] If what is true for evangelicals also extends to some nonevangelical groups, such as Orthodox Jewish congregations, then the causal link between religious identity and public good is even harder to establish.

Even if many churches and other religious groups contribute a great deal by way of philanthropy and other public goods, many also discriminate in ways that cannot be counted as publicly valuable. This conclusion would be unsurprising were it not for the fact that so many commentators generalize that religious associations are especially good or bad for democracies. As the comparison of different Protestant denominations in the United States demonstrates, the practices of religious associations have widely varying content and their content brings with it widely divergent contributions, both good and bad, to a democratic society. The public value of the practices of religious associations are better judged on the same terms as those of other voluntary associations in democracies rather than in terms of their religious character, which carries no guarantees of public value or lack thereof.

What about the public value of religious arguments made within democratic politics? The controversy over whether religiously based arguments are especially good or bad for democratic politics is generally not about tolerating religious speech. Opposing sides in this debate generally accept freedom of speech as a basic right. The more challenging debate is over the public value of bringing religiously based arguments to bear on considerations of law and public policy in democracies. Does politically valuable reasoning include religiously based arguments?

Some liberals say that religious arguments should be tolerated as long as they are not directly threatening but they should not be welcomed in democratic politics. Examples of religious arguments from Christians, Jews, and Muslims that are anathema to even the most minimally decent democracy are not hard to find. The (Christian) World Church of the Creator sports this message on its website:

> This Jewish-dominated government not only milks us of our hard-earned income to bankroll the Jews of Israel and elsewhere, but also is quite willing to force non-Jewish Americans to become

"human shields" when the righteous wrath of the Arab people towards America moves from rhetoric to violence.[31]

Based on his religious understanding, the "Lubavitcher Rabbi" Schneerson publicly argued that:

> . . . the body of a Jewish person is of a totally different quality from the body of [members] of all nations of the world . . . A non-Jew's entire reality is only vanity. It is written, "And the strangers shall guard and feed your flocks" (Isaiah 61:5). The entire creation [of a non-Jew] exists only for the sake of the Jews. . . .[32]

After September 11, 2001, Sheikh Al-Hawali, who uses the Internet to publish his religious rulings permitting the killing of entire groups and nations, issued a *fatwa* against all supporters of the United States, including the Northern Alliance:

> Support of any kind for the unbelievers against the Muslims, even if only verbal, constitutes blatant heresy and hypocrisy, and anyone doing so goes against Islam. . . . Members of the Afghan opposition or others who do so must repent, recant this loathsome deed, and support their Muslim brothers. . . .[33]

The *fatwa* also justified the September 11 attacks and killings as strictly "measure for measure" acts.

By focusing on religious hate speech of this sort, we can easily see the appeal of not welcoming religious arguments in politics. The problem with a simple stance toward religious arguments of "tolerate but do not welcome" is that it says too much and too little. Too much in suggesting that all religious arguments are of this sort, and too little in overlooking the need not to tolerate some speech, whether religious or secular, that directly threatens the lives of individuals, as does falsely shouting fire in a crowded theater, whether or not religious revelation happens to inspire the speaker's words. Not welcoming religious arguments in democratic politics is defensible when the arguments fail to respect basic human rights rather than when they fail to be secular.

Far from failing to respect basic human rights, some religious arguments have greatly contributed to furthering the cause of democratic justice. Many examples show how religiously based beliefs can contribute to combating injustice in the United States, although none quite as extraordinary in its ability to address a wide range of believers and nonbelievers as Martin Luther King's defense of civic rights. Among other notable examples of religious arguments that support basic human rights are the pastoral letters of the National Conference of Catholic Bishops, one criticizing nuclear proliferation and the other economic injustice.[34]

The arguments made by these thinkers are not uniquely tied to their faith, but they need not be common to all ethical perspectives to make an important public contribution. Commonality with all ethical perspectives is too much to expect of political argument and would silence everyone on some important political issues that need to be debated for democratic politics to work effectively. These examples suffice to show that religious claims can contribute something of significant public value to democratic discourse.

Democratic politics should not merely tolerate but welcome religiously based arguments in politics when they support reciprocity among citizens. Reciprocity does not require agreement among citizens or arguments on the same secular or religious terms. The importance of political arguments that strive for reciprocity lies not in whether we agree with them but rather in whether we can appreciate their moral force. If we support any kind of democracy, we must be able to appreciate the legitimate role of arguments in democratic politics with which we do not agree.

There is no formula for making an argument in reciprocal terms, and therefore we can expect reasonable disagreement here as well. Some religiously based understandings clearly converge enough to be appreciated (even if not accepted) by nonbelievers, and the same is true for some secularly based understandings. What is at stake, it bears emphasizing, is not free speech but the arguments that can become the basis for coercive laws and public policies. As long as striving for reciprocity is possible across different ethical identities, it is democratically desirable. The alternative is giving up on the aim of justifying coercive laws and public policies to the people who are bound by them. In democratic contexts, religious or secular arguments per se cannot be assumed to be publicly beneficial, but neither can they be assumed to be the reverse. The wide range of religious and secular arguments that accept the idea of civic equality, for example, may be among the best available means for pursuing democratic justice, especially when we take into account the dependency of democracy on the moral motivation of its citizenry.

CONSCIENCE AND ETHICAL IDENTITY: SECULAR AND RELIGIOUS

Religious arguments, I have just argued, cannot consistently be treated as special for their truth value or their public value in democracy. The religiously based arguments of Martin Luther King and the Catholic bishops are valuable because they are arguments for social justice, not because they are religious. But the religious arguments of these believers manifest something else that is a special feature of ethical personhood: conscience. Conscience, as I am using the term here, designates a person's ultimate ethical commitments: ethical precepts that are experienced as binding on those who believe in them. Their source is thought to be an ethical authority that is variously identified as God, nature, reason, or human individuality itself. Some of these sources are considered external and others internal to the conscientious person. A constant across different conceptions of conscience is that it is not mere whim or will. Conscience is law-like, not capricious, and it binds the will of a conscientious believer. When conscience fails to bind someone's will because the will is morally weak, the failure stands as a moral reproach to the conscientious believer.

Conscience was once thought to be uniquely tied to religion (and the particular religion of Protestantism) but has since become synonymous with ethical identity, both secular and religious. The idea of conscience predates modern democracy, but conscience and democracy share a fundamental premise: persons are ethical subjects.[35] The conscience of John Milton's God was nonpluralistic, but contemporary usage accommodates ethical pluralism.

Whereas Milton's "Umpire Conscience" originally presupposed "a *shared knowledge* of good and evil,"[36] democracies that have disestablished religion do not presume that an omniscient God imparts the same content to every person's conscience. Conscience can be variously based in divine revelation, on interpretations of sacred or secular texts, or on methods of moral reasoning that rely or eschew reliance on ethical authorities outside of the person. If conscience is to be treated as special in democracies, it cannot be because it is either exclusively religious or based on a single shared body of moral knowledge or commitments of faith.

Ultimate ethical commitments need not entail belief in God or an ethical power in the universe outside of persons themselves. Thoreau's conscience entailed neither belief. It was secular and bound him to act in ways, such as opposing the poll tax and helping runaway slaves, that democrats should urge their governments to respect. Thoreau's ultimate ethical commitments pitted him against the law at the time but put him in harmony with the only morally defensible interpretation of the United States Constitution. Many forms of pacifism and Immanuel Kant's categorical imperative do not depend on any distinctively religious beliefs, although they may share with religion reliance on a reasonable moral faith in the capacity of individuals to be bound by ethical precepts. Kant does invoke God in the latter part of the second critique. But he does so to claim that the categorical imperative is consistent with the idea of God's eternal benevolence. Human beings cannot know God's will but they can know the good, and conclude what is good based on their reason. The moral faith is similar in form although distinct in content from that of religious believers who bind themselves to the commands of God as best they can perceive them.

In a landmark Supreme Court case exempting Amish children from two years of (otherwise mandatory) high school, Justice Burger contrasted their religious convictions to the secular convictions of Henry David Thoreau, which Burger called "subjective" and "philosophical and personal" and therefore less deserving of judicial respect.[37] This contrast between religious and nonreligious convictions may be widely held but it is fundamentally indefensible. Thoreau's convictions are subjective and personal in one sense, but it is the very same sense in which the convictions of conscientious religious dissenters are subjective and personal. Conscientious convictions—whether they are religious or secular—are subjective in that they manifest themselves internally in individual lives rather than externally in democratic laws (unless the convictions happen to be instantiated in law, in which case the conscientious citizens have no reason to dissent). Conscientious convictions, whether religious or secular, are personal in that they are someone's, not everyone's, beliefs. In a more substantive sense, however, Thoreau's conscientious convictions—against treating persons as slaves, for example—were no more subjective or personal than the antislavery convictions of religious believers. In both cases, individuals are bound in a law-like way by their ultimate ethical commitments.

Although some religious and secular citizens diverge in what they view as the source of their ultimate ethical commitments, they still can converge in understanding and experiencing their ethical commitments as binding on their will. Religious believers themselves dramatically differ in how they understand the source and content of their ultimate ethical commitments. Some religious believers, like Neuhaus, think that publicly accessible reasons must mediate between God's will and democratic politics, whereas other religious believers think it ethically acceptable (or even mandatory) to rely on unmediated revelation. Differences among religious believers are often as great as those between secular and religious believers.

Some religious consciences demand that children be provided with lifesaving medical care and others demand the reverse. Some demand that violent aggression be resisted by proportional violence if necessary, and others demand that violence not be met with violence. To make a credible case that conscience should be treated as special in modern democratic contexts requires facing up to the fact of deep disagreement among conscientious people. A democratic government cannot possibly accommodate all conscientious beliefs, whatever they happen to be, and still remain democratic let alone committed to pursuing democratic justice. Even if it were possible for democratic governments to accommodate all conscientious beliefs, it would therefore be undesirable. Some conscientious beliefs require people to deny others basic freedoms and opportunities, which any democracy must defend.

Even in the face of divergent conscientious beliefs, what conscience manifests about persons is especially valuable in democratic societies. By contrast to people who are ruthlessly interested only in their own welfare, conscientious people try to live up to the ethical precepts or laws that they take to be good and just and therefore binding on their will. Conscience represents the distinctively human effort to conceive and to live an ethical life, which democracy presupposes when it is committed to the ideal of reciprocal respect for persons, manifest in the democratic ideals of civic equality, liberty and opportunity. Without an ethical capacity, it is unclear how anyone can command respect. The effort to live according to a sense of goodness and justice constitutes ethical personhood or identity.

Democratic governments demonstrate respect for ethical personhood when they try to protect freedom of conscience within the limits of protecting civic equality and other basic freedoms and opportunities for all individuals. Respect for conscience is a moral good because it reflects respect for the ethical identity of persons, a respect that democratic governments cannot consistently reject. But respect for conscience cannot be an absolute value for democratic governments because it can conflict with other basic democratic principles such as equal liberty. Therefore deference to conscience by itself offers no guarantee of producing greater justice in any given instance (or even over any period of time). Conscience is ethically fallible, and therefore respect for it may be overridden when it would clearly produce greater injustice.

In recognizing the fallibility of conscience, democrats can ill afford to neglect the fallibility of democratic decision making as well. Like respect for conscience, respect for the democratic authorization of laws also is part of what it means to treat people as civic equals. On the one hand, respect for conscience is no substitute for respect for democratically constituted governments that enforce laws authorized by a democratic (written or unwritten) constitution. On the other hand, a democratically constituted government is no substitute for respect for the conscientious commitments of citizens. Both are necessary; neither is sufficient for the pursuit of democratic justice.

Respect for persons is basic to democratic justice, and such respect, as we have discussed previously, implies respect both for individual conscience and for the duly constituted laws of a democracy that are the product of people's political freedom. The lives of conscientious (but fallible) people who refused to be governed by collectively agreed upon laws would be poor and short, even if they managed to avoid being solitary, nasty, and brutish. With a government to issue laws, the demands of conscience would produce conflict every bit as bloody—if not more so—than the demands of amoral self-interest. At the same time, blind obedience to democratic laws is dangerous. Conscientious commitments are necessary to counteract tendencies to tyranny that are ever-present in politics. Remove or repress conscientious objectors and tyranny is given freer reign in a nonideal democracy.

As an ethical instrument, conscientious objection itself is two-edged. At any given time, the conscientious commitments of citizens may push in the direction of greater justice or injustice. But conscientious objection is more than an instrument. The instrumental value of conscience in democracies is often hard to determine prospectively over time, but its intrinsic value in individual lives is ever-present: it is the ethical identity of persons. The commands of conscience are a basic part of the identity of conscientious persons. They serve as ultimate ethical guides in life. Conscience has special relevance for democratic politics because it can be ignored only at the expense of respect for persons, which is a fundamental tenet of democratic justice. Conscience therefore cannot be so starkly separated from politics as classical liberals like Locke thought that it could be.

Thoreau's refusal to pay the poll tax and King's civil disobedience to laws enforcing racial segregation illustrate how conscientious commitments that are directly relevant to politics can help push democracies in the direction of justice. One distinctive feature of these conscientious commitments is their support of the ideal of human equality. Not all conscientious commitments support this ideal, and this is one among many reasons why respect for conscience cannot be absolute or a substitute for political support for laws that enact democratic justice for all individuals.

Although respect for conscience is surely no substitute for democratically authorized laws, it provides a distinctively valuable supplement. When conscience contests a law, a democratic government cannot simply assume that the law or the conscience should take precedence. Consistent with equal regard for persons, democratic governments should try to respect conscientious objectors in one of two ways. When conscientious objectors show that a law is incompatible with democratic justice, a democratic government should revise the law through legitimate procedural means. When a law to which conscientious citizens object is justified, a democratic government should consider whether exempting the conscientious objectors would harm others. Judicial exemption of pacifists from conscription laws is the paradigmatic example of a legitimate exemption for conscientious objectors.[38] A more recent example is the revision by Oregon's legislature of a drug law that originally prohibited everyone from using peyote but now exempts citizens who use the drug for sacramental purposes.[39]

When conscience contests democratic laws, one imperfect ethics confronts the other, and no credible ideal of democratic justice can assume that the claim of law or conscience will always be more just. To insist on either form of one-way protection—law enforcement or conscientious exemption—makes little sense when the stakes are so high on both sides: respect for the rule of law on the one hand, upon which democratic justice depends, and respect for individual conscience on the other, upon which democratic justice also depends. Since neither the rule of law nor respect for conscience needs to be sacrificed in toto, neither should be completely sacrificed when more nuanced judgments are possible.

Nuanced judgments are possible even in a nonideal democracy, and they highlight the fact that conscientious objection to laws can be justice-friendly or unfriendly, as democratic laws also can be. It is therefore perfectly consistent for courts and legislatures to staunchly support the conscientious objection of Jehovah's Witness parents when they defend their children's right not to be forced to pledge allegiance to the American flag and yet adamantly oppose this group's conscientious objection to laws that require parents to provide their children with access to lifesaving health care.[40] Democratic institutions need some discerning judgment to respect conscientious citizenship without sacrificing their responsibility to further democratic justice.

The flag salute case illustrates a distinctively valuable yet commonly neglected feature of conscientious objection to democratic laws. *Conscientious* objection to a law is special. Recognizing a constitutional right of school children not to salute the flag against their will makes no sense if all that is at stake is ordinary dissent from a majoritarian policy. In order to distinguish between conscientious dissent and ordinary dissent, we need to imagine resistance to pledging allegiance coming from sophisticated school children who honestly say: "We do not want to pledge allegiance to this flag, not because we are conscientiously opposed to pledging allegiance, but because we do not think this flag is the best symbol for our democracy. We want to pledge allegiance to a flag of our own design. Our right to free speech means that no one—not even our duly authorized school teachers—may force us to say what we do not feel like saying." This example shows why it is misleading to say that a general right of free speech of school children was at issue in flag salute case, *Board of Education v Barnette*, since young school children do not have anything close to an unqualified right of free speech in the classroom. At stake in *Barnette* was a far more specific *freedom from forced profession of belief against conscience*. Respect for conscience is a basic form of respect for ethical commitment and identity.

When democratic governments exempt conscientious objectors, they need not also respect ordinary dissent from majoritarian laws. In *Barnette*, Justices Black and Douglas noted one way that the state can distinguish between conscientious and nonconscientious dissent, but it ironically requires the state to subject conscientious dissenters to the threat of persecution or punishment before accommodating their beliefs. "The devoutness of their belief," the Justices wrote of the children who refused to pledge allegiance to the flag, "is evidenced by their willingness to suffer persecution and punishment, rather than make the pledge."[41] The justices also observed that forced profession of belief may be counterproductive if the state's aim is true allegiance: "Words uttered under coercion are proof of loyalty to nothing but self-interest."[42] The mere fact that the children are willing to suffer persecution and punishment rather than make the pledge should be sufficient to show their conscientiousness. But if a willingness to suffer punishment is made a necessary condition for respecting conscience, then the democratic state will be punishing conscientious people as a condition of respecting them. Perhaps a better evidence of depth of the conscientiousness of dissenters is their willingness to take the lengthy and demanding path of legal procedure to state their perspective and receive acknowledgment and possibly legal exemption.

The state should not require individuals to show that they are willing to suffer punishment for their beliefs, but then as a practical matter it must be willing to exempt some nonconscientious people who are ordinary dissenters rather than conscientious objectors. There is rarely a sure way to discriminate between conscientious objectors, and merely willful ones, short of imposing unnecessary hardships on conscientious objectors. In order to respect conscientious objectors, democratic governments therefore also accommodate some people who are not, and this raises the issue of whether exemptions for conscientious objectors discriminate in favor of dishonest individuals who feign conscientious objection. As in many other decision making domains, democratic governments here have a choice between underinclusion and over-inclusion.

Conscientious objection to a bad law ideally leads to its abolition, as happened in the mandatory flag salute. The mandatory flag salute overreached the bounds of what any legitimate law should require. Conscientious objection publicly exposed the bad law. In such a case, there is no problem of discriminating in favor of non–conscientious objectors. As long as the law is unnecessary and officially recognized as such citizens need not be concerned that conscientious objectors are afforded a special standing over non–conscientious objectors. As a consequence of the conscientious challenge to democratic policy by Jehovah's Witnesses, children were no longer required to profess their belief at the risk of prosecution and punishment.

The abolition of laws requiring profession of belief highlights a special contribution of conscience to democracy. Conscientious challenges can help abolish bad public policies. Legitimate claims of conscience can thereby mitigate the threat of majority tyranny, as did the conscientious challenge by Jehovah's Witnesses to the mandatory flag salute in public schools. By abolishing laws that require profession of belief, democratic governments no longer need to distinguish between conscientious and non–conscientious dissent on this issue. Conscientious objection has done its work in the direction of a more justice-friendly democracy.

Since conscientious objection is not always directed against bad laws, governments would be irresponsible if they automatically exempted conscientious objectors from obedience to laws they found objectionable. An automatic exemption rule would permit conscientious parents to deny their children lifesaving medical care. The greatest challenge to democratic governments is to decide when conscientious objection should be accommodated, even though the law in question is legitimate. Two eminent legal scholars—Christopher Eisgruber and Lawrence Sager—defend a sensible standard of equal regard for conscientious objectors to laws.[43] Their defense raises the question of what equal regard for conscientious objectors entails. Out of equal regard for the ultimate ethical commitments of persons, should democratic governments exempt conscientious objectors from some or all legitimate laws? We can begin to answer this question by rejecting two extreme examples, each of which has only the virtue of simplicity.

One extreme would require democratic governments to exempt every conscientious objector from all laws that do not protect a basic democratic principle (such as civic equality or equal freedom). A blanket exception of this sort would effectively disestablish democracy in order to privilege the conscience of every individual above that of the majority, even when some members of the majority may have conscientious reasons to support the law in question. Automatic exemptions from legitimate laws on the basis of conscientious objection undermine the ability of duly constituted majorities to make law. Automatic exemptions also offer perverse incentives to non-conscientious citizens who would rather feign conscientious objection than contribute their share to the pursuit of legitimate democratic purposes. Conscientious objection therefore should not be treated as a *sufficient* condition for legal exemption.

The opposite extreme would be to oppose exempting *any* conscientious objectors from *any* laws no matter how great a burden the law in question places on a person's conscience or how small the public benefit of enforcing the law without the exemption in question. Because conscience represents ultimate ethical commitments, a democratic government that fails to consider exempting conscientious objectors from some laws also fails to take the ethical identities of persons as seriously as it can without sacrificing the democratic pursuit of public purposes. This was a problem with Oregon's drug law before the legislature made a concession for sacramental use of peyote by members of the Native American church. Almost every state alcohol law had made such concessions for mainstream Christian believers, so the absence of a concession for Native Americans also smacked of discrimination. When nonexemption in effect discriminates against some conscientious individuals, exemptions are all the more essential for the sake of treating people as civic equals, regardless (in this case) of their religion.

Conscience is therefore not so special that democratic governments should routinely defer to it, nor is it so ordinary that it should be routinely overridden. Respect for persons as civic equals opposes either extreme response. A nondiscrimination principle can also serve as a guide to judging when exemptions for conscientious persons are likely to be legitimate. In addition to protecting basic freedom (as in the flag salute case), exemptions should try to secure nondiscriminatory treatment of all persons rather than more favorable treatment for more mainstream consciences (as in Oregon prior to the legislature's revision of its drug law).

Two-way protection secures the legitimate demands of both individual conscience and democratic governance. Neither protection can be absolute, since the two sometimes conflict. Democratic justice pushes a democratic government away from routinely deferring to conscience at the same time as it pulls it toward respecting conscience whenever it is compatible with upholding a law's legitimate public purpose. Democratic governments should not exempt conscientious objectors from a legitimate law when exemption would undermine the law's legitimate purpose (if the exemption were extended on a nondiscriminatory basis to all relevant cases of conscientious objection). Democratic governments should exempt conscientious believers when this action is consistent with upholding the law's legitimate purpose and avoiding the discriminatory effects that some laws have against non–mainstream moral agents.

The alternatives to two-way protection are strict separation and one-way protection, which we encountered when we first considered the question of why religious identity is often treated as special. Strict separation goes beyond defending separation of church and state to defending separation of conscience and state. It therefore opposes any exemptions from legitimate laws on grounds of individual conscience. By contrast, one-way protection supports routine exemption of individual conscience from legitimate laws. Conscience is protected from democratic governance, but democratic governance is not reciprocally protected from conscience. Conscience trumps democratic governance except in cases where democratic governance is simply instrumental to protecting other people from direct harm.

By examining these alternatives to two-way protection, we see why two-way protection serves democratic justice by respecting conscience more than strict separation and by respecting democratic governance more than one-way protection.[44] One-way protection also falls prey to the same problem we encountered when discussing why a democratic state should not defer to the demands of cultural, voluntary, and ascriptive identity groups, which all provide homes (away from home) for conscientious citizens, religious and secular alike.

STRICT SEPARATION

Strict separation has the attraction of a certain theoretical simplicity: Democratic politics should separate itself from the conscientious commitments of believers because those commitments are particularistic, not publicly shared, and believers therefore should not expect special support from the state. State support carries with it interference that corrupts spiritual life. Strict separation of the spiritual realm and the political realm is defended for the sake of both.

The problem with the theoretical simplicity of strict separation is that it may not be possible, let alone desirable, for democratic politics to separate itself so strictly from the conscientious commitments of citizens, who after all are free to bring those commitments into politics. Strict separation requires the democratic state to strike a bargain with citizens: The state will protect your freedom of conscience and you will protect the state from being used for the particularistic purposes of your religious group. Classic liberals expected citizens to accept this bargain because they thought that Protestant Christianity in modern democracies had internalized these same terms, and most religions—like American Catholicism—would become "protestant" in this sense: They would accept separation as part of their own doctrinal creed.

Strict separationists count on the spiritual realm confining itself or else being confined by state force to areas apart from everyday politics. The prime area of the spiritual should be worship of the divine. According to Locke, the democratic state should:

> Accept all refusals to perform orthodox rites and all performances of unorthodox rites—short, of course, of such rites as human sacrifice or of performances which violate rules thought necessary for the general safety of the community.[45]

The state must not require a profession of conscientious belief from its citizens, including children, as the court upheld in *Board of Education v Barnette*.

The terms of strict separation go beyond placing restrictions on what the state can do to citizens. Strict separation also limits the legitimate expectations of citizens. They must not expect the state to support their spiritual commitments beyond what is generally available to all citizens in support of their preferred ways of life. No expectation of support means that religious activities must sustain themselves without state subsidies, which are common in democracies that veer toward the model of one-way protection.

The terms of strict separation also prevent the state from using the ultimate religious (or conscientious) commitments of its citizens as a reason for exempting them from laws or otherwise altering public policy. Since liberty is always within the limits of legitimate laws, freedom of conscience does not include the freedom to violate legitimate laws, such as laws against harming innocent people, even if conscience dictates withholding lifesaving support from one's children or engaging in ritual sacrifice.

A conscientious person still may feel bound to violate legitimate laws, but the state is not bound to lift its legal burden or give him any dispensation just because his conscience opposes the law.[46] When martyrs conscientiously choose to kill innocent people, they violate a basic right of others, and the democratic public has a duty not to defer to their conscientious commitment. Strict separation, like two-way protection, supports the state's duty to prevent harm to others even in the face of conscientious commitments that push in the reverse direction.

John Locke, along with many later liberal philosophers, thought

that toleration in matters of worship, religious rites, and doctrinal beliefs was enough to establish distinct spheres for church and state,
along with correspondingly separate roles for conscientious believers
and responsible citizens. "Nobody ought to be compelled in matters of
religion," he wrote, assuring his readers that: "The establishment of
this one thing would take away all grounds of complaints and tumults
upon account of conscience."[47] Locke was mistaken about this assurance and even about the Protestant conscience that he thought would
dominate. As Michael Walzer has observed, "The Protestant conscience resisted compulsion also in matters of politics—and . . . matters of politics were not so easily distinguishable from matters of religion as [Locke] thought."[48]

Strict separation never has been a reality, and even as an ideal it is
only rarely defended in its pure form by contemporary liberals.[49]
Locke himself recognized that there would be instances of conscientious objection to legitimate laws. What he did not foresee or recommend, however, was making legal exemptions for conscientious objectors. In cases of conscientious objection, Locke recommended that the
believer "abstain from the action that he judges unlawful, and . . .
undergo the punishment which it is not unlawful for him to bear."[50]
Under the strict separation view, conscientious citizens may feel obligated to dissent from laws they deem illegitimate, but then they should
suffer the full civil consequences of punishment.

Strict separation has fallen short from the start in not recognizing
that a stable democratic state can and should exempt conscientious
citizens from some legitimate laws and in so doing respect their conscientious objection without harming other innocent people. On this
score, political practice has outpaced political theory. Widely respected citizens—members of well-established religious groups like
the Quakers—have successfully asserted themselves in conscientious
refusal to fight for their state. The New York Constitution of 1777
exempted Quakers from military service, provided they pay "such
sums of money, in lieu of their personal service, as the same may, in
the judgements of the Legislature, be worth."

The New Hampshire Constitution of 1784 came closer to respecting conscientious refusal when it declared that "No person who is
conscientiously scrupulous about the lawfulness of bearing arms shall
be compelled to do so."[51] A remarkable feature of this clause is that

the exemption is not explicitly tied to religion (perhaps because its framers assumed that only religious persons could be conscientiously scrupulous). The clause gave secular conscience room to assert itself, successfully so in the case of conscientious refusal to fight wars for the state. Civic equality calls for nondiscrimination among citizens who have similar conscientious scruples, whether they be religious or secular in source.

Opening up conscientious refusal to selective refusal to fight unjust wars would be the next step, a step yet to be taken because it risks undermining the draft law itself when the state is fighting an unjust war. Undermining an illegitimate law—one that drafts citizens to fight an unjust war—would be a public good, although one that the government that is fighting the war is very unlikely to support. When more than 400 Israeli Army reservists publicly stated that they refuse to serve in the West Bank and Gaza Strip because their state's policy involves "dominating, expelling, starving, and humiliating an entire people," the official response by Prime Minister Ariel Sharon was that soldiers refusing to carry out the decisions of an elected government "will be the beginning of the end of democracy."[52] This response reveals a far too simple understanding of democracy as requiring citizens to do whatever an elected government requires of them. Even democratically elected governments do not retain unconstrained legitimate authority or absolute sovereignty to order their citizens to do whatever the government wishes. The question always remains as to whether the government's demands are legitimate, and conscientious refusal can be a check on the illegitimate use of democratic authority.

One of the most common objections to exempting conscientious objectors is fear of creating a slippery slope from conscientious to nonconscientious refusal. To avoid a slippery slope, the tests of conscientious refusal need to be serious, as they have been. Individuals need to appear before a review board and demonstrate by their past actions and affiliations that they hold a set of conscientious beliefs that can qualify them for the status of conscientious objector. This is a fair if not foolproof test, which demonstrates that strict separation of church and state is not essential in order to protect democratic justice. What is essential is the government's ability to make justifiable laws on grounds that are not specific to particular religions.

The problem with strict separation is that conscience is not confined to a separate sphere from politics, nor would it be good for democracy if it were. The formula of toleration within the limits of legitimate laws, while generally defensible, is therefore too simple. Democratic governments may give more than what strict separation affords by way of respect and accommodation of conscience.

ONE-WAY PROTECTION

One-way protection, by contrast to strict separation, tries to maximize accommodation of conscience. Its regime would "protect religion from the state, not the state from religion."[53] A nondiscriminatory regime would extend accommodation of religious freedom to freedom of conscience. Otherwise one-way protection would discriminate against equally conscientious citizens who are not religious. By granting exemption from the wartime draft to conscientious objectors who were nonreligious as well as religious, the Supreme Court moved toward a less discriminatory form of accommodation of conscience.[54] It treated conscience as special, consistently with equal regard for persons.[55] Support for this kind of accommodation is a strength of one-way protection.

One-way protection goes far beyond supporting conscientious objection to war, however, and the further it goes, the less defensible it gets. One-way protection wants to maximize accommodation of conscientious objectors, either by maximizing exemptions for individuals or by ceding political power to the plurality of subgroups within society with which most conscientious individuals identify. The first maximization is more individualistic and the second more communitarian, but both share the same aim. Both also recognize some limits on conscientious exemptions to protect people from being victimized by other people's conscientious commitments.

The main method of the first maximization is to exempt individual conscientious believers from laws to which they object. Conscience is special because it represents the ethical identity of citizens, and one-way protectionists therefore protect the ethical identity of citizens from the state. But they do not reciprocally protect other citizens of the state from the harms that can come from conscience. Accommodating conscientious objection becomes the rule rather than an exception that is justifiable under certain circumstances, where legitimate laws will not be undermined and innocent people will not be harmed.

What one-way protectionists are reluctant to recognize is that a democratic government cannot maximize respect for individual conscience, regardless of its content, without undermining the legitimate purposes of democratic government. If freedom of conscience is maximized, legitimate laws that pursue public purposes are undermined. Democratic decision making ceases to be meaningful along with the political freedoms, such as suffrage, that support it. This is a fundamental weakness of one-way protection: it does not give due regard to democratically authorized laws and the political freedoms that create them.

Sometimes, in order to avoid undermining the legitimate purpose of a democratic law, one-way protectionists tailor exemptions for conscientious objectors in a discriminatory way. Equally conscientious citizens are discriminated against so as to avoid undermining a legitimate public policy. In *Wisconsin v Yoder*, Justice Burger so narrowly tailored his reasoning as to exempt the Amish but no other group of equally conscientiously objecting citizens from mandatory schooling laws. He did so by making it necessary that the Amish not only be *religious* objectors to the law but also people whose *traditional, self-contained, peace-loving, agrarian community* depends for its survival on the exemption of their children from the law.

Exemptions from law for only religious convictions discriminate against secular conscientious believers, and they are doubly unjustified if they also discriminate among equally conscientious religious believers. This critique leaves open the question of whether the discriminatory character of the *Yoder* decision would have been better avoided by deciding against the Amish or by extending the decision over time to accommodate all conscientious parents. The price of extending *Yoder* by accommodating the children of all parents who are conscientious dissenters would be undoing democratic decision making over schooling. Maximizing accommodation of conscience means minimizing democratic self-government, and one-way protectionists fail to offer good reasons why conscience—regardless of its content—should be given priority over legitimate democratic laws. Legitimate democratic laws, after all, also reflect the ethical commitments of individuals as citizens concerning how their society should be governed. How collective goods like the democratic education of children should be distributed is an ethical question, and legitimate democratic answers to this question have ethical content. Better, therefore, for democrats to live with the exception for an isolated group like the Amish than to support one-way protectionists in undoing the discrimination by undermining democratic decision making over schooling.[56]

A communitarian version of one-way protection seeks to make democracy as safe as possible for conscientious group identities. The ideal is a pluralist democracy within which, in the words of an 1813 court decision, "Every citizen . . . is in his own country. To the protestant it is a protestant country; to the catholic, a catholic country; and the jew, if he pleases, may establish in it his New Jerusalem."[57] To avoid discrimination, one-way protectionists could add: "And to the atheist it is an atheist country, to the agnostic an agnostic country, and so on." The image captures a pluralist ideal that is historically associated with the millet system of the Ottoman Empire, which protected freedom of conscience only insofar as a person's conscience was represented by a state-recognized and communally governed group. One-way protectionists today imagine a democratic society that protects freedom of conscience but eschews separation of church and state. Every conscientious citizen may join a political subcommunity that is largely self-governing but not necessarily democratic.

Some local communities, for example, would be controlled by particular churches, pursuing the religious ends of the local majority with the aid of state power. Other local towns would be similarly controlled by secular groups, pursuing their own conscientious commitments, also with the aid of state power. No dissenting citizen would be coerced into any of the many political communities. This means that there also could be local communities of democratic individualists. The various conscientious communities would be free to regulate the schooling of children in the way that helps reproduce their conscientious world view. All citizens would be free to find the community that comes closest to pursuing their conscientious way of life, whether religious or not. Every citizen could feel as if she were living in her own country, as Michael McConnell writes approvingly: "To the Protestant it is a Protestant country, to the Catholic a Catholic country, to the Jew a Jewish country."[58]

But what would it mean for the United States to be a Jewish country to Jewish Americans? American Jews do not agree any more than Israeli Jews on what it would mean for their country to be Jewish.[59] Moreover, many Jewish Americans think it better that theirs is not a Jewish country, just as many other citizens morally approve of their country's not corresponding to their religious identity.

Unlike the United States, Israel is a Jewish country, religiously as well as culturally speaking, to some of its Jewish citizens.[60] Israel has traveled down the path of communitarian one-way protection for Orthodox Jews by exacting a high price in unequal personal and political freedoms. When the state speaks in the name of Judaism, it speaks in the name of an establishment interpretation of Orthodox Judaism against other interpretations. Israeli Jews must be married by Orthodox rabbis for their marriages to be respected under the state marriage law as Jewish. Israeli Jews who are Reform or Conservative must either agree to be married by an Orthodox rabbi or not have their marriages recognized (as Jewish or as official) by the state. (Or else they must leave the state to be married elsewhere, in which case the marriage will be officially recognized as a foreign marriage, as international treaty demands.) The cost of making the state more Jewish for Orthodox Jews is to make it less protective of other Jews and even less like a political home for non-Jews.[61]

Religious establishment even exacts a price from dissenting members of the Orthodox establishment who deny the possibility of a truly religious state because political power corrupts conscience. As one Orthodox critic of the Orthodox establishment writes:

> At no time have the religious leaders [in Israel] ever offered a concrete program for operating the existing state in accordance with the Torah. . . . There can be no greater logical and moral incoherence . . . than the appearance on the political scene of a religious bloc of parties demanding "a state in accordance with the

Torah," but lacking any concrete program for administering the state in accordance with halakhic norms. The result is mere clerical politics.[62]

For one-way protection to work on the communitarian model, authorities must be entrusted with exercising political and spiritual authority. Yet some of the most persistent threats of tyranny over individuals—sometimes over members of the group and other times over nonmembers—have come from groups entrusted with both spiritual and political authority.

It is also important to emphasize here what chapter 1 makes clear: Religion is not alone in threatening this kind of tyranny. Nonreligious cultural groups also threaten tyranny when they wield political power that they refuse to constrain by respect for the equal personal and political freedoms of individuals. They refuse to constrain their power by respect for basic freedoms because they claim to constitute the identity of their members so comprehensively that the perpetuation of the group represents their basic interests. This premise of a group so comprehensively constituting the identity of individuals is dangerous, whether the group is secular or religious. Such tyranny is commonly threatened in the name of a cultural group identity, which a shared religion like Judaism can help to constitute, but the content of the culture need not be religious for one-way protection to threaten tyranny both internally and over nonmembers.

One-way protection supports accommodating conscience far beyond the limits of legitimate laws. It thereby threatens to undermine basic freedoms, including democratic freedoms, all in the name of protecting conscience, regardless of whether its content is publicly defensible. One-way protection expects a democratic government to be one-sided in its accommodation of conscience and therefore does not expect conscientious citizens reciprocally to support democracy as democracy supports them, by abiding by laws that are legitimate and democratically authorized. The irony of one-way protection is that conscientious citizens who reject reciprocity have no public ground on which to stand in pleading their case for accommodation.

Accommodation of conscience should be a two-way street. Conscientious citizens have a general responsibility to democracy to respect those democratically authorized laws that are legitimate for the sake of supporting the society that supports them, just as the democratic society has a responsibility to them to accommodate their conscientious commitments to the extent that such accommodation does not inflict injustice on others or create discriminatory exemptions or otherwise undermine legitimate democratic decision-making. Two-way protection is the approach to accommodation that recognizes the importance of this reciprocity and the competing values that a democratic society therefore must support.

TWO-WAY PROTECTION

Under two-way protection, there is a reciprocal relationship between ethical identity and democratic politics. Ethical identity is accommodated when doing so pushes democracy in the direction of greater justice or at least avoids undermining legitimate democratic decision making. When exemptions for conscientious objectors threaten greater injustice, legitimate democratic laws are upheld without the exemptions. Religious commitments should have neither a privileged nor a disfavored position in democratic politics, but some exceptions may be made for conscientious objectors without sliding down a slippery slope toward one-way protection, which maximizes accommodation at the expense of minimizing legitimate democratic decision making.

Two-way protection lets reciprocity reign. When conscientious citizens invoke their ideas for political purposes, including the purpose of exempting themselves from laws, those ideas can be criticized on the same basis as any other ideas in politics. Seeking accommodation of one's conscience in democratic politics should not be without risk of criticism. Those who expect their conscientious commitments to be protected from political criticism have no better alternative than to keep their commitments out of politics.

Why should conscience and democratic politics each be willing to accommodate the other on occasion? First, because complete nonaccommodation on either side expresses disrespect for persons, whether as democratic decision makers or as conscientious objectors. Second, because nonaccommodation often discriminates against non-mainstream conscientious objectors; majoritarian laws more often tend to reflect the ethical commitments of mainstream consciences. Third, conscience cannot rule supreme without either threatening anarchy or (more likely) turning political power over to organized religious groups that substitute group tyranny for democratic decision making. Fourth, reciprocal accommodation aims to mitigate *on moral terms*— terms of reciprocity—the ineradicable conflict between conscientious citizens and democracy.

A politics of ethical recognition by which a state would strive to be a religious state to all believers and agnostic or atheist to all non-believers is impossible. Even if possible, it would be undesirable be-cause the road to such politics is lined with the tyranny of undemocra-tic groups that claim to represent the ultimate ethical commitments of their members, but whose members cannot hold their leaders account-able. To hold their leaders accountable, the subgroups would need to be democratic, but this would require the democratic state to shape these groups in its own democratic image, which is precisely what the communitarian version of one-way protection seeks to prohibit in the name of protecting conscientious group identities.

Voluntary associations should be permitted to be nondemocratic. An important part of their value in democracy, as discussed in chapter 2, depends on their separation from coercive state power, and their ability to offer alternative ways of associating to those institutionalized by the democratic state itself. If subgroups are permitted to wield po-litical power on behalf of a state, however, they cease to be voluntary and should be democratic. Two-way protection cautions democratic governments from becoming so entangled with organized religious groups or their secular equivalents that they wield the equivalent of political power in society.

The controversy over carving out a school district along religious lines, centered around the case of *Kiryas Joel v Grumet*,[63] illustrates why two-way protection should support a strong degree of separation of church and state against the claims of some one-way protectionists. Over a decade ago, the New York State legislature carved out of an existing school district—Monroe-Woodbury—a new one called Kiryas Joel to accommodate a small religious denomination. The statute that created the district did not directly violate anyone's freedom of conscience. There was no threat to the freedom of those residents of the Monroe-Woodbury School District who were not residents of Kiryas Joel. Members of the larger school district even favored carving out Kiryas Joel. Members of Kiryas Joel were an Ultra-Orthodox Jewish minority in the school district, and children in the public schools were taunting some of these children. "From all appearances," as one commentator writes, "this was a happy instance in which the political and cultural majority protected the practices of an unconventional minority without imposing any costs on other citizens."[64]

On closer inspection, the situation was not a happy convergence of costless protections. First, the village used "covenants to maintain religiously segregated and impermeable borders, [and] so the school district physically busse[d] students into (and, in theory, out of) Kiryas Joel in order to maintain religiously segregated schools."[65] Second, political dissent in the village was treated as religious heresy. When a resident tried to run for the first (and only) school board election without the Grand Rabbi's approval:

He was banished from the congregation, his tires were slashed, his windows broken, and several hundred people, including the Rabbi, marched outside his house chanting, "Death to Joseph Waldman!"

The more religious and political authority is entangled, the more religious and political dissidence is also tied together, as they were in Kiryas Joel. Dissidents in Kiryas Joel "faced showers of cold water, heckling, removal of their yarmulkes, and signs proclaiming their outcast status."[66] The most accessible source of legal recourse, the local source, was blocked by the entanglement of church and state in the village. Local entanglement considerably raises the costs of protecting each resident's basic right of political freedom.

Although holding the school board elections in the synagogue was illegal, they were held there nonetheless, which is what is likely to happen when a democracy carves out political districts in order to include only people who identify with one organized religious group. Over one hundred dissident villagers voted by absentee ballots because they were too intimidated to vote in the synagogue. They also filed a lawsuit to remove the voting booths from the synagogue to a neutral site, but local officials were unresponsive, not surprisingly, since they (along with state officials) had authorized the entanglement.[67]

State-church entanglement is opposed by two-way protection when it entails the ceding of state power to religious leaders, the ceding of religious power to state officials, or both. When state and church power become entangled, effective state action to protect civic equality, equal freedom, and opportunity becomes all the more important and all but impossible. Dissenting citizens at the local level might look to public authorities at a higher level to regulate and restrain their local religious-political officials. But why would a politics that permitted church-state entanglement at the local level not also permit it at the county and state level? An important advantage that two-way protection shares with strict separation is decreasing the state's need to regulate religious authorities to the extent that they do not wield political power.

Like strict separation, two-way protection seeks to protect religion from the state and the state from religion. But two-way protectionists recognize that neither protection can be absolute because each, taken to the extreme, would deny the importance of the other. I have already argued that separation should not be so strict as to exclude religiously based arguments from democratic politics or to preclude the state from accommodating conscientious objectors.

Now the question arises: Can two-way protection draw a defensible line between legitimate and illegitimate accommodation? A defensible line can be a permeable one. Defensible laws, as we have seen when we discussed accommodating conscientious objection, can become more defensible when they make room for exceptions for conscientious objectors whose dissent does no injustice to others. To show that two-way protection is a politically defensible position, we need to consider whether any principled line between legitimate and illegitimate accommodation can be defended on democratic grounds. Different democratic contexts may lead to significantly different defensible positions, since drawing a defensible line is a matter of both ethical argument and democratic deliberation. One line that democrats in the United States can defend, both ethically and politically, is a permeable wall of separation between church and state. The wall exists to ensure that publicly funded programs not be controlled by religious authorities or used for religious purposes. The wall is permitted to be permeable in order to protect the equal freedom and opportunity of conscientious citizens to influence and benefit from democratic politics.[68]

In sum: Freedom of religion, as I have argued, is a subclass of freedom of conscience, which is freedom to pursue one's ultimate ethical commitments within the limits of legitimate laws. Two-way protection suggests that the limits of legitimate laws should be expanded beyond what strict separation suggests to accommodate conscientious dissenters when doing so does not discriminate against other conscientious dissenters or undermine the legitimate purpose of the law. A great advantage of accommodating conscientious dissent is to publicly acknowledge the centrality of ethical commitments to the identity of persons, and the contribution that those commitments can make to democracy. Accommodating dissent based on ethical identity within the limits of nondiscrimination and respect for democratic governance recognizes reciprocity between conscientious citizens and the democratic governments that represent them. This reciprocity is the lifeblood of democratic justice.

Integrating Identity in Democracy

Identity groups abound in democratic politics, but their claims cannot be taken at face value as compatible with, let alone as conducive to, democratic justice. Democratic justice entails treating all individuals as civic equals with equal liberty and opportunity. Granting identity groups sovereignty or other significant political powers regardless of the way they treat individuals would mean subordinating individuals to their cause. Subordinating individuals to groups is another name for tyranny. One reason to be skeptical about identity groups in democracy is that they often enhance their own power at the expense of justice. So, too, do interest groups.

An assessment of identity groups must be nuanced because such groups aid as well as impede democratic justice. Democratic societies are sites of ongoing discrimination against individuals on the basis of their race, gender, sexual orientation, and other group identities. When feminist, African American, gay, lesbian, and bisexual identity groups, for example, publicly express a more positive interpretation of their group identities against prevailing negative stereotypes, they may be using identity politics to good effect. When they struggle for greater civic equality for a subordinated group, identity groups use their political power in defense of democratic justice.

Moreover, identity groups are typically far more than instruments of public policy for their members. They provide mutual support and a sense of belonging that would otherwise be lacking in many people's lives, and some do so without threatening injustice to outsiders. This means that quite apart from the demands of justice, we can appreciate people's wanting—indeed even needing—the mutual support and sense of belonging that identity groups can provide. Identifying with groups that provide mutual support on the basis of mutual identification also can help to mitigate the insecurities of social and economic life in competitive capitalist societies.

In democratic politics, identity groups are particularly important because the numbers count (at least when they are accurately counted). Without the ability to engage in coordinated group action, most individuals are far less politically influential and effective. Disadvantaged individuals who are treated unjustly cannot mount a successful struggle, let alone a social movement, without allies in their cause. Allies can be easier to organize based on mutual identification rather than self-interest, especially when collective goods are at stake. Individuals who do not identify with the cause have no self-interested reason to sacrifice for a social movement. Identification with a group can provide that reason and provide intangible benefits, such as social belonging, that motivate individuals to work together to combat injustice.

When women and minorities are negatively stereotyped because of their group identity, individuals acting alone are relatively powerless to effect change. Organized resistance is needed to supply a counterweight to prevailing negative stereotypes and to publicly express a more positive (and ideally more accurate) view of group identities. All views of group identities are in some sense stereotypes, but not all stereotypes are hostile to the democratic ideal of civic equality for all individuals. Identity groups of women and minorities that resist negative stereotyping are a valuable tool in the arsenal of democratic politics. In the absence of mutual identification, women and minorities would be far less able to combat negative stereotyping. When mutual identification serves this purpose, it is not a moral end in itself, but it is a justifiable means for disadvantaged individuals to fight against one of the more insidious forms of social injustice, the negative stereotyping of individuals. When identity groups aid such moral causes, we can consider them "justice-friendly."

Even identity groups that are justice-friendly should not be exempt from critical questioning. Critics ask: Must people identify around divisive categories such as race and gender rather than around unifying sympathies for those who are treated unjustly, whomever they happen to be? Logically speaking, people need not think and act in identity groups. But people commonly do identify with others on the basis of many kinds of social markers, and in a democracy they must be free to do so. Moreover, mutual identification makes political organization easier, so there is a built-in incentive in democratic politics for identity groups to form. Group identification in itself is not morally admirable in democracy since, as we have seen throughout this book, identity groups can impede and undermine as well as aid and express the cause of democratic justice. A democratic perspective therefore does not consider identity groups as good or bad in themselves but rather evaluates them according to what they publicly pursue and express.

Since individual freedom is an important part of democratic justice, an identity group is suspect to the extent that it attempts comprehensively to determine the identity of individuals rather than leave room for significant self-shaping. As long as group identities are neither comprehensive nor immune from interpretation, however, individuals can both identify with groups and live the lives of free people. An important underlying theme of this book is that group identities are best conceived as multiple and fluid; except under conditions of tyranny, they do not comprehensively determine the identities of individuals. Free people have multiple and alterable identities.

Identity groups are commonly evaluated by their type rather than their contribution to democratic justice. Critics call for the abolition of ascriptive groups, for example, while they praise voluntary associations. Such contrasts between groups, as we have seen, are far too crude for evaluative purposes. We need to combine considering kinds of identity groups with defending an evaluative standard that is relevant to their context and social role. My chosen context is democratic societies, and the standard I invoke is democratic. In order to do justice to different kinds of identity groups and the particular issues that arise for each kind, four major categories of identity groups are evaluated by standards of democratic justice, each category in a separate chapter: cultural, voluntary, ascriptive, and religious.

SEPARATING CULTURE AND SOVEREIGNTY

Chapter 1 focuses on cultural identity groups. The premise of some theorists of culture is that a societal culture, such as the Pueblo or Québécois, encompasses its members' identities. These theorists then build an argument for political sovereignty on the premise that culture encompasses individual identity. Because an encompassing culture provides the context of choice for its members, the political sovereignty of the cultural group is said to supply the justifiable context within which individual freedom can be adequately exercised and enjoyed.

One problem with this popular argument is its premise that a single culture, albeit a complex one, provides *the* context of choice for its members. Individuals can think, imagine, and aspire beyond what any single culture determines for them. Theorists of culture are right to point out that many national cultures, like the Québécois, that are not sovereign societies have no less of a right to be so than those cultures, like the Anglophone Canadian, that are sovereign societies. Where they tend to fall short is in recognizing how little of a right to sovereignty can be derived from the claims of any cultural groups to encompass the identities of their members. Nationalism, whether writ large or small, cannot be justified by subordinating the cultural identities of individuals to the political sovereignty of their group.

Both modern democracies and many individuals within them are multicultural. Democratic life is characterized more accurately by the intermixing and changing of cultures and the conflicting interpretations of cultures by creative individuals and groups than it is by the constitution of individual identity by a single, coherent cultural group. Yet democratic life is not without its dominant cultural cast. Every democratic society imposes some culture on its citizens by the very language, history, holidays, and customs within which its politics is conducted. The dominant culture does not completely constitute individuals, but neither does it provide equal freedom and opportunity to those people who would feel more at home in another cultural climate. This asymmetry in cultural belongingness places some legitimate demands on democratic societies for accommodating different cultural groups in ways that treat their members as equally free citizens as those who identify with the dominant culture. Securing the survival of cultures is not a recipe for treating all individuals as free and equal citizens because the moral claims of cultures are dependent on the claims of their members. When cultural institutions have suffered as a consequence of the historical injustices committed against members of the culture, claims to support cultural institutions take on a strength that they lack when abstracted from the justifiable claims of their members. Political claims of conquered indigenous groups, for example, therefore often justifiably extend to government support of their cultural practices and institutions, which would have flourished had it not been for the injustices committed against their members. Support for cultures under such circumstances, however, should not be confused with a general group right of cultures to survive.

Whatever culture or cultures are supported by democratic governments, if citizens are to be treated as even minimally free in today's world, they will have choices that extend beyond the context that any single culture provides. That is even more true for cultures within a democratic context, from which people can learn about other lives and possibilities when they exercise their freedom of speech, travel, and association and take advantage of the benefits of a free press. Even cultures that are often taken to be paradigmatically comprehensive—such as those of indigenous peoples—are not, as the intermingling of cultures by their members demonstrates. If the most encompassing cultures are taken to be those of the most powerful democracies, such as the United States, it is no less misleading to say that a single culture encompasses the identities of its members.

The claim that a single culture provides the context of choice for its members could become a self-fulfilling rationalization for cultural authority rather than a justification if the cultural authorities manage to seize absolute sovereignty over their members. Political sovereignty in this situation operates also as a kind of cultural tyranny and not as a context for individual freedom as sovereignty based on cultural coherence claims to be. The defense of political sovereignty based on comprehensive cultures is therefore dangerous. The more encompassing a group, the greater its capacity for tyranny if it gains sovereign political authority.

As a general rule, separating potentially oppressive centers of power in society rather than merging them is a better recipe for protecting basic rights. Chapter 4 defends separation of church and state but at the same time acknowledges that the strictest form of separation (of religious beliefs and politics) is neither possible nor desirable. Something similar holds for the separation of culture and politics. An absolutely strict separation is impossible and undesirable, because democracies must carry on a coherent politics in common languages, calendars, holidays, and histories, all of which are culturally specific, not neutral. Yet some significant degree of separation between organized cultural and political authorities still helps protect individual freedom.

When separation is not honored, political authorities tend to mandate a specific culture that limits individual freedom. In so doing, they may provide a sense of secure belonging and meaning for their members, but to grant a cultural group sovereignty for this reason is to neglect the serious threat of sovereign authority to the freedom of individuals. It is far more defensible to say that the more a cultural group constrains itself by considerations of justice, the greater the claims that group has to political sovereignty. The political challenge is then to support institutions that can constrain themselves or be constrained by considerations of justice.

Cultural identity groups may insist on enforcing marriage, divorce, inheritance, schooling, and other laws in ways that conflict with treating all members or nonmembers as civic equals with equal freedom and opportunity. The family law of some groups within a democratic society gives men an unfair advantage over women. Men are not only the dominant members but also the established authorities of the cultural group. Some theorists of culture, such as Taylor and Kymlicka, argue for limiting the legitimate authority of a cultural group in order to respect the basic rights of individuals. By contrast, other theorists of culture, such as Margalit and Halbertal, defend the group's authority over its members as long as the larger democracy ensures a legal right of individuals to exit the group. Margalit and Halbertal challenge democrats to articulate why a legal right to exit a powerful cultural group does not suffice to ensure democratic justice. I address this challenge in chapter 1 by arguing that for the very same reasons that a right to exit is necessary to secure individual freedom, it cannot be sufficient to justify depriving individuals of equal liberty and opportunity. Individuals cannot be considered consensual subjects of a group that denies them, for example, as children an education adequate to exercising equal freedom and opportunity as adults.

No one can justifiably infer informed consent from the fact that vulnerable individuals remain within a cultural group that denies them equal freedom and opportunity. For many women and other vulnerable individuals who stand to lose their families, friends, property, and means of livelihood if they exit the group, the price of exiting is exorbitant. Under these circumstances, a legal right to exit is insufficient to guarantee respect for persons as moral agents or to infer that they consent to deprivations of equal liberty and opportunity by their cultural group. Mutual respect or reciprocity entails equal freedom and opportunity. Equal freedom and opportunity extend well beyond a formal right to leave undemocratic cultural groups that make the cost of exiting exorbitantly and prohibitively high for vulnerable and disadvantaged people.

At their best, cultures are repositories of meaningful choices for individuals. Respect for human agency requires democracies to grant all individuals equal cultural freedom. For powerful majorities to restrict the cultural practices of less powerful minorities when those practices do no injustice to others constitutes a kind of tyranny, even less excusable than the tyranny that minority cultures exert when they prevent their members from adopting majority cultural practices that do no injustice to others. (Minority cultures have the excuse of worrying about the survival of their culture, although this excuse, as we have seen, does not justify repression of individual freedom.) Many restrictions of cultural freedom reflect parochial tastes rather than fair-minded principles of justice. Greater deliberation across cultural group lines can mitigate the tendency to enlist one's own parochial tastes to restrict other people's cultural freedom.

Cultural distance makes it more likely that powerful people will not understand the legitimacy of the claims of other cultural identities. Their failure to grant equal freedom to people whose cultural identities differ from their own is then reasonably viewed as a sign of disrespect and an unwillingness to understand other cultures on the same terms as they understand their own. The Seattle hospital should have been applauded when it arrived at a reasonable understanding through due deliberation with Somali immigrant parents as to how they could avoid subjecting their daughters to clitoridectomy and yet satisfy their sense of cultural identity. The agreed-upon alternative was a small incision on the clitoral hood, performed under anesthesia, which, unlike clitoridectomy and infibulation and other forms of female genital mutilation, would be as safe as male circumcision. It would not be more sexist or oppressive than cosmetic surgeries for adolescents, the legality of which is taken for granted in the United States. Nevertheless, the proposal provoked a storm of vehement opposition to the agreement by outsiders, who threatened a costly federal lawsuit. The threat undermined the agreement, along with the equal freedom of the Somali immigrants. Accepting the equal legitimacy of "other" cultural practices that are no less problematic than "ours" is as important as opposing cultural practices, whether "ours" or "theirs," when they violate basic rights.

Civic equality and equal freedom fairly applied across cultural identities require that distaste for cultural practices that strike us as offensive not become a pretext for suppressing those practices when we tolerate analogous ones in our own culture that are more familiar and therefore less jarring to our aesthetic sensibilities. By being open-minded toward foreign cultural practices that are more consistent with civic equality while criticizing those that are less so, we come closer to the possibility of mutual respect and reciprocity that paves the way to democratic justice.

DECREASING DISCRIMINATION

Living the life of a free person means being free to express one's identity and shape it through one's associations with others. Voluntary associations are valuable, as we saw in chapter 2, even when they are not themselves an instrumental means of combating injustice or securing a public good. Voluntary groups are valuable as manifestations of individual freedom of association, which is essential to free expression. Free association entails the freedom to exclude others (who want to join) from voluntary groups, but such exclusion need not be unjust. Many voluntary groups do no injustice by excluding various people; they support the ability of free individuals to live their own lives as they see fit. Free individuals must be able to associate as they see fit within the limits of doing no injustice to others. Problems arise, however, when exclusions are unjust, and especially when the excluded individuals are among the most vulnerable in society and lack the same expressive freedom as those who are excluding them.

The right of free association ends where injustice to others begins. Voluntary associations often discriminate against individuals based on grounds such as gender, race, sexual orientation, ethnicity, and religion that are unwarranted sources of civic inequality. It is unjust for institutions to discriminate in the distribution of a public good, such as education or economic opportunity, and therefore impede civic equality, equal freedom, or opportunity. A mitigating factor is the expressive freedom of individuals that voluntary associations manifest when their primary purpose is advocacy of a particular point of view that cannot be separated from excluding certain individuals from their group. A group that exists primarily to further the cause of advocating homosexuality or heterosexuality, for example, legitimately excludes heterosexuals or homosexuals, respectively, as part of its expressive freedom. Expressive freedom of a primarily expressive association therefore needs to be weighed against the public good of securing civic equality and equal freedom for all individuals, thereby preventing invidious discrimination as far as justice permits.

Free expression must not become an unconstrained license to discriminate. The Junior Chamber of Commerce, whose primary purpose was to introduce young men to the world of commerce by teaching them the relevant social skills, was rightly constrained not to discriminate against women because an association that teaches the social skills of commerce is distributing a public good that must be distributed fairly for democratic justice to be furthered. More recently, the Boy Scouts defended their associational right to discriminate against homosexuals on grounds of their expressive freedom. The expressive freedom of an association is the most powerful claim it can make to discriminate as it sees fit. But the claim alone surely does not dispose of cases of discrimination by voluntary associations. Competing considerations include whether the association itself is instrumental in affecting whether civic equality and equal freedom for all individuals is possible in a democracy, as the Boy Scouts arguably is. Another competing consideration must be how the association's exclusion of homosexuals affects the expressive freedom of those it excludes. Democratic justice aims for equal liberty, which includes the expressive freedom of individuals. A relevant consideration is therefore whether the exclusion by a powerful association leaves those who are excluded equally free to express their identities in other ways. In the case of the Boy Scouts, it is unlikely that such equal freedom of the excluded individuals could be obtained by joining another organization.

When a constitutional democracy permits voluntary associations to discriminate on grounds of their expressive freedom (whether rightly or wrongly), governmental agents have a correlative civic duty to dissociate themselves from the discrimination. Democratic governments should not support discrimination, even if they must tolerate some manifestations of it for the sake of supporting freedom of expression. It is most difficult to determine which manifestations they must tolerate when competing freedoms are at stake (freedom of expression and freedom from discrimination), as in the case of the Boy Scouts. When those who are excluded do not have equally prominent and powerful associations for publicly expressing themselves, expressive freedom itself then pulls in opposing directions. Democratic justice supports a general rule that democratic governments must not become the agents of discrimination by offering special support for discriminatory associations.

MOTIVATING POLITICAL ACTION BY ASCRIPTIVE IDENTITY

Associations that organize around ascriptive characteristics such as gender and race would seem to be primary targets of antidiscrimination law. Yet, as we saw in chapter 3, many ascriptive associations exist to fight gender and racial discrimination rather than to promote it. Many of these organizations, such as the NAACP, are also open to anyone who supports their cause regardless of gender or race. Some ascriptive associations, such as the National Association of the Deaf (NAD), are not as open for good reason: They offer their members mutual support that they would otherwise not find in a more diverse setting. When NAD provides mutual support for deaf individuals that they would otherwise not receive, it contributes to a just cause, not despite the fact but because it is an ascriptive association. When it opposed the legalization of cochlear implants for deaf children, however, it did not contribute to a just cause, and it was rightly criticized. NAD subsequently changed its position on cochlear implants, even as it continued to view itself as providing primary support for deaf individuals who sign rather than speak English.

Ascriptive identification, like other kinds of group identity, helps mobilize people in politics. Sometimes the motivation operates not to fight injustice or to provide mutual support for the group of which one is a part but rather to pursue one's own material gain. In this vain Skip Hayward adopted the identity of a Pequot Indian late in life and founded the Foxwoods Resort Casino by gaining valuable exemptions from state law available only to a descendant of the Pequot, which he was. Group identity was no less important to Hayward and his extended family because it served as an instrumental means for material gain. But unlike many other examples of individuals whose identities drive their interests in overcoming discrimination for their group, Hayward's interests in material gain seem to have driven his choice of an ascriptive identity. The Pequot identity had historically disadvantaged its members. However that ended, at least in material terms, for Hayward's extended family, and therefore Hayward's reversal of this situation was called the "revenge of the Pequots." Even when identity politics is employed as a not so subtle means for pursuing material interests, group identity still plays a causally independent role in shaping how the interests are pursued.

Ascriptive associations commonly mobilize in democratic politics to fight against discrimination directed against their group. Civic inequalities based on ascriptive identities are injustices that democracies should strive to overcome. The political morality of ascriptive identity groups can be assessed on the basis of whether they promote or impede civic equality, equal freedom, and opportunity. Trying to fight injustices associated with ascription by ascriptive association is controversial but no less so than refusing to fight injustices by ascriptive associations on the grounds that they perpetuate the pernicious idea that morally arbitrary characteristics such as gender and race are politically relevant.

Why should ascriptive identity groups be necessary to fight injustice? Regardless of one's group identity, one might say that every person should join with everyone else to pursue just causes. If everyone acted so impartially, there would be so many impartial people that democratic justice would be done. But not everyone acts impartially, and to rely on impartiality alone for the pursuit of justice is not only unrealistic but also morally unnecessary. Many people seem to be motivated to act morally as well as immorally by their identification with others. Since the immoral ways in which people act as groups are not likely to disappear, furthering the moral ways is a far better strategy than wishing group identification as a whole would go away. As we have seen, identification with others can be used in moral ways, and often (even if not often enough) it is.

One way of fighting injustice is for members of ascriptive identity groups to work together in associations to substitute the expression of positive social identities for the negatively stereotyped ones that have been imposed by others. Even positive identities are unlikely to be freely accepted by all members of the group, but a positive identity is better than a negative one, and a negotiated identity is better than an imposed one, given that some socially ascribed group identities are inescapable even in a just society.

Justice-friendly ascriptive associations such as the NAACP and NOW aim to oppose the kind of discrimination that would not exist in a just society. It is therefore rather senseless to evaluate them other than in their nonideal social context. The dire need to fight injustice flows from a historical record of discrimination and the fact that many people today still favor their own kind beyond what justice can sanction. Democracies institutionalize favoritism of some sort because no objective political authority exists that can be trusted with the (undemocratic) power to impose impartiality on everyone or to prevent partial people from having a say in self-government.

Justice-friendly ascriptive associations help to fight discrimination. These associations get good political mileage out of mutual identification around morally arbitrary characteristics such as gender and race. Who can blame them for doing so in the face of ongoing injustice? To do so would be to blame the victims of injustice for rallying together to oppose it. We can consistently support justice-friendly ascriptive associations at the same time as we would wish for and work for more effective action by associations that are not organized on ascriptive bases.

An ascriptive association is maximally justice-friendly if it struggles against discrimination and allies with other associations that share this aim. Ascriptive associations that are narrowly self-centered do not make such alliances, but many ascriptive associations have strategic as well as moral reasons not to be narrowly self-centered. The NAACP is a model in this regard; it explicitly aims to end discrimination for all individuals, even as it focuses its energies on African Americans. It is justice-friendly in the fullest sense, and no less so than a nonascriptive association like the American Civil Liberties Union (ACLU). The ACLU is not morally better simply because it has no ascriptive basis to its organization or mission. The analysis of this book suggests that the morally relevant feature of justice-friendly associations is that they similarly recognize all people, regardless of their ascriptive identities, as entitled to be treated as civic equals with equal freedom and opportunity.

Many ascriptive groups need to act for themselves because otherwise no one else will act for them, at least not now. If not now, they may legitimately ask, then when? If the answer is that the day will come when enough people think and act impartially rather than on the basis of their own identities to overcome discrimination, this is not a sufficient reason for ascriptive associations to delay their actions against discrimination.

Democrats therefore can consistently defend that part of political solidarity on the basis of ascriptive characteristics that fights against discrimination on the basis of ascription. Ascriptive associations that are justice-friendly do important work in nonideal democracies that would not be done without them. When they are most successful, they express the civic equality of their members, form coalitions with other justice-friendly associations across ascriptive lines, and successfully pressure governments to institute nondiscriminatory laws and public policies. When they are least successful, all ascriptive associations do is to perpetuate invidious divisions and distinctions, thereby exacerbating injustices in democracies. There is no simple case for or against all ascription associations on democratic grounds. The good associations further the cause of civic equality for individuals identified with subordinated groups, whereas the bad associations do just the reverse. Mixed cases abound.

The most morally jarring feature of any ascriptive association per se is its failure to express the idea that people should associate for political purposes on the basis of a general moral obligation and commitment to oppose injustice rather than on the basis of identification with particular others. The problem of injustice should be addressed by everyone, not primarily, let alone only, by people most closely identified with the victims or the victims themselves. Justice says: Act regardless of your particular identity to aid those in need; do not act out of identification only with your own kind. When justice becomes group specific, it adds insult to injury in the following sense. Special obligations are attributed to African Americans, women, and other members of less advantaged groups on the basis of their group identification. Middle-class blacks, for example, are singled out for criticism when they do not support African American causes. The perspective underlying this criticism saddles the most advantaged members of the least advantaged groups with the greatest obligations. Although the idea that they have greater obligations than their less advantaged peers is defensible, the overall perspective that singles them out for criticism is still morally indefensible. The greatest obligations should be attributed to and borne by the most advantaged individuals, regardless of their group identity.

Attributing obligations to others goes only so far in combating injustice. The world would be better off to the extent that people could identify their own interests with living in a society and world where other people were treated more justly than they are today. When we view our own interests as bound up with how others are treated, we aid just causes not only or even primarily out of obligation but out of identification. Our interests become bound up with our social identification as members of both a just society and a just world. Each of us contains multitudes because our identity includes our social memberships, which extend to the world with which our society is interdependent. We then identify with just causes both because they are just and also because our own lives go better by being part of a more just (or less unjust) society and world.

By identifying with just causes, we can make our lives go better at the same time as we can contribute to democratic justice. This motivating feature of the identification view is lacking in a perspective that focuses exclusively on the moral obligations of individuals, as if doing things to help others is necessarily or even usually a sacrifice. The identification view reminds us that individuals can reasonably view the goodness of their own lives as bound up with the justice of their society and world. When people identify their own good with the justice of the world within which they live, identification is a source of motivational content for the pursuit of democratic justice. It makes sense that our identities and well-being should be so bound up with justice because it is reasonable that we see ourselves joined together by the societies and world that we share. For the short time that we inhabit it, this is not only "the" world, it is "*our*" world.

Our identification with others best serves the cause of democratic justice when it is not exclusively based on ascription. Ideally, identification with other people who share an interest in democratic justice would be the basis of organizing against discrimination. Short of the ideal, any identification that motivates people to organize together to further civic equality is better than no motivating identification. The common suspicion of ascriptive identification seems less severe a critique of political organization once we remind ourselves that humanity itself is an ascriptive identity, and one that has both served just causes and also blinded people to the needs of other living beings. We should not therefore hold suspect ascriptive identity groups of human beings.

We should also consider how identity groups can avoid the common malady of obliviousness to the needs of others, both those outside the group and those dissenting within the group. Perhaps most important for any modern democracy to emphasize is that no single group identity completely constitutes a person and no person is only a generic human being. Even if we each contain multitudes, however, we should do our fair share to act out of identification with our fellow human beings. Democratic justice calls for more than identification alone. This is the most fundamental critique that democratic justice directs toward some instances of identity group politics. *Without ethical precepts to guide group identity, members of groups are blind and can just as easily tyrannize over others as aid them. When guided by ethical precepts, individuals can enlist group identity as a justifiable means for organizing in democratic politics.*

PROTECTING INDIVIDUAL CONSCIENCE AND DEMOCRATIC GOVERNANCE

Among group identities, religious identity is often said to be special because of its intimate relationship with ethical identity, where ethical identity entails the ultimate commitments of a person's life. There are many other ways in which religious identity is said to be special, which I examined in chapter 4, but I concentrated on the claims of conscience because those claims have the most relevance to democratic justice. I invoke a meaning of conscience that is broader than its Protestant origins sometimes suggest. I use conscience to capture the ultimate ethical commitments of persons, regardless of whether those commitments are religious or secular in origin. Conscience has been historically tied to having a religious identity. But once we recognize that people need not be religious to have a conscience—a set of ultimate commitments upon which their ethical identity is based—we must also recognize that religion is not special in this sense. What is special for democratic justice is ethical identity, whether it is religiously or secularly based. It is special precisely because it reflects the ultimate ethical commitments of a person.

The question then arises: What does the special nature of conscience demand of democratic governments? Since democratic justice itself is based on respect for persons and respect for persons entails taking a person's conscience seriously, democratic governments should try to protect freedom of conscience when justice permits. Conscience is fallible, and respect for one person's conscience can conflict with the equal liberty and opportunity of others. Democratic governments therefore should not simply defer to conscience. But neither should governments simply override dissenting consciences whenever legitimate laws would allow them to do so. Considering whether the law can accommodate individual conscience without unjust discrimination is an important way in which democratic governments express their respect for ethical personhood.

Democratic governments are also fallible, and conscientious objection is an important means of exposing unjust laws. Even when laws are legitimate, I have argued, exemptions for conscientious objectors are worthy of consideration. Exemptions are exemplary when they respect the ethical identities of individuals without doing any injustice to others. Respect for persons, at the root of democratic justice, entails taking a person's conscience seriously. Taking a person's conscience seriously is not radically different from taking personal identity seriously, since conscience is a fundamental part of personal identity. Democratic governments should accommodate diverse personal identities whenever possible provided the accommodation does no injustice. This proviso recognizes that not all conscientious commitments should be accommodated simply by virtue of being conscientious. Accommodating conscientious commitments that clearly entail injustice—to bomb the infidels or to burn heretics at the stake—would make a mockery of democratic justice by undermining it, not expressing or supporting it.

When a democratic government makes an exemption from a specific law for conscientious objectors who do not threaten injustice, it can still uphold the primary purpose of the law itself. In upholding the law but making an exemption for conscience, democracy respects deep ethical commitments of dissenting individuals along with the legitimacy of democratic governance in the face of opposing ethical commitments. Similarly, a democratic government can tolerate the degree of discrimination by expressive groups that does not threaten civic equality, consistent with a general policy of nondiscrimination in the distribution of public goods. Two-way protection of individual conscience and democratic justice aims at balancing the competing demands of free expression and nondiscrimination. How to strike the balance is often difficult to determine, but the centrality of both demands to democratic justice should not be denied. When expressive groups discriminate out of ethical conviction and their discrimination does not interfere with the pursuit of civic equality for all individuals, a democratic government can dissociate itself from their views while leaving them room to act upon them. A democratic government cannot dissociate itself from discriminations that threaten to undermine the basic principle of civic equality.

Honoring the legitimate demands of both individual conscience and democratic governance is what distinguishes two-way protection from one-way protection of either individual conscience or democratic governance to the exclusion of the other. Neither protection of conscience nor protection of democratic rule is ideally absolute because both reflect important yet sometimes competing freedoms, one personal and the other political. Both freedoms are important ways of protecting the basic elements of democratic justice: civic equality, equal freedom, and opportunity for all. Church and state need to be separated, but there also needs to be democratic discretion in exempting conscientious believers from legitimate laws for the sake of respecting their ethical identities. Two-way protection can consistently support exemptions for conscientious objectors that do no injustice while defending the legitimacy of democratic governance.

In making some exemptions for conscientious objectors, a just democratic government aims at expressing its respect for the ultimate ethical commitments of individuals. It also recognizes its own ethical fallibility. It does not expect to provide each citizen with a social environment that fulfills the demands of conscience. This expectation is unreasonable given the diverse commitments of conscientious persons. It is also undesirable in light of the content of some consciences. Conscientious diversity is unlikely to disappear in a democracy that grants equal freedom and opportunity to all individuals. This means that democratic justice is likely to be at odds with what some people take to be a basic element of their identities. It also means that even if identity politics at its best is a politics of shared conscience, democracies at their best should not strive to satisfy all the demands of identity politics.

The promise of democratic justice is to grant individuals equal freedom and opportunity to live their lives as they see fit rather than to see their identities writ large in their very own society. This promise is hard to realize, but it is defensible on democratic grounds. Deferring to each and every conscientious identity, regardless of content, is not defensible. Identity groups are one important means of furthering democratic justice, but they are not ends in themselves.

DELIBERATING ABOUT IDENTITY IN DEMOCRACY

In sum, many individuals form and join identity groups for many politically relevant reasons:

- To publicly express what they consider an important aspect of their identity;

- To conserve their culture, which they identify with the group;

- To gain more material (and other) goods for themselves and their group (whether justified or not);

- To fight in a group for or against discrimination and other injustices;

- To receive mutual support from others who share some part of their social identity; and

- To express and act upon ethical commitments that they share with a group.

These reasons alone do not tell us enough to know whether identity groups on balance aid or impede democratic justice. Since no democracy could defensibly abolish identity groups, no practical or moral purpose would be served by an all-things-considered judgment about identity groups as a whole. For the purpose of pursuing democratic justice, one needs to assess how different identity groups act within specific social contexts, drawing upon defensible standards. Since the pursuit of democratic justice is necessarily a public enterprise, deliberation in public contexts about identity groups and the relevant standards of assessment is needed.

This book is no substitute for such deliberation. All I hope to have offered here is a principled democratic way of understanding and evaluating identity groups in democracy. In a democracy, people must be free to ally themselves with a wide range of identity groups. Identity groups represent an important part of who people are, which in turn influences what they want. Consequently, identity groups allow individuals to express themselves in democratic politics, which they do for better and for worse. Citizens who are concerned about democratic justice need to distinguish the better from the worse while recognizing that the aims of abolishing identity groups or elevating them above basic individual rights would threaten the very cause of democratic justice that they wish to be defending.

NOTES

INTRODUCTION
The Good, the Bad, and the Ugly of Identity Politics

1. For a review of the relevant experiments, see Jonathan D. Brown Natalie D. Novick, Kelley A. Lord, and Jane M. Richards, "When Gulliver Travels: Social Context, Psychological Closeness, and Self-Appraisals," *Journal of Personality and Social Psychology* 62, no. 5 (1992): 717–27. For an overview of the psychological literature, see Margaret Wetherell, ed., *Identities, Groups, and Social Issues* (London: Sage, 1996); and Michael A. Hogg and Scott Tindale, eds., *Group Processes* (Oxford: Blackwell, 2001).

2. See Claude M. Steele and J. Aronson, "Stereotype Threat and the Test Performance of Academically Successful African Americans," in Jencks, C., and M. Phillips, eds. *Black-White Test Score Gap* (Washington, DC: Brookings Institution Press, 1998); J. Aronson, et al., "When White Men Can't Do Math: Necessary and Sufficient Factors in Stereotype Threat," *Journal of Experimental Social Psychology* 35: (1999) 29–46; and S. J. Spencer, C. M. Steele, and D. M. Quinn, "Stereotype Threat and Women's Math Performance," *Journal of Experimental Social Psychology* 35 (1999): 4–28. For an overview of the experimental evidence on African American college students, see Claude Steele, "Thin Ice: 'Stereotype Threat' and Black College Students," *The Atlantic Monthly* 284 (August 1999), no. 2: 44–47, 50–54.

3. David Truman, who helped establish interest group theory in political science, neglected identity groups because he used the term interest group to include every group that "makes certain claims upon other groups for the establishment, maintenance or enhancement of forms of behavior that are implied by the[ir] shared attitudes." *The Governmental Process*, 2d ed. (New York: Knopf, 1971), 33.

So broadly used, interest groups include what today we call identity groups, but they were invisible at the time Truman wrote partly because no term captured the politically significant phenomenon of people joining together out of mutual identification, which interest group theorists call a "solidary" incentive.

4. For a hypercritique of identity groups in the American context, see Ward Connerly, "Are Ethnic and Gender-based Special-Interest Groups Good for America?" *Insight on the News*, July 7, 1997: 30 paragraphs. Lexis Academic Universe. News. General News. Magazines & Journals. Part Symposium, 25. (Accessed October 18, 2000.)

Connerly's claim that identity politics "was not envisioned by our Founders" is belied by the *Federalist 10*, which suggests precisely the contrary. Madison's understanding of factions is very broad, subsuming both interest and identity groups as the terms are used today: "The latent causes of faction are thus sown in the nature of man; and we see them everywhere brought into different degrees of activity. A zeal for different opinions concerning religion, concerning government, and many other points, as well of speculation as of practice . . ." (25).

5. See Yael Tamir, *Liberal Nationalism* (Princeton, NJ: Princeton University Press, 1985).

6. Bruce E. Keith *The Myth of the Independent Voter* (Berkeley: University of California Press, 1992), 38ff.

7. Angus Campbell, Philip E. Converse, Warren E. Miller, and Donald E. Stokes, *The American Voter* (New York: John Wiley and Sons, 1960), pp. 143–44.

8. Larry Bartels, "Partisanship and Voting Behavior, 1952–1996," *American Journal of Political Science* 44, no. 1 (January 2000): 35–50.

9. See, e.g., Philip E. Converse and Roy Pierce, *Political Representation in France* (Cambridge, MA: Harvard University Press, 1986), especially 120–67.

10. For a vivid portrayal of this march, see *Women of the Wall*, a film by Faye Lederman. This description is borrowed from the description of the film. For a discussion of the legal struggle by the Women of the Wall, see Pnina Lahav, "The Women-of-the-Wall Decision." *Israel Studies Bulletin* 16, no. 1 (Fall 2000): 19–22.

11. *Boy Scouts of America et al. v Dale*, 530 US 696 (June 28, 2000).

12. Unorganized identity groups are also an important phenomenon but not as directly connected to democratic politics. They include, for example, "jocks" and "geeks." When the identities of these groups are negatively stereotyped, they raise the political question of whether the negative stereotyping can realistically be overcome without the identity groups themselves organizing in some way to do so. The political problems raised by informal (or "nominal") identity groups therefore overlap substantially with those discussed in this book.

13. See, e.g., the review of the literature in Margaret Wetherell, ed., *Identities, Groups, and Social Issues* (London: Sage, 1996); and Michael A. Hogg and Scott Tindale, eds., *Group Processes* (Oxford: Blackwell, 2001).

14. A feminist is not only a feminist. As Iris Marion Young writes: "A person's identity is her own, formed in active relation to social positions, among other things, rather than [completely] constituted by them." *Inclusion and Democracy* (Oxford: Oxford University Press, 2000), 99. We therefore should distinguish between whether group identities can partially constitute individual identities or completely constitute them. An active agent can be partially constituted by many group identities but not fully constituted by any or all of them. The idea that being a woman and a feminist partially constitutes my identity is also completely consistent with my standing in an active relationship to what these identities mean to me and their implications for my life.

15. Many American women who identify as feminists, for example, join NOW or some other feminist group. Like feminism, other social markers are identifiable

independently of any single person's interpretation of them. My interpretation of feminism does not determine what feminism means to most people. And yet I can interpret what it means for me to be a feminist in a way that is comprehensibly to others. My identity as a feminist therefore is not completely determined by the dominant social meaning. But it is influenced by that meaning if only by requiring me to dissent if I want to publicly distinguish my interpretation from the dominant one. Over time within a social context, the interpretation of social markers by individuals can make a difference in how the dominant social meanings of the markers change or not. See also Iris Marion Young, *Inclusion and Democracy*, 87–120.

16. For an insightful new account, see K. Anthony Appiah, "The State and the Shaping of Identity," unpublished Tanner Lectures, 2001.

17. For a similar understanding, see James Fearon, "What Is Identity (As We Now Use the Word)?," unpublished manuscript, 1999.

18. For an interest group theory that is typical in recognizing the importance of solidary incentives without recognizing the phenomenon of identity groups, see Allan J. Cigler and Burdett A. Loomis, eds. *Interest Group Politics*, 4th ed. (Washington, DC: Congressional Quarterly Press, 1995), 9.

19. Mancur Olson, *The Logic of Collective Action* (Cambridge, MA: Harvard University Press, 1971).

20. Rogers Brubaker and Frederick Cooper, "Beyond 'Identity,'" *Theory and Society* 29(1) (2000): 8.

21. Terrence M. Moe, *The Organization of Interests* (Chicago: University of Chicago, 1980).

22. For an extensive critique along these lines, see Brian M. Barry, *Culture and Equality: An Egalitarian Critique of Multiculturalism* (Cambridge, MA: Harvard University Press, 2001).

23. John Rawls, *A Theory of Justice* (Cambridge, MA: Harvard University Press, 1999), 65–73.

24. Barry claims that trying to satisfy the demands of cultural identity groups not only "diverts political effort away from universalistic goals" but also destroys the political conditions that would favor "across-the-board equalization of opportunities and resources" (*Culture and Equality*, 325). But he does not suggest what political conditions favorable to egalitarianism existed and were actually destroyed by feminist, African American, Latin American, Native American, and other identity groups in the United States, whose members and supporters have been among the more egalitarian forces in American politics.

25. Todd Gitlin, *The Twilight of Common Dreams: Why America Is Wracked by Culture Wars* (New York: Henry Holt, 1995), 237. See also Barry, *Culture and Equality*, 326.

26. Brian Barry, *Culture and Equality*, 326.

27. William G. Bowen and Derek Bok, *The Shape of the River* (Princeton, NJ: Princeton University Press, 1998).

28. See William Julius Wilson, *The Bridge over the Racial Divide* (Berkeley: University of California Press, 1999); and William Julius Wilson, *The Truly Disad-*

vantaged: The Inner City, the Underclass, and Public Policy (Chicago: University of Chicago Press, 1987).

29. *Federalist 10.*

30. Barry, *Culture and Equality*, 326–327 and passim.

31. For a general discussion of Barry's critique of multiculturalism, see Ayelet Shachar, "Two Critiques of Multiculturalim," *Cardozo Law Review* 23:1 (November 2001): 253–297, especially 275–287.

32. Ibid., 8 and 292–328. Compare Nancy Fraser's critique of the relationship between the two approaches in "From Redistribution to Recognition? Dilemmas of Justice in a 'Post-Socialist' Age," *New Left Review* (1995): 68–93.

33. See, e.g., Stuart White, "Trade Unionism in a Liberal State," in *Freedom of Association*, edited by Amy Gutmann (Princeton, NJ: Princeton University Press, 1999), 330–356.

34. For a defense of deliberation and other principles of democratic justice, see Amy Gutmann and Dennis Thompson, *Democracy and Disagreement* (Cambridge, MA: Harvard University Press, 1996).

35. For a sampling of recent books that propose conceptions of democratic justice that defend a version of equal freedom, opportunity, and civic equality, see Seyla Benhabib, ed., *Democracy and Difference* (Princeton, NJ: Princeton University Press, 1996); Ronald Dworkin, *Sovereign Virtue* (Cambridge, MA: Harvard University Press, 2000); Amy Gutmann and Dennis Thompson, *Democracy and Disagreement*; Jurgen Habermas, *The Inclusion of the Other* (Cambridge, MA: MIT Press, 1998); Russell Hardin, *Liberalism, Constitutionalism and Democracy* (Oxford: Oxford University Press, 2000); George Kateb, *The Inner Ocean: Individualism and Democratic Culture* (Ithaca, NY: Cornell University Press, 1992); David Miller, *Principles of Social Justice* (Cambridge, MA: Harvard University Press, 1999); Carlos Santiago Nino, *The Constitution of Deliberative Democracy* (New Haven: Yale University Press, 1996); Philip Pettit, *Republicanism: A Theory of Freedom and Government* (Oxford: Clarendon Press, 1997); John Rawls, *A Theory of Justice*; and Ian Shapiro, *Democratic Justice* (New Haven, CT: Yale University Press, 1999).

36. A culture "provides its members with meaningful ways of life across the full range of human activities, including social, educational, religious, recreational, and economic life, encompassing both public and private spheres." Will Kymlicka, *Multicultural Citizenship: A Liberal Theory of Minority Rights* (Oxford: Clarendon Press, 1995), 76. A culture, as Avishai Margalit and Joseph Raz put it, "defines or marks a variety of forms or styles of life, types of activity, occupation, pursuit, and relationship. With national groups we expect to find national cuisines, distinctive architectural styles, a common language, distinctive literary and artistic traditions, national music, customs, dress, ceremonies and holidays, etc." From Avishai Margalit and Joseph Raz, "National Self-Determination," in *Ethics in the Public Domain: Essays in the Morality of Law and Politics*, edited by Joseph Raz (New York: Oxford University Press, 1994), 114. See also Will Kymlicka, *Liberalism, Community, and Culture* (Oxford: Clarendon Press, 1989), 162–78, who identifies culture with a "context of choice" (164, 166).

37. Alexis de Tocqueville, *Democracy in America*, edited by J. P. Mayer (New York: Doubleday Anchor ed., 1969), 513.

38. George Kateb, "The Value of Association," in *Freedom of Association*, edited by Amy Gutmann (Princeton, NJ: Princeton University Press, 1998), 37–38.

39. See K. Anthony Appiah, "Race, Culture, Identity," in K. Anthony Appiah and Amy Gutmann, *Color Conscious: The Political Morality of Race* (Princeton, NJ: Princeton University Press, 1996), 97–104.

CHAPTER ONE
Claims of Cultural Identity Groups

1. See, e.g., Iris Marion Young's influential *Justice and the Politics of Difference* (Princeton, NJ: Princeton University Press, 1990), 23–24, 152–55, and passim.

2. Iris Marion Young's work on the politics of difference tends to assimilate all disadvantaged identity groups to cultural groups, leading Young to a call to end cultural imperialism through a cultural revolution. Many disadvantaged (and advantaged) groups are not distinguished by a single culture. The oppression of women, for example, may be enhanced by their integration into some of the same cultures as men. A symptom of this problem of analysis is Young's call for a cultural revolution without due regard for the injustices that such a call may reasonably conjure up in the wake of Mao's Cultural Revolution. See ibid., 152–55, and the critique by Brian Barry, *Culture and Equality* (Cambridge, MA: Harvard University Press, 2001), 15, 269.

3. "Familiarity with a culture determines the boundaries of the imaginable. Sharing in a culture, being part of it, determines the limits of the feasible." Joseph Raz and Avishai Margalit, "National Self-Determination," in *Ethics in the Public Domain: Essays in the Morality of Law and Politics*, edited by Joseph Raz (New York: Oxford University Press, 1994), 119.

4. Ibid., 118.

5. Whereas the ETA, an armed group of separatist Basque nationalists, engages in terrorist activities that threaten the basic security of people who peacefully oppose them, Catalan nationalists peacefully coexist with non-Catalans in a federated Spain that gives both national minorities considerable political autonomy. The comparison between Basques and Catalans provides a striking example of why it would be a mistake to think that even a single category of cultural identity groups—national minorities—makes a single set of claims on democracy. Basque nationalists are themselves internally divided, and radically so, in their claims, some of which are entirely compatible and others completely incompatible with basic liberty and civic equality for all individuals.

6. Will Kymlicka, *Liberalism, Community, and Culture* (Oxford: Clarendon Press, 1989), 175.

7. Margalit and Raz, "National Self-Determination," 114.

8. See Will Kymlicka, *Multicultural Citizenship: A Liberal Theory of Minority Rights* (Oxford: Clarendon Press, 1995), 18, 76, and Margalit and Raz, "National

Self-Determination," 114. What Kymlicka calls a societal culture Margalit and Raz call a pervasive culture. People who share or come close to sharing a pervasive culture and whose "identity is determined at least in part by their culture" are "serious candidates for the right to self-determination" according to the account offered by Margalit and Raz ("National Self-Determination," 114).

9. Margalit and Raz, "National Self-Determination," 118.

10. Will Kymlicka, *Liberalism, Community, and Culture*, 164.

11. Margalit and Raz, "National Self-Determination," 118.

12. Ibid., 117.

13. As Margalit and Raz write: "Although accomplishments play their role in people's sense of their own identity, it would seem that at the most fundamental level our sense of our own identity depends on criteria of belonging rather than on those of accomplishment. Secure identification at that level [of cultural membership] is particularly important to one's well-being." Ibid, 117.

14. Raz, *Ethics in the Public Domain*, 162.

15. The seminal contemporary work on this subject is Charles Taylor's *Multiculturalism*, edited by Amy Gutmann (Princeton, NJ: Princeton University Press, 1994).

16. Ibid., 50.

17. For a philosophical basis for the toleration view, see Bruce Ackerman, *Social Justice in the Liberal State* (New Haven: Yale University Press, 1980), 139–141.

18. See Axel Honneth, *The Struggle for Recognition: The Moral Grammar of Social Conflicts* (Cambridge, MA: MIT Press, 1996); and Axel Honneth, "Integrity and Disrespect: Principles of a Conception of Morality Based on a Theory of Recognition," in *The Fragmented World of the Social: Essays in Social and Political Philosophy*, edited by Charles W. Wright (Albany: State University of New York Press, 1995), 255–56.

19. *Goldman v Weinberger*, 475 US 503 (1986). See discussions of these cases in Kymlicka, *Multicultural Citizenship*, 108–15; and Jacob T. Levy, *The Multiculturalism of Fear* (New York: Oxford University Press, 2000), 129–30.

20. See Levy, *The Multiculturalism of Fear*, for a clear and useful categorization of claims on behalf of cultural identity groups, which he subsumes under the rubric of "rights" (although not all of the claims by cultural identity groups are made in the name of rights), 125–60.

21. Cited in *Martinez v Santa Clara Pueblo*, 540 F2d 1039, 1042 (10th Cir 1976).

22. *Martinez v Romney*, 402F, Supp 5, 19 (D NM 1975). Emphasis added. By putting the "good" in scare quotes, the Court conveys the idea that no reason could be a good reason. The Court also makes explicit its own faulty reasoning, that upholding the discriminatory law saves a valued cultural identity of Pueblo women, while upholding Martinez's plea for being treated as a civic equal would destroy her valued cultural identity. In a tautological sense, deferring to any existing cultural practice "saves" the cultural identities that depend on the practice. But Martinez and the other

plaintiffs reasonably wanted to remain Pueblo but not labor under the burden of a discriminatory membership law.

23. For a discussion of the Martinez case from a legal and humanistic perspective, see Ayelet Shachar, *Multicultural Jurisdictions: Cultural Differences and Women's Rights* (Cambridge: Cambridge University Press, 2001), 18–20. Shachar's legal analysis concludes that "the group's collective interest in preserving its *nomos* is achieved, in part, through the imposition of severe and disproportionate burdens upon a particular class of group members [women] (19)."

24. Kymlicka, *Multicultural Citizenship*, 163–70. For a case made against one group's imposing rights on another group that it has a tradition of oppressing, see Jeff Spinner-Halev, "Feminism, Multiculturalism, Oppression, and the State," *Ethics* 112 (October 2001): 84–113. Spinner-Halev's argument does not rest on assuming the comprehensiveness of cultures but it does rest on an unargued assumption that groups will come to accept the basic rights of their members more quickly if they are not pressured from the outside to reform. Even if this assumption is sometimes correct, when it is not, the basic rights of individuals should not be violated out of deference to a group. In the Martinez case, as in many others, members of the culture are asking to have their rights vindicated. The case therefore cannot be reduced to one of external imposition of a human rights regime by an oppressive outside group when Pueblo women are the plaintiffs.

25. Taylor, *Multiculturalism*, 54–61, and Kymlicka, *Liberalism, Community, and Culture*, 135–61; 253–57.

26. See, for example, Taylor, *Multiculturalism*, 59. For a more recent discussion of basic rights in an international context, see Michael Ignatieff, *Human Rights as Politics and Idolatry*, edited by A. Gutmann (Princeton, NJ: Princeton University Press, 2001).

27. "I was born an Indian, and not only an Indian, but a Bombayite. . . . My writing and thought have . . . been as deeply influenced by Hindu myths and attitudes as Muslim ones. . . . Nor is the West absent from Bombay. . . . The point is this: Muslim culture has been very important to me, but it is not by any means the only shaping factor." Salman Rushdie, "In Good Faith," in *Imaginary Homelands: Essays and Criticism 1981–1991* (London: Penguin Books, 1991), 404. For a defense of cosmopolitanism based on Rushdie's example, see Jeremy Waldron, "Multiculturalism and Melange," in *Public Education in a Multicultural Society: Policy, Theory, Critique*, edited by Robert K. Fullinwider (Cambridge, England: Cambridge University Press, 1996), 90–118.

28. Amartya Sen, "Other People." *The New Republic*, December 18, 2000, 28.

29. Amy Gutmann, "Challenges of Multiculturalism in Education," in *Public Education in a Multicultural Society: Policy, Theory, Critique*, edited by Robert Fullinwider (Cambridge, England: Cambridge University Press, 1996), 156–79.

30. See Bryna Jocheved Levy, "Sense and Sensibilities: Women and Talmud Torah," *Jewish Action* magazine, *http://www.ou.org/publications/ja/5759winter/sense.htm.*

31. Still more facts of Martinez's case undermine the assumption that the Pueblo are an encompassing group. Not only was the 1939 law approved by the federal government of the United States, but Martinez was a citizen of both the Santa Clara Pueblo and the United States. She invoked a law in her defense—the Indian Civil Rights Act (ICRA) of 1968—which was ratified by both Congress and the Pueblo. The United States Supreme Court never questioned its own authority to interpret the ICRA. It interpreted the ICRA in a way that granted authority to the Pueblo to violate the civic equality of women. The Court's review subordinated the civic equality of Pueblo women to the tribe's authority, but the opposite decision would not have abolished the political sovereignty of the tribe; it would have constrained it by respect for an equal right of women. The tribe's authority was already constrained, in some cases in far less justifiable ways. Martinez's unequal treatment as a woman therefore cannot be attributed to her encompassing cultural identity as a Pueblo but rather to the refusal of two sets of political institutions to place the civic equality of women above the authority of a cultural group.

32. *Martinez v Santa Clara Pueblo*, 540 F2d 1039, 1047 (10th Cir 1976).

33. The dissenting opinion by Justice White in the *Martinez* case suggests how the court could have invalidated the tribe's violation of Martinez's constitutional right without substituting its own judgment of what alternative course of action the tribe should take to vindicate the right. See *Santa Clara Pueblo v Martinez*, 436 US at 76: "The federal district court's duty would be limited to determining whether the challenged tribal action violated one of the enumerated rights. If found to be in violation, the action would be invalidated; if not, it would be allowed to stand. In no event would the court be authorized, as in a *de novo* proceeding, to substitute its judgment concerning the wisdom of the action taken for that of the tribal authorities." For an extended and insightful commentary on the case, see Judith Resnick, "Dependent Sovereign: Indian Tribes, States, and the Federal Courts," 56 *University of Chicago Law Review* 671 (1989): 675–686. Resnick writes that the 1939 General Allotment Act that codified unequal citizenship rights for Pueblo women and men, far from being indigenous to the Pueblo, "seems to have been supported, if not influenced and encouraged, by the traditions of the United States." Recognizing the permeability of cultures would lead us to challenge those who defer to the legitimacy of the Act on grounds of cultural preservation and to wonder: "Whose culture is this culture? Is male supremacy sacred because it has become a tribal tradition?" Catharine A. MacKinnon, *Feminism Unmodified: Discourses on Life and Law* (Cambridge, MA: Harvard University Press, 1987), 67.

34. Justice White's dissent in *Santa Clara Pueblo v Martinez*, 436 US at 83.

35. The United States government should not be granted the authority to violate individual rights if an established legal tribunal could prevent it from so doing without any violence. There was an established and potentially effective tribunal in place that could have vindicated Martinez's right without any violence. When no established tribunal exists, political theorists need to consider the case for establishing one.

36. From text of President Bill Clinton's statement authorizing the United States to sign the Treaty on the International Criminal Court. *The New York Times*, January 1, 2001, A6.

37. Kymlicka, *Multicultural Citizenship*, 167.

38. For a useful and more comprehensive typology of group rights, see Jacob Levy, "Classifying Cultural Rights," in *NOMOS XXXIX: Ethincity and Group Rights*, edited by Will Kymlicka and Ian Shapiro (New York: New York University Press, 1997), 22–66. Steven Lukes provides an alternative typology, distinguishing between calls for enhancement of status through the removal of discriminatory barriers to individual access and demands for recognition of difference ranging from public assertion to "the State's granting of significant claims." Lukes, "Toleration and Recognition," *Ratio Juris* 10, no. 2 (1997): 217–18.

39. Bhikhu Parekh, *Rethinking Multiculturalism: Cultural Diversity and Political Theory* (Basingstoke, Hampshire, England: Macmillan, 2000), 215.

40. For a more extensive analysis of this distinction, see Joseph Raz, *The Morality of Freedom* (New York: Oxford University Press, 1986), 207–8; and Peter Jones, "Political Theory and Cultural Diversity," *Critical Review of International Social and Political Philosophy*, 1, no. 1 (Spring 1998): 46–50. Jones's larger analysis is instructive except insofar as it conflates fairness with cultural neutrality and makes a dichotomous distinction between legitimizing and justifying laws. He therefore views public deliberation as having a role only in legitimizing but not in justifying laws and public policies. If justification requires interpersonal demonstration, then deliberation is important for both justifying and legitimizing laws, which is not to say that it is sufficient for either (and in some extreme cases may not even be necessary). In cases of reasonable disagreement, deliberation is necessary. Jones himself supplies competing interpretations of what impartiality may reasonably be taken to mean with regard to cultural diversity, but he suggests that it is simply up to philosophy and philosophers to come up with the single justifiable resolution of actual conflicts among these interpretations.

41. Jones, "Political Theory and Cultural Diversity," 49.

42. Avishai Margalit and Moshe Halbertal, "Liberalism and the Right to Culture," *Social Research* 61, no. 3 (1994): 491.

43. Shachar, *Multicultural Jurisdictions*, p. 43.

44. Ultra-Orthodox Jewish girls and boys in Israel are educated at state expense in such a way that certainly limits (and is intended by the group to limit) their opportunities to live outside of the Ultra-Orthodox Jewish community. "The school curriculum is controlled exclusively by the [Ultra-Orthodox Jewish] community," as Margalit and Halbertal recognize, "and there is a clear discrimination between the education of girls and of boys." Discrimination against women is reinforced by state support for grossly unequal conditions of marriage, divorce, and inheritance rights. Under these conditions, one can reasonably wonder whether consent is really a solid ground on which to obligate the democratic state to support publicly accredited schooling and other institutions that are demanded by the cultural group. Ibid., 493.

45. This claim is another example of a general conflation of what a person's identity is and what that person ought to do. For a critique of this conflation, see Russell Hardin, *One for All: The Logic of Group Conflict* (Princeton, NJ: Princeton University Press, 1995), 6–10.

46. John Stuart Mill emphasized this point. See Mill, *On Liberty*, edited by David Spitz (New York: Norton, 1975), 451–456.

47. Richard Shweder, "What about Female Genital Mutilation? And Why Understanding Culture Matters in the First Place," in *Engaging Cultural Differences: Multicultural Challenge in Liberal Democracies*, edited by Richard A. Shweder, Martha Minow, and Hazel R. Markus (New York: Russell Sage Foundation Press, 2002), 222–26.

48. Ibid., 223, 235–36.

49. Carla Makhlouf Obermeyer, "Female Genital Surgeries: The Known, the Unknown, and the Unknowable," *Medical Anthropology Quarterly* 13, no. 1 (1999): 92.

50. Ibid., 94. Obermeyer's article offers the most thorough analysis of the available evidence, 79–106.

51. A wide range of political theorists defend the compatibility of mutual respect and partisanship. See, e.g., the commentaries by William Galston, Robert George, Jane Mansbridge, Cass Sunstein, Amy Gutmann, and Dennis Thompson in *Deliberative Politics: Essays on Democracy and Disagreement*, edited by Stephen Macedo (New York: Oxford University Press, 1999). See also Amy Gutmann and Dennis Thompson, *Democracy and Disagreement* (Cambridge, MA: Belknap Press, 1996).

52. For an extended defense of the basic rights of women against cultural practices that clearly threaten those rights, see Susan Moller Okin (Joshua Cohen, Matthew Howard, and Martha C. Nussbaum, eds) *Is Multiculturalism Bad for Women?* (Princeton, NJ: Princeton University Press, 1999); Martha C. Nussbaum and Jonathan Glover, eds., *Women, Culture, and Development: A Study of Human Capabilities* (New York: Oxford University Press, 1994); and Martha C. Nussbaum, *Sex and Social Justice* (New York: Oxford University Press, 1999).

53. I discuss the "Affair of the Scarf" in "Challenges of Multiculturalism in Democratic Education," in *Public Education in a Multicultural Society*, edited by Robert K. Fullinwider (New York: Cambridge University Press, 1996), 156–79. For an insightful and extended discussion of this controversy connected to a set of arguments for democratically deliberating about its resolution, see Seyla Benhabib, *The Claims of Culture: Equality and Diversity in the Global Era* (Princeton, NJ: Princeton University Press, 2002).

54. Anne Fadiman, *The Spirit Catches You and You Fall Down* (New York: Farrar, Straus and Giroux, 1999).

55. D. L. Coleman, "The Seattle Compromise: Multicultural Sensitivity and Americanization," *Duke Law Review* 47 (1998): 717–782. See also Richard Shweder, *Engaging Cultural Differences*, 231.

56. I am not suggesting, however, that the negative reactions to the hospital's proposal are culturally determined. An activist Ethiopian immigrant, for example,

told the *Seattle Times* that "How dare it even cross their mind [to perform female circumcision]? What the Somalis, what the immigrants like me need is an education, not sensitivity to culture." Quoted in Levy, *The Multiculturalism of Fear*, 55. See Levy's discussion, 53–57.

57. Another defense of deliberation about cultural diversity, which draws upon some similar democratic principles but focuses on different cultures, can be found in Seyla Benhabib, *The Claims of Culture: Equality and Diversity in the Global Era* (Princeton, NJ: Princeton University Press, 2002).

58. For discussions of the claims for descriptive representation for identity groups, see Anne Phillips, *Engendering Democracy* (University Park, PA: Pennsylvania State University Press, 1991); and Melissa Williams, *Voice, Trust, and Memory* (Princeton, NJ: Princeton University Press, 1998).

59. Taylor, *Multiculturalism*, 61.

60. Ibid., 59.

61. For a case made for the distinctive standing in democratic societies of aboriginal groups relative to other minority cultures based on the historical injustices committed against these groups, see John R. Danley, "Liberalism, Aboriginal Rights, and Cultural Minorities," *Philosophy and Public Affairs* 20, no. 2 (Spring 1991): 168–85.

62. "Cultural groups have no moral claim to eternal existence, especially as against the rights and choices of their own individual members—let alone their children and their children's children. What they do have is a right to be free from circumstances under which their continued existence is made impossible because of injustices such as those faced by aboriginal communities throughout the world." Michael Blake, "Rights for People, Not for Cultures," *Civilization* (August/September 2000): 50–54.

63. Some critics of Taylor suggest that he values the group above the individuals who constitute it, but this misrepresents Taylor's perspective at its strongest, which is a critique of liberal neutralists who claim that for political purposes individual interests must be viewed as independent of particular cultures. Taylor argues, by contrast, that individual interests are laden with particular cultural goods and understandings, including language and a sense of valuable callings, careers, and customs. Taylor also attributes to individuals an interest in their culture's surviving over time, since people want to be assured that their descendants will share their culture. These are controversial claims about how we should understand the basic interests of individuals, but the claims are not that a group's interest takes precedence over the interests of its members. See Taylor, *Multiculturalism*, 51–73. For a sense of how heated the controversy about culturalism can be, see the exchange between David Bromwich, Michael Walzer, and Taylor in *Dissent* 42, no. 1 (Winter 1995): 89–106.

64. See, e.g., Judith Butler, "Restaging the Universal," in Judith Butler, Ernesto Laclau and Slavoj Zizek, *Contingency, Hegemony, Universality: Contemporary Dialogues on the Left* (London and New York: Verso, 2000), 35: "A recent resurgence of Anglofeminism in the academy has sought to restate the importance of making universal

claims about the conditions and rights of women (Okin, Nussbaum) without regard to the prevailing norms in local cultures, and without taking up the task of cultural translation. This effort to override the problem that local cultures pose for international feminism does not understand the parochial character of its own norms. . . ." Butler combines two criticisms here that are separable. The first is that critiques of cultural practices should take up "the task of cultural translation" and therefore be sure to attend to the context in which cultural practices take place. The second is that the norm of basic rights is "parochial." All norms are parochial in the sense of resting on claims and cultures that are not universally accepted. But this is not the same as saying that all norms find their defense solely in a single culture (or that they are objectionably parochial). Butler seems to agree that being culturally specific is not a criticism, and I agree that the task of cultural translation is important, as my defense of the Seattle Hospital proposal indicates. Cultural translation does not imply acceptance but it is often a precondition for acceptance of unfamiliar cultural practices that are no worse than far more familiar ones that are justifiably accepted within one's culture.

65. See, for example, Antonio Cassese, "The General Assembly: Historical Perspective, 1945–1989," in *The United Nations and Human Rights: A Critical Appraisal*, edited by Philip Alston (Oxford: Clarendon Press, 1992), 31. See also William Alford, "Making a Goddess of Democracy from Loose Sand: Thoughts on Human Rights in the Peoples Republic of China," in *Human Rights in Cross-Cultural Perspectives: A Quest for Consensus*, edited by Abdullahi Ahmed An-Na'im (Philadelphia: University of Pennsylvania Press, 1992), 75.

66. Johannes Morsink, *The Universal Declaration of Human Rights: Origins, Drafting, and Intent* (Philadelphia: University of Pennsylvania Press, 1999), xii.

67. See "Introduction" to Michael Ignatieff, *Human Rights as Politics and Idolatry*, edited by Amy Gutmann (Princeton, NJ: Princeton University Press, 2001): vii–xxxvii.

68. Morsink, *The Universal Declaration of Human Rights*, x.

69. See John Rawls, *Political Liberalism* (New York: Columbia University Press, 1993), especially 195–200.

70. Margalit and Halbertal, "Liberalism and the Right to Culture," 491.

CHAPTER TWO
The Value of Voluntary Groups

1. Alexis de Toqueville, *Democracy in America*, edited by J. P. Mayer (New York: Doubleday Anchor ed, 1969), p. 517.

2. The seminal study is Robert D. Putnam, *Bowling Alone: The Collapse and Revival of American Community* (New York: Simon & Schuster, 2000). For challenges (provoked by his article "Bowling Alone: America's Declining Social Capital," *Journal of Democracy* 6, no. 1 [1995]: 65–78) to Putnam's empirical claims concerning the decline in associational memberships, see Sheri Berman, "Civic Society and the Col-

lapse of the Weimar Republic," *World Politics* 49, no. 3 (1997): 401–29; and Pamela Paxton, "Is Social Capital Declining in the United States? A Multiple Indicator Assessment," *American Journal of Sociology* 105, no. 1 (July 1999): 88–127.

3. We can value individual freedom for a variety of reasons that find their source in many comprehensive philosophies of life as well as in democratic theories of politics that do not depend on a particular comprehensive philosophy of life. Among the principles that support individual freedom, each of which has several cultural and philosophical sources, are the dignity of persons, their equality before God, mutual respect for persons as self-originating sources of moral worth in society, and free and equal citizenship in democratic society. From each of these starting points emanates a defense of the freedom to live one's life according to one's own best lights consistent with respecting the equal freedom of others.

4. Nancy Rosenblum, *Membership and Morals* (Princeton, NJ: Princeton University Press, 1998), 32.

5. Kateb, "The Value of Association," 39.

6. Brian M. Barry, *Culture and Equality: An Egalitarian Critique of Multiculturalism* (Cambridge, England: Polity Press, 2001), 155–93.

7. See Rosenblum, *Membership and Morals*, 101ff; and Will Kymlicka, *Multicultural Citizenship: A Liberal Theory of Minority Rights* (New York: Oxford University Press, 1995), 234 n18.

8. Rosenblum, *Membership and Morals*, 4.

9. *Hofer v Hofer* 13 DLR (3d)1 (SCC), 984 (1970).

10. For a justification of unions, see Stuart White, "Trade Unionism in a Liberal State," in *Freedom of Association*, edited by Amy Gutmann (Princeton, NJ: Princeton University Press, 1998), 330–56.

11. George Kateb, "The Value of Association," in Freedom of Association, edited by Amy Gutmann (Princeton, NJ: Princeton University Press, 1998), 60. Emphasis added. The various standards offered by theorists of choice bear a strong family resemblance to one another. Many are versions of John Stuart Mill's "harm principle": "the sole end for which mankind are warranted, individually or collectively, in interfering with the liberty of action of any of their number is self-protection . . . to prevent harm to others" (Mill, "Introductory," 13). Brennan's case against the Jaycees draws on the Millean harm principle. Kateb's standard is in the same family; it recognizes that liberty may be limited for the sake of protecting an equally or more valuable liberty or another "vital claim" of individuals. In all these cases, the harm can be treatment as a civic unequal, rather than a separate harm that is caused by civic inequality.

12. "The mutual adjustment of the basic liberties is justified," Rawls writes, "on grounds allowed by the priority of these liberties as a family, no one of which is in itself absolute." Rawls, *Political Liberalism* (New York: Columbia University Press, 1993), 358.

13. John Rawls, *A Theory of Justice* (Cambridge, MA: Belknap Press of Harvard University Press, 1999), 202.

14. *Nixon v Condon*, 286 US 73, 83 (1932). Emphasis added.

15. Robert Post, "Prejudicial Appearances: The Logic of American Antidiscrimination Law," *California Law Review* 88, no. 1 (January 2000): 1–40.

16. Minnesota Human Rights Act, cited in *Roberts v United States Jaycees*, 468 US at 615 (1984).

17. Minnesota Statute 363.03, subd 3 (1982). The term "place of public accommodation" is defined in the act as "a business, accommodation, refreshment, entertainment, recreation, or transportation facility of any kind, whether licensed or not, whose goods, services, facilities, privileges, advantages or accommodations are extended, offered, sold, or otherwise made available to the public" (363.01, subd 18). Quoted in *Roberts v United States Jaycees*, 468 US at 615 (1984).

18. *Roberts v United States Jaycees*, 468 US at 624 (1984).

19. Ibid., at 625.

20. "Different opinions about the value of the liberties will, of course, affect how different persons think the full scheme of freedom should be arranged." Rawls, *A Theory of Justice*, 202. Different opinions are often part of the realm of reasonable disagreement. For a cogent explanation of the democratic search for fair terms of social cooperation and the Rawlsian concept of the reasonable, see Joshua Cohen, "A More Democratic Liberalism," *Michigan Law Review* 92, no. 6 (1994): 1521–1543.

21. *Roberts v United States Jaycees*, 468 US at 639. The Jaycees, like almost all associations, have some significant expressive purposes. If it were sufficient for a voluntary association to claim some significant expressive purpose to immunize itself from state regulation, then almost all associations would have immunity from nondiscrimination laws, rendering these laws impotent to protect civic equality.

22. Judith Shklar, *American Citizenship: The Quest for Inclusion* (Cambridge: Harvard University Press, 1991), 84. Opening up the informal associational channels of commerce to women is an extension of opening up occupations themselves. One way of undermining equal economic opportunity for women would be to keep the informal associational channels of commerce closed to young women or open to them only as the subordinate associates of young men, which is what the Jaycees had institutionalized before the *Roberts* decision, quite in keeping with the longstanding civic inequality of women.

23. Rosenblum, "Compelled Association," in *Freedom of Association*, 87.

24. Ibid., 90.

25. Ibid., 84.

26. For a call for a sociological account of employment discrimination, see Robert Post, "Prejudicial Appearances," 31–40.

27. Rosenblum, "Compelled Association," 87.

28. From the Boy Scouts Handbook, quoted in *Boy Scouts of America v Dale*, 530 US at 667 (2000). The dissenting opinion by Justice Stevens (joined by Justices Souter, Ginsburg, and Breyer) points out that prior to the expulsion of James Dale, the Boy Scouts had never explicitly associated being morally straight or clean with not being homosexual. But when pressed to defend their exclusion, the organization's

leadership made explicit the view that being homosexual is inconsistent with being a civic equal because homosexuals cannot be morally clean in some civic (and explicitly not religious) sense of moral cleanliness.

29. *Boy Scouts of America v Dale*, 530 US at 696 (2000).

30. Ibid.

31. Rawls, *A Theory of Justice*, 230.

32. Richard Epstein, "Free Association: The Incoherence of Antidiscrimination Laws," *National Review* LII, no. 19 (October 9, 2000): 38–40.

33. Ibid.

34. Laura Parker and Guillermo X. Garcia, "Boy Scout Troops Lose Funds, Meeting Places." *USA Today*, October 10, 2000, 1A.

35. Ibid.

36. For a defense of nondiscrimination in public schooling, see Amy Gutmann, *Democratic Education* (Princeton, NJ: Princeton University Press, 1999).

37. See Robert D. Putnam, Robert Leonardi, and Raffaella Y. Nanetti, *Making Democracy Work* (Princeton, NJ: Princeton University Press, 1994); and *Bowling Alone*, 66.

38. These and other social problems associated with declining membership in voluntary groups may be real even if Putnam somewhat overstates his empirically sustainable case when he claims, far more generally, that "social capital makes us smarter, healthier, safer, richer, and better able to govern a just and stable democracy." Putnam, *Bowling Alone*, 290.

39. Ibid., 353–56.

40. Ibid., 352. Over the last three decades of the twentieth century, increased toleration of diverse religious faiths and practices, greater gender equality, more racial integration, more equal rights for gays and lesbians, and more equal rights generally have meant that the vast majority of Americans have been "increasingly liberated from stigma and oppression." The liberation is far from complete, but the gain in liberty could well be worth the cost in community were trade-off a practical necessity, which it may not be.

CHAPTER THREE
Identification by Ascription

1. See Carol Padden and Tom Humphries, *Deaf in America: Voices from the Culture* (Cambridge, MA: Harvard University Press, 1988), 2 and passim.

2. Kim Isaac Eisler, *Revenge of the Pequots: How a Small American Tribe Created the World's Most Profitable Casino* (New York: Simon & Schuster, 2001).

3. David D. Laitin, *Identity in Formation: The Russian-Speaking Populations in the Near Abroad* (Ithaca, NY: Cornell University Press, 1998), 21.

4. Ibid., 20.

5. See, for example, K. Anthony Appiah, "Race, Culture, Identity," in Appiah and Gutmann, *Color Conscious: The Political Morality of Race* (Princeton, NJ: Princeton University Press, 1996), 30–105.

6. See Susan Moller Okin, *Justice, Gender and the Family* (New York: Basic Books, 1991); Iris Marion Young, *Intersecting Voices* (Princeton, NJ: Princeton University Press, 1997); Judith Butler, *Gender Trouble* (New York: Routledge, 1999); and Catharine A. Mackinnon, *Feminism Unmodified* (Cambridge, MA: Harvard University Press, 1987).

7. See Ian Shapiro and Will Kymlicka, *Ethnicity and Group Rights* (New York: New York University Press, 1997); and Nathan Glazer, *Ethnic Dilemmas: 1964–1982* (Cambridge, MA: Harvard University Press, 1983).

8. See Benedict Anderson, *Imagined Communities* (London: Verso, 1991).

9. For general theoretical statements about social construction of identity, see Ernesto Laclau, ed., *The Making of Political Identities* (London: Verso, 1994); and Judith Butler, Ernesto Laclau, and Slavoj Zizek, *Contingency, Hegemony, Universality* (London: Verso, 2000).

10. Eisler, *Revenge of the Pequots.*

11. See Amartya Sen, "Goals, Commitment, and Identity," *Journal of Law, Economics, & Organization* 1, no. 2 (Fall 1985): 347. Sen offers a trilogy of ways that economists think about motives of reasonable action, all of which are "private." The three are self-centered welfare, self-welfare goal, and self-goal choice. He then argues that there are nonprivate ways of thinking and acting based on identification with others and commitment to the welfare of others. Identity and commitment also can be manifest in ascriptive identity group politics.

12. The debate between defenders of interest-driven and identity-driven politics therefore suffers from a problem parallel to the one that plagues the debate between primordial and constructivist views of ascriptive identity: "Neither side comprehends that each is looking at only one face of Janus." Laitin, *Identity in Formation*, 20.

13. There is also another argument against those who would differentiate between groups like the KKK and NAACP on grounds that only one represents the interests of a subordinated group. Even the KKK can credibly claim to represent a subordinated group: nonaffluent white Southern men who feel themselves to be increasingly marginalized in society and may in fact be increasingly marginalized. This is not a major argument against the asymmetry view, however, because it does not recommend supporting any ascriptive group simply because it represents subordinated individuals.

14. David B. Wilkins, "Identities and Roles: Race, Recognition, and Professional Responsibility," *Maryland Law Review*, 57, no. 4 (1998): 1521–1522.

15. James T. Patterson, *Brown v Board of Education: A Civil Rights Milestone and Its Troubled Legacy* (Oxford: Oxford University Press, 2001), 73.

16. Ibid.

17. Ibid., 74.

18. Ibid., 80.

19. Ibid., 81.

20. "Status Report on Probe of Election Practices in Florida during the 2000 Presidential Election," *http://www.usccr.gov* [accessed June 28, 2001].

21. For the importance of distinguishing between misfortune and injustice, see Judith N. Shklar, *The Faces of Injustice* (New Haven, CT: Yale University Press, 1990).

22. The NAACP's explicit aim is consistent with this best case scenario. It is "to ensure the political, educational, social and economic equality of minority group citizens of the United States and eliminate race prejudice. "NAACP online," *http://www.naacp.org/* [accessed June 28, 2001].

23. Hazel Rose Markus, Claude M. Steele, and Dorothy M. Steele, "Color-blindness as a Barrier to Exclusion," in "The End of Tolerance: Engaging Cultural Differences." *Daedalus* 129, no. 4 (Fall 2000): 248.

24. Jason Lamberton, *The NewsHour with Jim Lehrer*, transcript, February 19, 2001.

25. NAD now explicitly recognizes the diversity of its ascriptive group: it "recognizes that diversity within the deaf community itself, and within the deaf experience, has not been acknowledged or explained very clearly in the public forum." "NAD Position Statement on Cochlear Implants," October 6, 2000. *http://www.nad.org/infocenter/newsroom/papers/Cochlear Implants.html* [accessed June 28, 2001].

26. For theories and principles of obligation, see Michael Walzer, *Obligations: Essays on Disobedience, War and Citizenship* (Cambridge, MA: Harvard University Press, 1970); and A. John Simmons, *Justification and Legitimacy: Essays on Rights and Obligations* (New York: Cambridge University Press, 2001). For arguments about special obligations as applied to the example of African American professionals, see Wilkins, "Identities and Roles," 1502–1594.

27. See also Appiah and Gutmann, *Color Conscious: The Political Morality of Race.*

28. James Baldwin, "Introduction to *Notes of a Native Son, 1984*," in James Baldwin, *Collected Essays*, edited by Toni Morrison (New York: Literary Classics of the United States, 1998), 810.

29. See, for example, John Rawls, *A Theory of Justice* (Cambridge, MA: Harvard University Press, 1999), 293–301.

30. For a related perspective, see Ronald Dworkin, *Sovereign Virtue: The Theory and Practice of Equality* (Cambridge, MA: Harvard University Press, 2000), 231–36.

31. See John Stuart Mill, "Introductory" and "Of Individuality" in *On Liberty*.

CHAPTER FOUR
Is Religious Identity Special?

1. "With all due respect, and in all good fellowship," DiIulio replied to Falwell, "predominantly white, exurban, evangelical and national para-church leaders should be careful not to presume to speak for any persons other than themselves and their own churches." He continued that in contrast to "predominantly exurban, white evangelical churches, urban African American and Latino Faith communities have benevolent traditions and histories that make them generally more dedicated to com-

munity-serving missions, and generally more confident about engaging public and secular partners in achieving those missions without enervating their spiritual identities or religious characters." Thomas B. Edsal and Dana Milbank, "Blunt Defense of 'Faith-Based' Aid; Bush Aide Rebukes Evangelical Critics of Administration Plan." *Washington Post*, March 8, 2001, A8.

2. I examine alternative interpretations of the Establishment Clause coupled with the Free Exercise Clause in "Religion and State in the United States: A Defense of Two-Way Protection," in *Obligations of Citizenship and Demands of Faith: Religious Accommodation in Pluralist Democracies*, edited by Nancy L. Rosenblum (Princeton, NJ: Princeton University Press, 2000), 127–64.

3. My use of conscience in this context refers broadly to all ultimate ethical commitments, not only those that are "Protestant" in their content. The use of the term now ranges far beyond its Protestant origins. The ultimate ethical commitments of Catholics, Muslims, Jews, Buddhists, and atheists, for example, all count as conscience. A person's conscience may dictate that she abide by the principles enunciated by a religious authority. Although the content of conscience will help determine whether a democratic government should defer to it, the content should not determine whether we can understand a person's ultimate ethical commitments to be a matter of conscience. As I shall argue below, a democratic government should defer to conscience only if it does so on a nondiscriminatory basis and the particular dictates of the conscience in question are compatible with protecting everyone's basic rights.

4. Kent Greenawalt, "Five Questions about Religion Judges are Afraid to Ask," in Rosenblum, ed., *Obligations of Citizenship*, 198.

5. Richard John Neuhaus, *The Naked Public Square: Religion and Democracy in America* (Grand Rapids, MI: William B. Eerdmans, 1984), 36.

6. Ibid.

7. By secularly based arguments I mean nonreligiously based arguments. John Rawls also contrasts secular with religious arguments. He uses secular to mean nonreligious arguments that are rooted in a comprehensive conception of the good, since he assumes that religiously based arguments are rooted in a comprehensive conception. But neither secular nor religious arguments need to be so comprehensively rooted. Both religious and secular arguments may or may not overlap with public reason, which in Rawls' view is not a comprehensive conception of morality. For a more detailed discussion of the distinction between religious, secular, and public reasons, see Amy Gutmann, "Two-Way Protection," in *Freedom of Association*, edited by Amy Gutmann (Princeton, NJ: Princeton University Press, 1998), 142–143. John Rawls defines secular reasoning as "reasoning in terms of comprehensive nonreligious doctrines." Rawls, "The Idea of Public Reason Revisited." 64 *The University of Chicago Law Review* (Summer 1997): 775, 776.

8. Rawls, *Political Liberalism* (New York: Columbia University Press, 1993), 212–254.

9. Robert Merrihew Adams, "Moral Faith," *The Journal of Philosophy* 92, no. 2 (February 1995): 77.

10. Rawls, *A Theory of Justice* (Cambridge, MA: Harvard University Press, 1999), 42–44.

11. Adams, "Moral Faith," 81.

12. Ibid., 75.

13. Rawls, *Political Liberalism*, 131–254.

14. King's famous "I Have a Dream" speech is exemplary in this regard. See Martin Luther King, Jr., *A Testament of Hope: the Essential Writings of Martin Luther King, Jr.*, edited by James M. Washington (New York: HarperCollins, 1991), 217–20.

15. See Gutmann, "Religion and State in the United States: A Defense of Two-Way Protection," in Rosenblum, ed., *Religion and Law*, 127–64.

16. King, *A Testament of Hope*, 293.

17. Ibid., 294.

18. For a typical example of an appeal to constitutional principles in the context of a publication intended for a religious readership, see King, "The Current Crisis in Race Relations," in *A Testament of Hope*, 89–90.

19. Alexis de Tocqueville, *Democracy in America*, edited by J. P. Mayer (New York: Doubleday Anchor ed., 1969), 448.

20. Michael McConnell, "Accommodation of Religion: An Update and a Response to Critics," 60 *George Washington Law Review* 60 no. 3 (March 1992): 685–742, 739.

21. Ibid.

22. *http://www.ppc.net/index.html* [accessed October 31, 2001].

23. Aldon D. Morris, *The Origins of the Civil Rights Movement: Black Communities Organizing for Change* (New York: Free Press, 1984), 4. See also Doug McAdam, *Freedom Summer* (New York: Oxford University Press, 1988); and McAdam, *Political Process and the Development of Black Insurgency, 1930–1970* (Chicago: University of Chicago Press, 1982).

24. Examples of the connection between charity and a separatist politics span major religious groups, including some Christian fundamentalist movements in the United States that are antiblack, some Black Muslim fundamentalist groups that are antiwhite, the Israeli party of Shas, and the Islamic Jihad. All provide significant welfare goods as a means of effectively maintaining their political power over their constituents (whether or not by intention).

25. Putnam, *Bowling Alone*, 66.

26. Ibid., 67.

27. For a discussion on the federal government's role in creating and supporting major civic associations in the United States, see Theda Skocpol, Marshall Ganz, and Ziad Munson "How Americans Became Civic," in *Civic Engagement in American Democracy*, edited by Theda Skocpol and Morris Fiorina (New York: Russell Sage Foundation, 1999), 27–71; especially 47, 49.

28. Robert Wuthnow, "Mobilizing Civic Engagement: The Changing Impact of Religious Involvement," in Skocpol and Fiorina, eds., *Civic Engagement*, 338.

29. Ibid., 346.

30. Putnam, *Bowling Alone*, 77.

31. World Church of the Creator website, press release of October 29, 2001, *http://www.wcotc.com/* [accessed February 5, 2002].

32. Rabbi Menachem Mendel Schneerson, *http://www.washington-report.org/backissues/0300/0003105.html* [accessed February 5, 2002].

33. Sheikh Safar Abd Al-Rahman Al-Hawali, *http://www.memri.org/* [accessed February 5, 2002].

34. For the former, see National Conference of Catholic Bishops, *The Challenge of Peace* (Washington, DC: National Conference of Catholic Bishops/United States Catholic Conference, 1983), and for the latter, see *Pastoral Letter of Catholic Social Teaching and the U.S. Economy* (Washington, DC: National Conference of Catholic Bishops/United States Catholic Conference, 1985).

35. Michael Walzer, *Obligations: Essays on Disobedience, War, and Citizenship*, (Cambridge, MA: Harvard University Press, 1970), 121.

36. Ibid.

37. *Wisconsin v Yoder*, 406 US 205 (1972).

38. For a discussion of the justification of conscientious refusal, see Rawls, *A Theory of Justice*, 331–35.

39. *Employment Division, Department of Human Resources of Oregon v Smith*, 494 US 872 (1990). To say that an exemption is desirable, on grounds of nondiscrimination, is not yet to say that it is constitutionally required, although it is a step in that direction. Whether legislatures or courts are the best agents for deciding upon such exemptions is a question worthy of further analysis.

40. *West Virginia State Board of Education v Barnette*, 319 US 624 (1943).

41. Ibid. at 643.

42. Ibid. at 644.

43. For arguments against privileging religion and conscience, see Christopher L. Eisgruber and Lawrence G. Sager, "The Vulnerability of Conscience: The Constitutional Basis for Protecting Religious Conduct," 61 *University of Chicago Law Review* (Fall 1994): 1245–1316. Their constitutional arguments establish a strong case against generally privileging conscience above the law but not against the greater claims to respect of conscientious objection over ordinary objection to laws.

44. Two-way protection recognizes competing values. Eisgruber and Kramer reject balancing tests, which "purport to balance secular and religious needs against each other [but] are at best fronts for more substantive but obscure intuitions about how particular claims for religious exemptions ought to come out" (ibid., 1259). Two-way protection calls for adjudicating between competing values on a principled basis. Since neither respect for conscience nor democratic decision-making should take precedence in all cases, we have no better alternative but to find a reasonable way of adjudicating between them. Equal regard for persons is a necessary but not always sufficient guide to such adjudication.

45. Walzer, *Obligations*, 123.

46. I develop this argument in "Religious Freedom and Civic Responsibility," *Washington and Lee Law Review* 56, no. 3 (Summer 1999): 907–22.

47. John Locke, *A Letter Concerning Toleration* (Indianapolis, IN: Library of Liberal Arts, 1955), 52.

48. Walzer, *Obligations*, 123–24.

49. The contemporary philosopher Robert Audi defends strict separation in "Liberal Democracy and the Place of Religion in Politics," in Audi and Nicholas Wolterstorff, *Religion in the Public Square: The Place of Religious Convictions in Political Debate* (Lanham, MD: Rowman & Littlefield Publishers, 1997), 1–66.

50. Locke, A *Letter Concerning Toleration*, 48.

51. New Hampshire Constitution of 1784 in F. N. Thorpe, *The Federal and State Constitutions, Colonial Charters and Other Organic Laws of the States, Territories, and Colonies Now or Heretofore Forming the United States of America* (Washington, DC, 1909), vol IV (*New Hampshire*).

52. Joel Greenberg, "Protesting Tactics in West Bank, Israeli Reservists Refuse to Serve." *The New York Times* (Saturday February 2, 2002), A1.

53. Stephen L. Carter, *The Culture of Disbelief* (New York: Basic Books, 1993), 105–6.

54. *Welsh v United States*, 398 US 333 (1970). The extension to nonreligious citizens in an overwhelmingly religious society is hard won, as in *Welsh*, which was a 5 to 4 decision without a majority opinion. An earlier decision, *United States v Seeger*, 380 US 163 (1965), paved the way by subsuming religious citizens who did not believe in a Supreme Being under the conscientious objection provision of the Universal Military Training and Service Act of 1948.

55. Carter, *The Culture of Disbelief*, 106.

56. Of course, if one thinks that democratic decision-making over schooling is illegitimate, then one will want the exception to become the rule. But recognize that this is not for the sake of respecting conscientious objection; it is for the sake of substituting parental for democratic decision-making. I argue against such substitution in *Democratic Education* (Princeton, NJ: Princeton University Press, 1999), 64–70, 292–303.

57. William Sampson, *People v Philips* [Court of General Sessions, City of New York 1813], excerpted in "Privileged Communications to Clergymen," 1 *Catholic Lawyer* 199 (1955). Quoted by McConnell in "Believers as Equal Citizens," in Rosenblum, ed., *Obligations of Citizenship*, 103.

58. McConnell, "Believers as Equal Citizens," 103. Note that McConnell's vision of the United States is significantly different from the original quote by Sampson, who did not say that "to the Jew, it is a Jewish country." Rather, he said, "the Jew, if he pleases, may establish in it his New Jerusalem." Establishing a New Jerusalem *in* this country can be consistent with two-way protection to the extent that its members do not depend on state power for maintaining or sustaining their religious community.

59. I discuss the implications for political morality of diversity within cultural and religious groups in "The Challenge of Multiculturalism in Political Ethics," *Philosophy & Public Affairs* 22, no. 3 (Summer 1993): 171–206.

60. A large part of what makes Israel a Jewish state is cultural rather than reli-

gious, but I focus here on the religious part, which is tied to the institutionalized political power of the Orthodox Jewish rabbinate. For an account of the nature of the Israeli state with respect to the closely related issue of toleration, see Michael Walzer, *On Toleration* (New Haven, CT: Yale University Press, 1997), 40–43.

61. Some Orthodox Jews also oppose state enforcement of Orthodox Jewish marriage because they distrust the state in matters of religion. As one Orthodox Jewish scholar suggests, by vesting religious power in the state, "Men and women are led into a far more serious halakhic transgression [violation of Jewish law] than that of living together without religious marriage." Yeshayahu Leibowitz, *Judaism, Human Values, and the Jewish State* (Cambridge, MA: Harvard University Press, 1992), 181.

62. Ibid., 169–70.

63. *Board of Education of Kiryas Joel Village School District v. Louis Grumet*, 512 US 687, 129 L.Ed. 2d 546 (1994).

64. Thomas C. Berg, "Slouching Toward Secularism: A Comment on *Kiryas Joel School District v. Grumet*," 44 *Emory Law Journal* 433, 434 (1995).

65. Jeffrey Rosen, "*Kiryas Joel* and *Shaw v. Reno*: A Text-Bound Interpretivist Approach," 26 *Cumberland Law Review* 387, 392 (1996).

66. Ibid.

67. *Kiryas Joel*, 512 US 687 at 710

68. See *Rachel Agostini, et al v Betty-Louise Felton, et al*, 521 US 203 (1997).

INDEX